THE IRONY TOWER

THE IRONY TOWER

SOVIET ARTISTS
IN A TIME OF GLASNOST

Andrew Solomon

ALFRED A. KNOPF
NEW YORK 1991

THIS IS A BORZOI BOOK
PUBLISHED BY ALFRED A. KNOPF, INC.

Copyright © 1991 by Andrew Solomon
All rights reserved under International and Pan-American
Copyright Conventions. Published in the United States by
Alfred A. Knopf, Inc., New York, and simultaneously in
Canada by Random House of Canada Limited, Toronto.
Distributed by Random House, Inc., New York.

Library of Congress Cataloging-in-Publication Data

Solomon, Andrew [*date*]
   The irony tower: Soviet artists in a time of glasnost /
Andrew Solomon. — 1st ed.
      p.   cm.
   Includes index.
   ISBN 0-394-58513-5
   1. Art, Soviet.   2. Avant-garde (Aesthetics)—Soviet
Union—History—20th century.   3. Glasnost.   I. Title.
N6988.S62   1991
709'.47'09048—dc20   90-53414
                                                            CIP

Manufactured in the United States of America
First Edition

For my mother,
who is also one of the survivors

You see for us, even when we come to the West,
we remain like academics,
looking out at the world from an irony tower.

—KOSTYA ZVEZDOCHETOV

Contents

Illustrations

Acknowledgments

This book could not have come into being without the help of dozens of people, so many that I hardly know how to begin to thank them. First and foremost, I am grateful to the artists themselves, whose insight and integrity are the reason for this project, whose warmth and enthusiasm blurred for me the line between work and pleasure, and whose friendship during the last few years has made me very happy. I must also thank Lisa Schmitz for her persistent generosity, which has been on a scale I have not encountered before and do not expect to encounter again. Without her, I would never have had the energy to pursue the subject of Soviet art, and I would never have conceived of writing this book. Her dedication has been altogether fantastic. Galina Main saw to it that I had fun all the time, and dealt with every crisis as though it were the merest bagatelle—which, in her hands, it proved to be. Viktoria Ivleva skillfully negotiated the impossible on dozens of occasions, and proved a better courier than the most eager employees of Federal Express. The Bomba Colori artists —Andrea Sunder-Plassmann, Dési Baumeister, Werner Zein, Mario Radina, Gaby Rets, and Enzo Enzel—offered their friendship, their time, and their perspicacity whenever I looked for it, and sustained me through more dark hours than I would care to remember, as did Marie Mannschatz.

I have had endless negotiations with dealers, some pleasant and some unpleasant, and I must thank for their constant graciousness Phyllis and Rachel Kind, Ronald Feldman, Paul Alan Judelson, and Thomas Krings-Ernst. The critics who have written in this field have without exception been patient and kind, and I have benefited enormously from conversations with them and from their writings. No one can discuss Soviet art now without reference to Margarita Tupitsyn's *Margins of Soviet Art,* and to her regular publications on the subject for the last ten years; and I must thank her and her husband, Viktor, for giving me regular access to their invaluable archives. One also looks inevitably to Jamey Gambrell's articles in *Art in America* as a reference source, and to the superb writings of Boris Groys. Viktor Miziano has crafted fine articles and essays; I am grateful to him for encouraging me, when I came to Moscow for the first time, to learn about and specialize in this field.

I must thank Meredith Etherington-Smith and Nicholas Coleridge for becoming excited about this project when it was still only a pipe dream, and for arranging to fund my trip to the Sotheby's sale in 1988. Meredith deserves further thanks for her constant encouragement, and for the advice she so often gave on how to proceed in the tricky world of writing and publishing. Ida Panicelli encouraged me to look beyond the surface from the very start, and it was she who first suggested that I see the work of Kabakov; without her advice, I would not have engaged with these artists. Roderic Grierson provided information by the bushel, and he and Dee Smith were generous with knowledge, time, and connections. Timothy Greenfield-Sanders's excitement about this whole project has been much appreciated. Hans Dyhlén has provided enthusiastic support for and help with my research, as have Kathryn Blee, Marianne Gourary, Nina Lobanov-Rostovsky, and Barbara Herbich. Sally Laird has permitted me to reprint her translations of Dmitriy Prigov's poetry (on pages 51 and 95), and I am grateful to her for this.

Katherine Keenum and James Wood merit star-spangled thanks for reading every draft of every chapter, frequently in the course of just two or three days, and providing notes and marginalia equivalent in bulk to this volume as it now stands. Their intelligence and their love have been rare and magnificent. Thanks must go also to my editor, Susan Ralston, whose sympathy and excitement gave me the impetus to write, and who helped me to feel that my subject could be of interest far beyond what initially seemed to me to be its obvious circle.

Deborah Karl and Andrew Wylie have been endlessly patient and supportive as well. Several friends have devoted themselves unstintingly to this undertaking and have given gloriously thorough and rigorous responses to the onslaught of text to which I have subjected them: Maggie Robbins, Cornelia Pearsall, Talcott Camp, Jamie Meyer, Max Cavitch, Claudia Swan, Mary Marks, Mandy Smithson, and Christian Caryl have all been remarkable. Others have also been generous readers and advisers: Rachel Eisler, Betsy Joly de Lotbinière, Polly Shulman, Liz Hollander, Janet Malcolm, Naomi Wolf, Anna Christina Buchmann, Claire Messud, Ingrid Sischy, Leonard Sussman, Neroli Lawson, Jaime Wolf, and Anne Malcolm have all commented on this book in whole or in part, and have offered frequent encouragement. Alain Branchey provided invaluable help at the last minute and allowed me to submit my manuscript on time.

I must also thank all the friends who have fed, housed, or entertained Soviet friends: Christian Caryl, Michael Lee, Brian d'Amato, Vanessa Devereux, Cheryl Henson, John Rogers, Jamie Meyer, James Wood, Elizabeth Messud, Chopper Golob, Melanie Payne, and, most of all, Sue Macartney-Snape, who came with me on my first trip to the U.S.S.R., bore patiently with my long disappearances to performances and Actions during that visit, and believed from the start that I was an authority on Soviet art.

My brother David has been a loyal supporter, has read this book with sustained enthusiasm, and has made many extremely helpful comments. My father has read it over and over and over again with close attention and deep, unfailing affection; it has been a great comfort to find, among the critics, one voice of unexceptioned succor. If this is a book about nobility of spirit, human integrity, and the importance of the courage of conviction, then I must thank my parents for the values their whole lives have taught me. I wanted to write in praise of people who turned their circumstances of adversity into occasions for dignity and honesty, because the ability to do that seemed to me as many-splendored as any ability there is. During the year I have spent writing, my mother has battled a terrible illness with a deep strength I never knew she possessed—which has taught me that I, like Dorothy Gale from Kansas, could find what I valued most in a world of glorious fantasy and characters larger than life, or in my own backyard. I thank my mother here and now for the inspiration she has provided since before my memory began.

Introduction

The popular media in the West seem to suffer under the misapprehension that communism is something that happens to people, that it is a sort of airborne infection that chanced to be carried in the early years of this century to Russia and that happened not to be carried to, say, France, or Britain, or the United States. Mikhail Gorbachev is seen in this context as the man with the vaccine, a doctor liberating his people from a seventy-year bout of an extreme form of influenza. How fortunate for them that someone has come along with the cure; and how fortunate for us that the disease never spread so far as to infect us, that by dint of our vigilance and luck we managed not to turn into a communist state, where human rights are compromised and the mechanisms of productivity do not function. We believe, in this vein, that Soviets cured of communism will turn into something not so different from Americans.

It is not fashionable to speak of national character these days; such discourse has been associated too strongly and for too long with racism and chauvinism. But it is ignorant to suggest that the economic internationalism uniting Europe, and the broad distribution systems that bring the same consumer products to Tokyo, Nairobi, and New York, have in fact eliminated national character. Nor would it be a good thing if they had; it may be self-evident that all men are created equal, but it is equally evident that all men are not created the same, and that their homogenization would be both creepy and dreary. One of the favorite debates among Soviets today is whether the people of the U.S.S.R. are Soviet in character because they have lived in a Soviet system, or whether they created a Soviet system because they had a Soviet turn of character in the first place. The answer lies somewhere between the two; and so it is important to realize that the relative democracy Gorbachev is bringing to his people is perceived by many of them to run against the national grain. "We want democracy in principle," one of the vanguard artists who are the subject of this book said to me, "but we feel very uncomfortable with it." That discomfort comes most immediately from the novelty of the new system, but it comes also from its deeper strangeness, the sense that it will remain, by definition, alien. Perestroika is part of a continuing tradition of looking to the West, a tradition of pomp and circumstance which has wrought few changes. Ivan the Terrible tried to make Russia into a Western country in the sixteenth century; Peter the Great tried in the late seventeenth and early eighteenth centuries; Catherine the Great tried at the end of the eighteenth century. Lenin tried to make Russia a model for the West in 1917. Gorbachev takes his place in a distinguished line.

Democracy, in the eyes of many Russians, becomes too easily a matter of the consensus of the populace about its own convenience and self-interest, and not, as they believe government should be, a master plan to effect universal good and reveal the truth. Freedom and prosperity (life, liberty, and the pursuit of happiness) are seen as secondary rights, not primary objectives; communism must be shunted out because it failed to effect universal good—not in order to give everyone the American life. This is just as well, because the American life is unlikely to be in the offing. In my own experience, the flip side of the idealism of the Russian Soviets is often sloth; the most ordinary events of daily life regularly demonstrate that ambition and self-motivation are not operative concepts in the U.S.S.R. Many a time I found myself in Moscow in the rain desperate to go somewhere and hailed a taxi. Taxis in Moscow are not legally required to take you where you wish, and nothing is more frustrating than the experience of hailing one cab after another, naming your destination, and getting a look from each driver that says not only that he will not take you to that place, but also that he cannot believe that *you* are going to that place, cannot believe that you actually made him stop even to *discuss* going to that place. On more than one occasion, knowing that it was a fifteen-minute cab ride to where I was going and that it simply could not be that much trouble for a working cabdriver to drive there in an unengaged taxi, I offered Western currency to the drivers, sometimes as much (at the universal black market rate) as they earned in two months. A few would snatch greedily for it, but more would just shrug their shoulders—not out of pride, but out of lack of interest. The driver didn't feel like driving to Avtozavodskaya, and he wasn't going to drive to Avtozavodskaya, and there was no point discussing it further. What had money to do with anything?

There seem to be reasons why communism—as both an economic and a political reality—happened in Russia and not in France, or England, or the United States. There are things that French, English, and American people simply wouldn't stand for that Russians seem to accept with equanimity. There is also an emotive moral rhetoric that motivates Russians, but that seems naive, and therefore politically irrelevant, in the West. Life in a communist country is grim and implacably dreary. And yet for years and years and years, in the face of that drear, and of disaster, poverty, and misery, the Russian Soviets went on believing in communism. If they hadn't believed in the notion of enforceable human equality on which communism is founded, the system would never have risen, and it was that belief that sustained communism once it was in place. The Russian intelligentsia believes in truth and in the importance of locating and communicating that truth. Once, a long time ago, they thought that truth was communism, and now they know they were wrong; but it is their faith in communism that has dimmed, and not their faith in truth itself, a manifest abstract, a thing as palpable as the kitchen table if one could only locate it. The fate of members of the Russian Soviet intelligentsia has been harsher than the fate of almost anyone in the West, but despite all the endemic grumbling, their outlook is still, in its serious engagement with the idea of utopia, shimmeringly bright. It is that brightness that is so inspiring and so compelling.

The natural result of this mix of visionary idealism and idleness is an inability to formulate or realize the simplest goals. Sir Donald Mackenzie Wallace, an English traveler to Russia in the nineteenth century, described visiting a town in which everyone was dying of a ghastly disease that came from the water they drank. With dour pride, the people there described the stages of the illness that afflicted almost all of them. Meanwhile, they were waiting for a council to come from the Tsar and make certain measurements and calculations to determine the best place to dig a well which might provide a new and better source of water. Wallace was amazed that none of them had taken it upon themselves to dig a well more expeditiously, to put an end to this terrible thing that was happening to them. But this, he found, was typical Russian behavior: to retain a nobility of spirit and a dignity of bearing in the face of difficulties, to explain their situation in its tragic light to their visitor and wait for a great miracle arranged by those more important and more powerful than they, rather than to take the small practical steps that would have saved them.

Shortly after I returned from my first trip to the Soviet Union, I went to see a production of *The Three Sisters*. "When will we ever get to Moscow?" the Sisters ask one another again and again. "But when, when will we ever get to Moscow?" they sigh as they continue with all the busy routines of their lives. The tragedy of the play is that they never get to Moscow, that circumstances are so overwhelming that they never contrive even to leave their town. Before I had been to the Soviet Union, I was moved by their plight, which seemed to me to be a metaphor for every human being's inevitable realization of his destiny. After I had been to the Soviet Union, I found that the play was all about the Russian inability to take control of a controllable situation, and it took all my restraint not to run up onto the stage and say: "Listen, there's a train to Moscow; it leaves from this town every day at four o'clock; get on it. Throw some clothes in a bag and just go. I'll buy your tickets if you'll only stop whining and *do* something."

I restrained myself, partly in deference to the actors, but more significantly in deference to the Sisters' dignity. Even if you are driven to the brink of distraction by the Three Sisters, you cannot help also admiring them, loving them, even. Though the marriage of idealism and idleness engenders an inability to function, it also occasions a spectacular generosity of spirit, an attribute as moving as the other is infuriating. You really wouldn't mind buying the Sisters' tickets for them, because they are so good, so fervent in their sustained belief in ideals that their own miserable experience should surely have killed long ago. Of course they are maddening; but they are also capable of such great joy, even in their village, where nothing ever happens, given to such outbursts of strong emotion, that one's heart goes out to them despite all one's irritation. Moreover, as though each of them had opened Pandora's box herself, they are sustained through every increasing agony by a hope so enormous, so disproportionate, so optimistic as to bring tears to the eyes. How can they go on hoping and hoping and hoping in the face of so much evidence that things will only get worse?

Everything about Soviet communism, including its failures, has been on a grand scale. The Soviet people hate compromise, the middle path, the line that comes closest to suiting the most people. Stalin wanted to rebuild Moscow as a city of great boulevards and monuments to the workers' state. He therefore reconceived its entire scheme, putting together plans so enormous and far-reaching as to be impossible; the city today is a patchwork of his unrealized objectives, but it is also a monument to the scale of his ambitions. The package in which a common brand of *papirosy* cigarettes are sold shows an entire network of canals crisscrossing the Soviet Union; these too were proposed by Stalin, though only a few of them were built by forced labor before he had to abandon what was clearly a glorious but absurd idea. And so with perestroika. No one I have met ever thought it would work; the attitude of the Soviet people is one of patience with suffering, which, as they have always predicted, only becomes worse through change. An acquisitive few have set up cooperatives and are making lots of money, but more don't care or don't think in those terms, and sit, instead, griping and complaining about the difficulty of their lives and passing up the opportunities around them. The United States and the U.S.S.R. are friends now, and bread costs several times what it cost a few years ago; capitalists can now speak out in public, and so can fascists. Is this progress? No one in the Soviet Union has much faith in the idea that things will gradually ameliorate; that sounds too much like compromise. They want everything to be different overnight. If you don't dismantle the party and get rid of every existing administrator and destroy completely the existing system to pave the way for a wholly new one, you're wasting your time. And yet like the Three Sisters—who would like to go to Moscow more than anything in the world, but not enough to break out of their own lives, pack up their furniture, and buy tickets—the citizens of the Soviet Union whom I have encountered, though they would like perestroika to work, would not in most instances like it enough to take their lives in hand and help it. They are nonetheless, like the Sisters, suffused with a hope whose power can hardly be overestimated. It is the grandeur and idealism of perestroika, as radical change, that may let it carry the day, and not the practical promise of a capitalist economy: it is perestroika's iconoclasm that fires the hearts of the Soviet people I have come to know.

If I tell the story of the art and artists of the Soviet vanguard largely in terms of myself and my own history, I do so in part because I have had my own experiences and not others, and in part because the sequence of my activities describes the sequence of those of the artists. More importantly, however, I do so because that is a valid, perhaps the most valid, way to approach such a history. My version of these people and their lives is shaped by my esteem, affection, biases, and foreignness, by my ignorance, and by my sometime frustration. There are many ways in which my knowledge is inadequate: I still do not speak enough Russian to have a meaningful conversation in that language, and the many hours of discourse that form the basis of this book took place in English, in French, or very occasionally in the translations one artist made of another's remarks. It is my good fortune that almost everyone discussed here is reasonably fluent in some Western tongue. But I am no more ignorant of these men and women than they were, for most of their history, of a life uncompromised by the indignities of post-Stalinism. Their lives and work are about the importance of making moral choices that are not fully informed, about the need to judge whatever you believe is, in humane terms, worth judging—with or without information and qualifications. Reserving judgment on people or acts is the most common excuse of the functionaries of brutality; waiting to be well informed before you begin to speak is a means of remaining dumb, and it is, by the standards of these people, unconscionable. In seeking out the terms of what was unknown to them and was likely to remain in many ways unknowable, they came to great insights and constructed an impressive ethical paradigm; I can only model my writing on their original. Where I have used the moral/aesthetic rhetoric of nineteenth-century humanism, I have done so because the nature of Soviet work, and my relation to it, seemed to me to require such language. Though this vocabulary has been often and reasonably challenged in the last thirty years, its aspiring universalism is more apposite to work born out of the resistance to ideology than is the rarified and often morally neutral or even morally defensive diction of much contemporary criticism.

Though refusing to make moral and human judgments on grounds of inadequate information may be foolish, making artistic judgments on the basis of inadequate information is obviously idiotic; and whereas the West has tended in recent years to avoid the former, we have rushed headlong into the latter. This book is more a moral than an aesthetic tract; I have tried to describe a situation without dwelling on individual works of art except as they elucidate larger points or demonstrate the artists' priorities and biases. I have chosen not to illustrate paintings or installations discussed in the text because I did not want to imply by my choice that certain works were the landmarks of vanguard Soviet art—which, I would suggest, does not have landmarks. In this area, it seemed best to let the artists make their own choices, and so, following a suggestion that they made to me, I have asked each of those whom I discuss at greatest length to do a quick black-and-white drawing or graphic. The works published here in most instances serve more as signatures than as representations of entire artistic visions. Some of these are detailed; some are not. Some of the artists spent an enormous amount of time on these works; others did not. What is important is that they have created something themselves for this book which is about them. Sven Gundlakh said: "In this era, Gorbachev is forcing the people to assume financial responsibility, so that if they do not have enough to eat they will have only themselves to blame; similarly, if the work we do for your book does not say what we would wish to say in conjunction with your text, we will have only ourselves to blame. I think it's a good policy for artists in a time of perestroika."

This is at one level a book about a particular community, about their adventures and accomplishments in the course of the last few years; it is about their particular philosophies and experiences. But I hope it is more fundamentally and more importantly a book about the difference between communication in the West and communication in the East, a comment on how the West and East communicate with one another, a close reading of the contact of two very different cultures, in which the explication of one group of experiences serves as an emblem for a larger experience that is shaping the world today. It is difficult for the West to respond to perestroika and glasnost in terms other than those of triumph: all too often one reads that we have won the Cold War at last, that the people of the U.S.S.R. have seen the error of their ways—that they have decided to become like us. That is simply untrue. Soviet life and Western life will remain different; Soviet values and Western values will remain different; and if the West can absorb as much from the U.S.S.R. as the Soviets are now trying to absorb from the West, then something that cannot be overestimated will have taken place. The seriousness and the urgency and the ideological optimism of people in the U.S.S.R., the profound commitment to truth in the abstract (despite the corruptions that thrive in the specific), the hope that endures inhuman evils and yet is as fine as it has ever been—it would be a shame to leave these benefactions unclaimed in a rage of complacence and self-satisfaction.

THE IRONY TOWER

CHAPTER I

We Came to Moscow

I began to understand about Soviet artists on the day I was stood up by the Ministry of Culture. Indeed, I began to understand in large part *because* I was stood up by the Ministry; it would not be wholly inaccurate to say that being stood up by the Ministry was the best thing that happened to me in Moscow. At ten o'clock in the morning on July 9, 1988, I was at the Ministry office in the Mezhdunarodnaya Hotel, where the Ministry had based itself for the duration of the Sotheby's Sale of Contemporary and Avant-Garde Soviet Art—the event I had ostensibly come to Moscow to cover for a British magazine. The office was locked and dark; through its glass wall I could just distinguish the desk where I had sat the previous day, making arrangements for my visit to some artists' studios. "We will organize most definitely that you have a translator," Sergey Popov, Deputy General Director of the U.S.S.R. Ministry of Culture and All Union Artistic Production Association Named after E. Vuchetich, had absolutely assured me. Lena Olikheyko, the liaison between the Ministry and the artists included in the sale, had added, "It will be one of our very good translators, who understands art." But at ten o'clock in the morning, there was no sign of a translator, or of either Sergey Popov or Lena Olikheyko. I decided to wait; I couldn't think what else to do, and I had been told that people often wait in Moscow.

At about ten-thirty, a pinched-looking woman appeared with a key to the Ministry office. I greeted her with joy, certain that she must be the promised translator, and began making anxious but friendly noises about the interviews I had arranged for the day. She looked at me blankly, shrugged her shoulders, and then went into the office, where she began rifling through papers. When I tried to follow her, I found that she had locked the door behind her. I knocked, tentatively at first, and then with rather more energy. There was no response. Through the wall of glass, I could see her reading something. She picked up the phone to make a call. I wondered whether she was calling about my problem. I waited—rather politely, I thought—until her phone conversation was over, and then I knocked once more. She lit a cigarette and started reading, occasionally looking out through the wall of glass with an expression of mild distaste and lack of interest, as though I were a not-unusual insect buzzing on a screen. I banged on the door again. She glowered, and then came and opened the door.

"I'm just slightly anxious," I started, but I got no further. She opened her mouth and let flow a river of hostility, the devastating current of which rendered me totally inarticulate. There were bits of English thrown in for emphasis, but most of what she said was in Russian. "I don't think you realize," was the opening of my response; but before the words were out, she had slammed the door in my face again. I was left staring through the wall of glass; and whereas I had earlier received the look appropriate to a housefly, I now received a more threatening glower of the sort that the Romans, persuaded of their superiority, might well have directed toward the oncoming Huns.

About ten minutes later, another woman appeared, smiled at me, nodded, and disappeared into the office. With some trepidation, I once more knocked at the door, and this woman came out and smiled again, in an extremely friendly sort of way. I explained my predicament, which was beginning to seem quite severe. It was now eleven o'clock; I had made an appointment to see a group of seven artists at half-past ten. They had agreed to assemble specifically for my benefit. I was afraid that they might give up on me and leave, but I was more afraid that they would think I was uninterested in them and their work, that they might suppose I was treating them in an offhand and superior way. I knew very little about Moscow at that time.

The second woman to arrive at the Ministry office could not have been more different from the first. She agreed that the situation was terrible, expressed absolute stupefaction at the news that I didn't have a translator, and agreed that something should be done immediately. She asked me to wait, and went back into the office, where I could see her making telephone calls and talking quickly. I settled down outside the office, feeling satisfied that the situation was under control. After another quarter of an hour, she came out and said, "There is no translator." I patiently explained all over again that I had made extensive arrangements, and that I had been promised a translator by no less a figure than Sergey Popov. She listened to this explanation and then nodded. "Yes," she said. "I understand that. But there is no translator." I said that I would be glad to wait while they telephoned a translator; after all, this was the Ministry of Culture, and there must be dozens of translators in the wings. The woman smiled at me, and said, "If you like, you may wait here, but there is no translator." Would a translator perhaps come later? "Maybe," said the woman, and went back into the office.

I waited, my hopes balanced precariously on the word "maybe." In Moscow, "maybe" means "probably not"—not a deeply comforting phrase at the best of times, but better by far than a categorical "no." "Maybe," a word used more often than almost any other, is not a final term, because the Soviet Union is a country of sudden miracles. Maybe the rain will stop before we have to go out this afternoon, maybe the elevator will be fixed, maybe I'll get a visa and go to the West, maybe there will be freedom for everyone, maybe perestroika will work, maybe I'll be an artist the rest of my life. It is the standard form for any arrangement that is made, because no arrangement can be much more than tentative in Moscow; though I did not remember it at the time, I have little doubt that the appointment I had made had been couched in a maybe—"Maybe you'll come to interview me with six other artists on Saturday at half-past ten?" was no doubt what Vadim Zakharov had said two days earlier. It must have been I, versed in different habits, who said, "Yes. I will be here, at your studio, at half-past ten on Saturday."

As I sat outside the Ministry office, I understood none of this, and I was becoming frantic. I was more than an hour late for an appointment in a building I didn't think I could find in a country by which I felt altogether overwhelmed in a city too large to negotiate in a language I couldn't even read. And the people on whom I had thought I could depend—since I at that time saw the Ministry of Culture as a sort of public service and public relations organization—had proved totally unreliable. What could I do but wait? And so I continued to sit outside the Ministry office, on a narrow balcony, peering in through the glass door at the two women, who were chatting and reading and paying not a modicum of attention to my nervous expressions.

I think I might have given up then if an American woman curator, on wholly unrelated business, had not shown up at the Ministry office at the stroke of noon and taken pity on me. I flung myself at her, and explained the whole saga in garbled words. "Which artists are you meeting?" she asked. I gave her a few names. "The Mironenkos speak French," she said. "Do you?" I said that I spoke French adequately. "That's fine," she said. "I'll come with you; I have to stop by and see some of those guys anyway."

We found a taxi in front of the Mezhdunarodnaya and set off for Furmanny Lane, the nexus of Moscow art and artists, a large, dilapidated building just inside the inner ring road of Moscow. Had someone told me then that a year later I would be living there, drinking harsh pale cognac at night, sleeping on the floor, and trudging through the courtyard of cracked concrete every morning wrapped in a towel, I would no doubt have laughed. Or perhaps not—perhaps I would only have paid more attention to the ways in which an alien world eventually comes to make more sense than one whose familiarity is bred into the habits of childhood. Perhaps I would have noticed how strong but indistinct the line between fascination and affection is, and perhaps I would have seen that nothing is so winning as mutual understanding and recognition, especially when they are forged across what seem, to the untutored eye, to be insurmountable barriers.

When I first arrived at Furmanny, I thought none of these things. I was relieved that I had at least made it to the studios. I followed the American woman up the stairs, and we were duly admitted. I started to explain and apologize in slightly incoherent French—but the Mironenkos, the ones who spoke French, were not there. The American woman spoke no Russian. Someone had a friend who spoke some English, we gathered after a lot of sign language had passed; maybe she could come. Meanwhile, we were told to sit down and drink tea. We went into a small room, and we sat with a half-dozen artists in a ring. Everyone chatted in Russian; I talked a bit to the American woman, who hoped to organize some exhibitions of Soviet art in California. Periodically one of the Soviets would make an attempt to piece together a sentence in English, but it was usually at an advanced level of incoherence, and there was little one could do by way of response except nod and smile. I managed to get across, "Good tea!" (which it distinctly was not), but that was about it.

The building we were in was falling down. We had climbed up flights of stairs which stank and then entered the artists' studios, large rooms with big windows at one end. No one sat in these open rooms with their stacks of paintings and their clear daylight; the room we were in was tiny and had a small window at one end, half-obscured by a large canvas resting in front of it, and so dirty that only the faintest light managed to filter through the part of it that was exposed. We were on broken chairs and stools of various heights. On a shelf above our heads was a group of little figures modeled in clay and painted in bright colors; they looked to me like meso-American folk art. The tea leaves floated in glasses or in cracked white teacups with a cheery pattern of orange polka dots. In the middle of the table there was a gray cardboard box full of sugar cubes—which, though I did not know it, were items of great luxury, a sign of contact with wealthy foreigners, who were the only ones with access to sugar.

One seldom needs to search for ironies in Moscow; more often than not, they are given like gifts. These artists were in studios obtained through the Union of Artists in some unoccupied space above the Institute for the Blind. They were allowed to use the telephone only at night; if you called by day to ask for Yuriy Albert or Andrey Filippov, you would reach the Institute itself and be sharply reprimanded, as though it were an affront to the blind for anyone to remind them of their proximity to these masters of color and painted shape. Assuming in my Western way that all meaning is planned, I asked later whether the government was driving home some point by surrounding these contentious artists, who told forbidden truths with visual signs, with people unable to see. "Not at all," said Andrey Filippov. "Maybe," said Kostya Zvezdochetov, and smiled because what he had said—or else what I had said—might have been a joke.

In retrospect, it's rather difficult to chart what happened that day. I arrived at Furmanny at about one o'clock in the afternoon, and I stayed until almost six o'clock the following morning. At some point the friend who spoke English came and did some translating. At some later point, the Mironenkos, who spoke French, returned. A lot of the time, I sat unable to communicate, listening to the artists talk to one another in Russian, and looking at the paintings, a few of which I recognized from the Western art press, but most of which were like ciphers, totally incomprehensible to me. In the course of the day, all seven of the artists whose studios were there—Vadim Zakharov, Yuriy Albert, Vladimir (Volodya) and Sergey Mironenko (the twins), Andrey Filippov, Kostya Zvezdochetov, Sven Gundlakh—made appearances. Later on, the artists told me that they had liked me that day because I seemed so lost—because I kept saying that the more they explained, the less I understood. But I did not say that to make them like me; I said it only because it was true. That day in Furmanny, no one actually showed me work in an organized or carefully conceived way, and no one explained his own particular artistic ideas to me. They asked me a few questions, about galleries in the West, and Sotheby's, and about the kinds of things I was in the habit of writing; but they didn't press me much, and I don't think I told them much. Mostly we talked about ways of communicating, what the West thought of Soviet art, and what the Soviets thought of Western art and art criticism. I could not help being fascinated by their interest in communicating and understanding, because our conversation was an ample study in those very difficulties; I suppose that we were talking about art both explicitly and implicitly.

Being stood up by the Ministry of Culture was the best thing that could have happened; had I not been stood up, I would have seen an entirely different side of this group of artists, and we would have spoken of very different things. Later on, I would see curators and critics file in with their Ministry translators, and I would hear the translators lucidly repeating information with all the energy of enumerative dirges. The curators and critics would ask questions, wondering what on earth to make of the convoluted, impenetrable, but somehow unarguable explanations with which they had been provided. Surely there was something more to all this, they would ask. Surely these strange swirling gray forms must have some significance less baroque and more vivid than Vadim Zakharov was letting on? Surely the childlike fairy stories told by Kostya Zvezdochetov couldn't be all there was to his paintings? And could this Yuriy Albert, about whom everyone seemed to be so enthusiastic, really be nothing more than a short, plump jokester?

It was not my natural inclination, when I arrived in Moscow, to eschew formalities. I knew that I was not interested in the historic "official" artists, members of the Union of Artists whose status had been granted for party political reasons, without reference to their

SERGEY MIRONENKO: *Untitled*

artistic abilities. I knew that the artists I did want to meet opposed the structure that had excluded them for many years, but I liked, for my own purposes, the idea of negotiating with ministries and ministers. I liked having a diplomatic-type visa and a room in the Mezhdunarodnaya, bastion of exclusivity and power. I liked the idea of hiring a car with a driver and a translator so that I could go and see the maximum number of artists in the minimum amount of time, so that I could ask them elaborate questions in my own language and get back their responses. I thought the best way to write about artists was to say: "When you take images from the past, are you commenting on the impossibility of formulating original images in a society which does not tolerate individuality?" and to make careful note of what they said in response. Had the Ministry not been in relative shambles on July 9, 1988, and had I not felt compelled to keep my appointment for fear of being rude, I would have spent the three weeks of my first trip to the Soviet Union writing down the responses to questions like that. It would probably have been my only trip, and I would have left knowing nothing, like many who went to Moscow that summer and did not have so fateful a bit of luck.

What is meaningful in Moscow is the community of artists; the friendships of the artists are both the subject and the object of their work. Only the sociology of the Moscow scene explains its meanings; only by knowing the artists can one know their work. Through the many years of oppression, the circle of the Soviet vanguard were unable to exhibit their work in public, and so they would hang it on their walls and invite people to come and look at it. The only people who ever saw their work were their friends, their acquaintances, the friends of their friends—the other members of the vanguard. They were, in their own phrase, "like the early Christians, or like Freemasons." They could recognize one another almost at a glance, and they stuck by one another—more or less—and did not betray the members of the circle. They believed that they knew a higher truth than was vouchsafed to the rest of the Soviet people, and from their circumstances of difficulty they learned integrity, and built a world of mutuality. This world was shot through with intense ironies and with petty conflicts, of course, but it was still a life-force for them, giving urgency to existence in a country where for so many people all gesture had come to seem futile. It was in the face of misery that they learned both the joy of secrecy and the joy of their own secrets, and the constant surprise of such delight taught them the value of their talent.

And that talent was formidable. The joy may have been great, but the passage to it was too fraught with travail to tempt anyone who was not able to achieve some transcendence, and the frustration of battling a system as all-encompassing as the Soviet one with an inadequate intellect quickly defeated the fools who came to this ship. The Moscow artistic community had no room for the passive observer; it was made up of people whose commitment was immense. And since the experience of their work always coincided with the experience of them as people, since the forty or fifty or maybe sixty people who made up the circle of the vanguard were both the creators of Soviet art and its audience, the personalities of the artists came to be a key to what they painted. They have strong personalities, defined in part by the place they fill within the vanguard and in part by the proclivities with which they came to it; but their genius is, of necessity, the genius not only of the painter or sculptor, but also of the poet and the actor, and it is this curious concatenation that makes them compelling, irresistible, implacable, and, ultimately, impenetrable. It is why they combine that rigorous trait of integrity with a sly elusiveness that all too often can masquerade as dishonesty.

But it is not dishonesty in our simple and straightforward sense of the word. Remember that it was necessary for serious artists working in the Soviet Union to communicate their truths in fragments, because whole and simple acts of communication—given the subversive inclinations behind those acts—would have won their authors governmental disapprobation, with all its attendant punishments. The artists did not show their work in public, but it was seen by the omnipresent eyes of power, and official people could have made the lives of artists very difficult if their work had been too obviously contentious. In a nation in which the state constantly readjusted the facts of history to give the appearance of logic to developments wholly alien to reason, progress, and humanitarianism, truth itself took on the status of a forbidden indulgence. The idea of much of the art created in the Soviet Union under Khrushchev and Brezhnev was to give voice to truths in terms that were incomprehensible to the bodies responsible for alienating truth itself. It was necessary, then, that these truths be given the status of fiction which the bodies of power—including, of course, the Ministry of Culture—had appointed as acceptable. The great difference between the fictions perpetrated by artists and the fictions perpetrated by the Ministry was that the artistic fictions were constructed specifically to be penetrated; whereas they were emblems for the truth which could be decoded by anyone initiated into an understanding of them, the somewhat random nature of the Ministry's fictions meant that they were as shallow as they appeared to be. Whereas the artists were willing to accept fiction as an extension of or marker for truth, the Ministry insisted that it be a substitute. It is for that reason that the work of the important unofficial artists, though it was held in suspicion, did not have the confrontational bearing of dissident literature, and did not subject its creators to quite the same kind of oppression that Soviet poets and novelists suffered before the advent of glasnost.

How, then, was the deep meaning of these ostensibly fictional works of art conveyed to those to whom it was urgent that truth be made apparent? This community had lines of communication explicitly dependent on its status as a community; meaning emerged along the lines of interdependence that give any community its internal strength. The extreme narrowness of the audience during the years when the artists were unable to show their work publicly forced them to lead their lives as extensions of their art, so that each encounter with them was a clue to the category of reference operating in it, each exposition not so much a statement of a single meaning as an instruction on the all-important escape from fictionality.

Meaning in their work lies in the recognition of the way visual and accessible truths fail to live up to their apparent promises, and in the acceptance of each personality and the collective personality as artworks without which the companion paintings, albums, sculptures, performances, and installations are stripped of significance. The encoded truths emerge not only from the relationship of the works of one artist to those of another, but also, by extension, from the relationship of the artists' personalities. The artists depend on one another not only for recognition of their personalities but for the establishment of them in the first place. The work, at its strongest, is always half illustration and half manifestation (raison d'être) of these personalities; the works influence one another, and that influence is carried back into the personalities. It would be reductive and inaccurate to suggest, of course, that personal biography can offer all the keys to artistic meaning; both the artists and their intended audience recognized any such intentional fallacy as both simpleminded and Stalinist. But this circumstance turned each experience an artist had of another artist's work into the occasion for mutual unraveling of codified experience and intentions. And so meaning in these works emerged via a process of what we might call loyal embezzlement, since only viewers who had been entrusted with an intimate knowledge of each personality— and thus, in a sense, with the collective personality forged out of everyone's mutual dependence on and dialogue with one another— were empowered to place these works into the context without which they were stripped of significance. The art as a body functioned to declare its own labyrinthine complexity.

Enter the West. At first there were occasional junior diplomats and some nosy journalists; later on, there were individuals who tried to steal paintings; but none of these people had much influence on what they touched. By the time I arrived in Moscow in July 1988, however, that had all changed. I was stood up by the Ministry of Culture, but hundreds were not, and they came in hordes to the studios of these artists. Suddenly the works were being seen by people unfamiliar not only with the artists' personalities, but also with the geography and circumstances of life in the Soviet Union. "Our small rooms here," Sven Gundlakh told me, "are now a more popular tourist destination than the Pushkin Museum, and a visit to them on one's first trip to Moscow is in better taste than a visit to the tomb of Lenin. After the return home, it is a more prestigious thing to mention." What to say to these people who came, wanting endless explication and explanation, wanting a half-hour talk that would make everything perfectly clear to them so that they could put together their exhibitions and their collections and their articles?

The ironies of the situation were not lost on the artists. In the studio of every artist who was discovering popularity in the West, there emerged a vocabulary of explication that was individual and stunning and, though not false, intentionally limited and distracting. Each artist had a sort of aesthetic/political patter-song to perform in which all the mysteries were revealed, in which the work was explained. The idea was that after some hours or pages of explanation, the viewer might understand what had been entirely shrouded in mystery. But these performances, in fact, represented the artists' attempts to resist the hierarchization of Western canon-formation, and were a technique for maintaining independence in the face of the threat of alien artistic—and moral—values. For, like the apparent fictions they replaced, these explications ultimately served to maintain the mystery.

And in this sense, the solution went beyond practicality; it became an absolute necessity. The artists found that many Western viewers were confounded by the fictive aspect of their work, and found most of its subtle evasions incomprehensible. Such viewers insisted that untruthfulness must always be tropological, the basis of a system of images, and they tended to approach Soviet paintings with the unfair demand that their fictive nature signal only what was already familiar in Western painting; they expected the fictions themselves to align into cohesive systems of meaning. These people failed to realize that the first question to be considered is not the nature of the fictions conveyed, but the very significance of fiction itself. They could not see that to tell a truth by way of a lie is as basic to Soviet artists as the telling of a lie in the vocabulary of truth has historically been to Soviet bureaucrats. One painter who repaints images from the past was at that time favorably compared by New York critics with the appropriationists; because the work looks a bit like appropriationism, the impulse was to assume that it was just that. And his work continues to sell more easily in the West than the work of other equally good painters since it appears—because of this chance resemblance—to be accessible. Unofficial Soviet artists work within a tradition in which the very act of producing a painting is political, no matter what the content of that painting, and in which many visual or theoretical questions are therefore moot; elusiveness and quotation have their own tradition in Soviet art. They in no sense signal exhaustion, as they do for Western appropriationist artists. The work has always told the story of its own secrecy in far too many rich ways to allow systematization. Indeed it has been empowered by its eccentricity; each artist's primary arena for originality has been the variety and particularity of his own disguises. The tightness of the community was based on the diversity of its members; in a communist society, those who are nonconformist have their nonconformity in common, no matter how different their values may be.

These things emerged very naturally with time. The reason I stayed for so long on that first day at Furmanny was not that I understood any of this; at that moment, I had no idea where instinct might begin. I stayed because no one asked me to go—because the artists seemed to be glad I was there and glad to talk to me. I stayed for reasons only marginally less banal and egotistical than the reasons for my original trip: I had gone to Moscow hoping to meet the artists of the vanguard, and I found to my surprise that I had done exactly that. It was the double exhilaration of liking one another and of finding that we could understand one another, that what we had to say to one another made sense.

Volodya Mironenko volunteered to drive me back to my hotel when the first streaks of grayish dawn penetrated the narrow window and interrupted our convocation. "Meet us at the train station at noon tomorrow," Andrey Filippov said to me as I left, and he gave me a piece of paper with the name of a station written in Cyrillic characters. I went back to the Mezhdunarodnaya, amused by the suspicious glower of the night guard, and then on to sleep enthralled.

All this occurred just after the Sotheby's sale, at a time when the Moscow art world was in a state of uproar, when it was more easily penetrable because it had been so disrupted that its defenses were down. The sale was a sort of paradigm for glasnost; it had the same level of good intention disrupted by the same amount of greed, and it was in equal measure a triumph and a disaster, a gift to the people it touched and also their ruination. Had it not been for the excess of publicity that surrounded Sotheby's, the Soviet artistic community might have escaped some of the bitterness that overtook it thereafter; but had it not been for that overeager promotion, the artists might never have escaped their circumstances of isolation.

I first heard about the sale in March 1988, at a lunch given by the Sotheby's press office. At the time, I was writing a regular column on the London auction world for a British glossy magazine, and so it was my business to hear auction gossip before the general public did. I was told that the sale would be among the most glamorous events ever, that there was a fabulously expensive grand tour planned, and that everyone who was anyone would be there. I decided at once to try to go. I had twice before scheduled trips to the Soviet Union: one slated for the spring of 1980 had had to be canceled when Soviet troops invaded Afghanistan; the second, to have taken place in the spring of 1986, had been deferred because of Chernobyl. I was determined to visit the U.S.S.R. and thought the Sotheby's sale sounded an ideal opportunity. In this consumerist spirit I began.

I was immediately suspicious, of course, of the hue and cry that surrounded the sale, and I assumed that such extravagant hyperbole as had been called into action would be appropriate only if its object were of almost no real value. I looked at transparencies of some of the Soviet works, and found them uninspiring; I suggested an exposé to the editors of my magazine, and it was on that basis that they agreed to send me to Moscow. In New York, a month later, I saw the editor of an American art magazine for which I was also writing; she sent me to see the Ilya Kabakov show then on at Ronald Feldman Fine Arts. "A lot of hype," she conceded, "but what makes you think that's it?"

The Kabakov show astonished me. I had already seen slides of some works of his that were to be included in the sale: large canvases with dense writing in black, like elegantly lettered Cyrillic shopping lists. One of them had a coat hanger, a nail, and a blue plastic toy gratuitously placed on its right side; one was half blank; the third was painted on a checkerboard background of blue, yellow, and beige. They had said and meant nothing to me. But this exhibition was entirely different. It was called *Ten Characters,* and it was an installation, a recreation of a Moscow communal apartment, where each of ten people had been given a single room in which to lead out his life, sharing hallway and kitchen. Each character had been driven to a curious obsession by this congested setup, and in the sum of their various ways of suffering and escaping, Kabakov located all the misery of Soviet life, strange and palpable and deeply moving.

The communal apartment is a commonplace in the Soviet Union, where housing is always in short supply. After the Revolution, the grand sixteen-room homes of prosperous Muscovites were given to the proletariat, who were usually allotted one room each. In that room they housed themselves and, as time went on, their families. The tradition has been sustained and magnified. Today, only the most fortunate in Moscow have places of their own; almost no one has control over where he lives, and friends, members of a community like the one that forms the subject of this book, are almost invariably assigned rooms at opposite ends of the city. As for living near the center—it is in principle a matter of luck, and in fact a matter of connections and bribes.

The people in communal apartments do not get to choose their cohabitants, and so people with no point of contact find themselves in constant overlap. Long after I saw *Ten Characters,* when I was not in New York but in Moscow, I visited many such places, and found that Kabakov had been, perhaps, less imaginative than I had at first supposed; the horror of communal living tends to drive people to extreme behavior, and the incompatibility of those who are randomly assigned to live together often throws even their most ordinary acts into sharp relief, so that they seem like a violation of human decency. A photographer I met some months later invited me to her room for tea, but warned me to enter quietly lest I bring down the wrath of her neighbor. We took the usual urine-splattered elevator to the sixth floor. As she unlocked the front door, she touched my arm. "Hold your nose; it will take only a moment," she said. I did not take her words literally, but I should have: I found myself in a dark, narrow hallway in which an unbearable stench hung like a forbidding shade between me and the room at the end of the hall—Vika's room—which was spotlessly clean, with pretty white curtains. Vika explained that one of the residents of her apartment was a woman of eighty who kept fourteen cats in her room and refused to wash them or the room or herself. When we went, a few minutes later, to get cheese from the kitchen, I saw that the floor was covered with cat hair; the sink was clogged with cat hair; the stove was covered in ancient burned pans and rotting cat food. Vika took some cheese from the refrigerator. She had wrapped it in layers of paper and cloth to protect it. "If I touch any of these things," she told me, gesturing at the mess, "I lay myself open to attack. I'm glad you've come in the summertime, because in winter I cannot keep my window open all day, and it becomes unbearable in my room also. But now in my room it is all right." I agreed with her as we hastened back down the dark hallway toward the white curtains.

But that came later. In May 1988, I had never been to Moscow, and the Kabakov exhibition in some senses brought me closer to the life experience of Muscovites than I had any reason to hope my visit would. The residents of his fantasy apartment, like Vika's neighbor, had approached madness by dint of their proximity to one another. In one room lived the Man Who Never Threw Anything Away; in another lived the Man Who Collects the Opinions of Others; in another, the Man Who Flew into Space from His Apartment; in yet another, the Person Who Describes His Life Through Characters. The glut of detail rendered these people with painful clarity: in each room were all the accessories for the chosen mania, and a long text to describe its precise manifestations. In the room of the Man Who Never Threw Anything Away, for example, there were stacks of cards with tiny objects mounted on them, labeled in tiny letters: "lint from my pocket," "dust from the hall," "paper from the streets." Back and forth along the center of the room hung lines, like washlines, with the same words attached to the same sorts of objects: "a paperclip," "small rag," "pencil stub." The text hung at the entrance to the room told a story about a plumber who came after many years and needed access to it; receiving no answer to his persistent knocking, he broke down the door:

> The entire room, from the floor to the ceiling, was filled with heaps of different types of garbage. But this wasn't a disgusting, stinking junkyard like the one in our yard or in the large bins near the gates of our building, but rather a gigantic warehouse of the most varied things, arranged in a special, one might say, in a carefully maintained order. Flat things formed a pyramid in one corner, all types of containers and jars were placed in appropriate boxes along the walls. In between hanging bunches of garbage stood all sorts of shelves, upon which myriad boxes, rags and sticks were set out in strict order. . . . Almost all the shelves where these things were placed were accurately labeled, and each item had a five- or six-digit number glued on it and a label attached to it from below. There were also lots of things on a big table standing in the middle of the room, but these didn't have numbers or labels on them yet: piles of paper, manuscripts. . . .

That was the room itself. But why and how had this man acquired and arranged these things, and where did his obsessiveness begin? This is what was written on one of the piles of paper in the middle of the room:

> Usually, everybody has heaps of accumulated piles of paper under their table, their desk, magazines and telephone notices which stream into our homes each day. Our home literally stands under a paper rain: magazines, letters, addresses, receipts, notes, envelopes, invitations, catalogs, programs, telegrams, wrapping paper, and others. These streams, waterfalls of paper, we periodically sort and arrange into groups, and for every person these groups are different: a group of valuable papers, a group for memory's sake, a group of pleasant recollections, a group for every unforeseen occasion—every person has his own principle. The rest, of course, is thrown out on the rubbish heap. It is precisely this division of important papers from unimportant that is particularly difficult and tedious, but everyone knows it is necessary, and after the sorting everything is more or less in order until the next deluge.
>
> But if you don't do these sortings . . . wouldn't that be insan-

ity? . . . To deprive ourselves of any of these paper symbols and testimonies is to deprive ourselves somewhat of our memories.

To deprive ourselves of all this means to part with who we were in the past, and in a certain sense, it means to cease to exist.

Kabakov's world comes through these strange episodes, and his work makes us wonder what is real, and what is fantasy, until we are utterly defeated by the task of trying to sort the threads from one another. Instead, we accept the glut with which he provides us, with all its fascinating twists and turnings. We return to the problem of history: what Kabakov gives us to remember is as valid as anything we have to remember, and the fact that it is not our own experience becomes irrelevant. He validates his whimsy by locating his most fundamental truths in the self-sufficient worlds he creates, conveying a moral rigor through the most persuasive of deliberate fictions. In *Ten Characters* there is an additional element to his wit. Kabakov knew, at the time that he designed the installation, that he was working for a Western audience, and for the first time he had to try to communicate over the great barriers of bias and experience that separate the U.S.S.R. from the rest of the world. He turned his vision just far enough toward the West to captivate his viewers. We cannot understand the tangle of arguing voices in the kitchen; we do not see any of the people. What did the Man Who Flew into Space from His Apartment find when he reached the layer of the stratosphere he believed contained the strong currents of freedom? It would be unlike Kabakov to be too precise. *Ten Characters* is full of opened secrets and closed ones, and it is a work, as befits an elder statesman of the Soviet vanguard, in which what is most easily divulged is the unknowable quantity of the undivulged.

I was disturbed by it, and though I still did not have a very clear idea of the different levels on which it was operating, of what it really meant, I did begin to see that there was a puzzle, that there were secrets to unfold. I realized that contemporary unofficial Soviet art was perhaps not a hoax; and in the month that remained before my trip, I read everything I could find on the subject. The essays I found suggested to me that this art was provincial, eccentric, and very complex; what I eventually found was different not only in type but also in category. At the time, however, I set about busily accruing names, hoping to make and confirm judgments when I reached the U.S.S.R.

Visas and hotel rooms for that summer were unavailable through ordinary channels, so I had to obtain both through Sotheby's, which was organizing the be-all and end-all of Soviet tours, a package involving diplomatic entertainments, singing gypsies, and seats at the sale; endless private viewings and meetings, visits to icons upon which Western eyes had never before gazed, and meetings with important persons of every description; cases of champagne imported specially for the occasion and caviar of a rare and exquisite flavor previously reserved for the tsars and their ilk. The billing was jet-set; we were not going to an auction but to one of the most important events in the new communication between East and West. Anyone reading the advance material would have thought this was an occurrence beside which the signing of the Treaty of Versailles was shoddy and insignificant. The glory was reflected in the price—$3,975 (not including airfare) for the long tour of eight days or marginally less for the four-day version, designed for people interested only in the sale. There was a drop-dead-smart brochure on which the word "Sotheby's" blazed red in Latin and Cyrillic type against the sienna tones of an ancient map lettered in unreadable hand. The purists among us, charmed though we were by the prospect of caviar and rare views of sanctified icons, were somewhat taken aback when we realized that this map—which became the logo of the trip and was reproduced time and again in the international press—was actually a colonial map of Bermuda. "It's what sprang to hand," one of the auction house's directors told me.

That's rather what the tour was like. We met at Heathrow, where a charming man assisted us with check-in—an activity one usually negotiates quite successfully on one's own. "When you get to Moscow," he said, "just ask for the Sotheby's representative, who will see you through everything. A diplomatic channel has been cleared for your arrival." We filled the business-class part of the British Airways flight, as chic a group of people as one might hope to find on a plane. At the front of the cabin, several women in identical Valentino suits laughed and babbled. "We're going to be swarmed by the press again," said one of them. "Photographed at every party; it's so exhausting!"

At Sheremetyevo Airport, things were in a predictable state of disarray, and the Sotheby's representative, having made a picturesque showing at the door to the plane, disappeared altogether until the following day. It's an impossible airport. It is illegal to enter the Soviet Union with Soviet currency, and it is impossible to get Soviet currency until after you have left customs, but in the baggage-claim area there is a man with baggage carts available for one ruble. Since you have no rubles—or would be ill-advised to show them if you had —you must revert to conventional forms of bribery. Cigarettes will get you a cart, unless, of course, the carts have run out. Wise people travel with luggage they can lift themselves. On the afternoon of July 5, 1988, there was madness at Sheremetyevo. Elegant suitcases were coming up on the wrong carousels; no one could find anything; there was no sign of the diplomatic channel that was to allow us to circumvent customs. At the far side of customs, after many of us had been treated to protracted interviews with obstreperous border guards, we found one another: a crew of lost-looking people. After an hour of confused milling, we were led onto a bus, which drove us through Moscow and then dropped us a block away from our hotel. Elderly Swedish countesses stood over dark blue leather-bound trunks with helpless looks, while the stormy waters of the Moskva River swirled behind them. There were no porters. We set up a sort of relay, the strong and the young passing bags to one another the whole way back to the hotel. Check-in was without rhyme or reason. Irritation was running high.

The Mezhdunarodnaya—commonly called the Mezh—was built in 1980, and looks much like any business hotel/convention center in the West. It's too large, with an enormous atrium lobby in which a five-story-high rooster clock crows out the hour and the half-hour. People on important business to the U.S.S.R. are put there, industrialists and lesser diplomats, and the powers that be expect them to be impressed by it. The hundreds of small rooms have private baths with toilets and bathtubs made by American Standard, which in Moscow is luxury beyond the dreams of avarice. Our rooms were stocked with Evian water, which had been flown in for the occasion. We took it as evidence that the rooms were tapped—though it may have been only coincidence—that anyone who said loudly, "We did not receive a welcoming bunch of roses! I think Peter and Kathryn did!" would within moments be given the appropriate flowers.

We were shown to our rooms, did some hasty unpacking, took showers, and then reassembled downstairs, suitably dressed for an evening out in London or Paris. What followed was dreamlike, sometimes nightmarish, sometimes wondrous, and sometimes just risible. Draped in quantities of couture and flashing sapphires, a collection of jet-set cultural peripherals wended their way through the streets of

Moscow. Some of these people had titles; some were regulars at the Salzburg festival, or at Bayreuth; some hailed from Newport or Palm Beach; others were tax refugees from minor principalities. A few were serious art dealers keen to have a good time, hoping they could mingle with clients and acquire some work and get some fine drink all in one fell swoop. There was a smattering of lost-looking families who were playing it grand. Some of these people were terribly nice, and a few of them were genuinely interested in the Soviet Union, glasnost, perestroika, and even art. Some of the people were bright; this was by no means a convocation of fools. But the overall effect of the crowd that descended for the Sotheby's sale was a trifle grotesque.

On my second night in Moscow, I was seated at a table with a prominent member of a Middle-Eastern royal family, the manager of an internationally famous rock star, a divorced countess, a retired pro baseball player, and at least a dozen others. When we sat down, there was caviar on the table. We instantly began to eat it, thinking it was a sort of *amuse-gueule* to precede our actual dinner. A few minutes later, a waiter came over with blini. "I'm afraid," someone said to him, "that we really can't eat these without caviar." The waiter looked confused and anxious; he gave us our blini and went off in search of more caviar. "Quickly," said a prominent British society figure. "Everyone, eat your blini." Everyone ate the blini, and when the waiter returned with the caviar, she looked at him and said, in the haughtiest tone she could muster, "We cannot eat that without blini. Bring us more blini." These people promptly devoured the caviar. And so the game went on, until everyone had consumed an indecent quantity of caviar, and the waiter had—who knows?

Games like the caviar game are typical of a particular stratum of British society, and they are unappealing at, for example, an extravagantly expensive charity ball in the presence of some member of the Royal Family at the Savoy. But we were not at the Savoy. The waiter was clearly getting into trouble for his inability to keep these Westerners in check; the hotel was running through its reserve caviar; Sotheby's was being made to look ridiculous. What would have been totally unacceptable at the Savoy was gross in Moscow. Were these people to be the salvation of the fragile world of genius that grew from artistic resistance to the terrors—and also the banalities—of Stalinism? The very idea seemed laughable.

The following day, the people on the tour were taken to see the studios of artists whose work was coming up for auction. Everyone had been randomly assigned to bus groups, and each group was to visit three artists, to see their work and their milieu and the way they lived. From my research I knew that some of these artists were members of the powerful Union of Artists—the people whose work had been accepted by Khrushchev and Brezhnev, the ones whose needs had been catered to by the society around them—and that others were part of the unofficial movement. I very much wanted to see Ilya Kabakov, of course, but he had just returned from New York, and was rather depressed; he refused to see anyone. So I negotiated my way onto the bus tour that included a visit to Vadim Zakharov at the Furmanny studios; I knew from my advance reading that this was one of the places I wanted to go.

At Vadim Zakharov's studio, we listened to an amazing and complex description of a system that defeats itself in an unending cycle of collapsed inspiration. Zakharov spelled out elaborate puns and discussed the way that color tones could sign for words, words for images, images, at last, for tones. He showed us canvases unlike anything I had seen, on which gray one-eyed men battled with elephantlike figures. As our translator explained all this, people took snapshots, interrupting the artist in midstream with their flashbulbs, as though he were, perhaps, an elephant at the zoo, or a one-eyed man in a freak show. When, breathless after a forty-five-minute monologue, Zakharov finally stopped to ask for questions, there was silence. Then the first question came from a wealthy German collector. "How many paintings do you do per year?" he asked, with an eye to values. The second came from a lady from Nice, "Do you paint in black and white and gray because it's hard to get colored paint in this country?"

You could see that Zakharov was crushed. It was as though he had recited train timetables for the previous forty-five minutes. He wasn't sure how many paintings. He used black and white because they fitted with his program. If these were the people who would buy his work, then why bother to have a program, an agenda, a theoretical construct at all? Other painters, having similar experiences that day, would laugh, but Vadim Zakharov, possessed though he is of both genius and generosity of spirit, is not one for laughing at the way the world is; his work is built on his seriousness. Sitting in Furmanny for the first time, three days before my amazing long day in the same studios, I tried to remember exactly what I had read about Zakharov, and I recalled that he had quoted Dostoevsky in an article in *Flash Art* as saying that beauty saves the world; I had not understood the beauty of his paintings, but I saw that there was a beauty to his system and asked about it.

Zakharov talked about beauty for a minute. Afterward, the translator helped me to make an appointment to see him on Saturday (it was then Wednesday) at ten-thirty. "I will get my friends also to be here," he said, "so that we can all talk together." And as I have remarked, he must have said, "Maybe." And I must have replied, "Saturday, at ten-thirty, I will be here."

After we left Zakharov we went on to see Ira Nakhova, and her sometime husband, art critic Josif Bakshteyn, who several days later would lead a boat ride and then an Action, each in its way a protest of Western commercialism. I had never heard of Ira or of Josif, and I found her art less immediately compelling than Zakharov's. But I liked Josif. And one could not help liking Ira, beautiful and gracious as she is, self-possessed, but full also of girlish enthusiasms. She explained her work, the way it reorders the world. Then we all sat down for food and conversation. We had brought a box lunch with us from the Mezhdunarodnaya to eat in her studio, but she had bought substantial supplements to it. An enormous amount of time and money had gone into acquiring these: there was lovely fresh fruit, and there was lettuce, and good bread with butter, and there was cheese, all attractively arranged on big earthenware plates.

We sat in silence while she brought everything out for us. Now that I have lived in Moscow, I know that Ira must have spent two days waiting in queues, buying on the black market food that ought to have gone elsewhere, putting together a table for these guests such as she seldom or never put together for herself; I now know also that she hates to cook, slice, arrange, and serve. We all took our plates and went quietly to the table. The first words to break the silence were: "D'you have any mustard?" Ira's grasp of English wavered. "Mustard?" she repeated. "Yeah, y'know, it's yellow, you put it on bread, for sandwiches." Ira shook her head. "No mustard. What a place," said the man, an American curator of contemporary art.

That's what the people on the Sotheby's tour were like. Or at least that's what enough of them were like so that they dominated the scene. The people from Sotheby's itself, on the other hand, were impeccable to the point of tragic grandeur. The three at the helm were Grey Gowrie (The Rt. Hon. The Earl of Gowrie), chairman of Sotheby's, Julian Barran, director of Sotheby's Paris, and Simon de Pury, chairman of Sotheby's Switzerland. Simon de Pury had been

VADIM ZAKHAROV: *Andrew! I order you to live a long life!*
V. Zakharov 2.8.90 Madam Shluz

personal curator to Baron Thyssen von Bornemisza for a number of years, and it was through this activity that he had become involved in cultural exchange with the Soviets and had come to see the work of contemporary Soviet artists; the Moscow sale was his idea in the first place. "Do you know that we had a list, culled from many sources," he said at dinner one night later that week, "of who all the good underground artists were supposed to be. We submitted it to the Ministry, and they said to us, 'This list is the same list we always get from people in the West. We know that it is actually the same list because one of these people is not an artist. He's a pianist. Please put out the word that people who want to see art should stop asking to meet him.' For us too, this is all a wonderful, giant risk, and we know so little about this work we are buying, except that we know it's worth buying, because it does so many new things. You can feel the originality here."

Y ou could feel the originality. So we come at last to the night of July 7, 1988, a Thursday, a day perhaps not so exalted as June 28, 1919, when the Treaty of Versailles was signed, but a day, despite all, that would change the history it touched. It was the day that brought together a group no previous circumstance could have brought together. Like the climactic sequence of a Bergman film, it was a scene in which people doing as they always do, in a room in which none of them felt entirely at home, changed one another forever. This is the rhetoric of melodrama, but the situation was one in which melodrama was the only vocabulary.

This is what happened: at six-thirty, the Sotheby's tour members began to file into the sale room, the great conference chamber of the Mezh. They stopped by the registration desk to collect numbered paddles for bidding, and then walked to the seats at the front of the auction room that had been reserved for them. They looked terrific, and by that time they had been at enough events together so that they could meet one another with the delicate nods of familiarity. "Are you really going to buy that one?" someone asked someone else. "At any price," came the response with a chuckle. A thin woman with diamonds at her throat and an oversized crocodile handbag kept flipping back and forth between two pictures by two different artists. "I just can't decide, I can't decide," she moaned, and asked a neighbor, "Which of these do you like better?"

Behind the people from the Sotheby's tour came Westerners resident in Moscow and certain powerful Soviets, all of them also highly overdressed. The American ambassador, Jack F. Matlock, was there, with his wife, Rebecca, and his son, David. Someone senior from the *Time* magazine bureau was there, not covering the sale but interested in it. The sons and daughters of wealthy foreign businessmen stationed in the U.S.S.R. were there. Exactly who the Soviets were who came was difficult to say, but they were people of some note and station, looking fat and easy among Americans abroad and Western Europeans on holiday. Some of them were from the Union of Artists, some from the Ministry of Culture, and others, no doubt, from the other ministries involved.

The press were there in spades, with notebooks and cameras and TV equipment, filming everything, documenting and documenting and documenting for all they were worth. This was not art press flown in for the event; it was the political press, everyone's Moscow bureau covering a day in history. They took sweeping shots of the audience, and must have wondered who all these people were, decked to the nines, in the Mezh, on a Thursday in July.

The artists included in the sale were there. Not all of them: Ira Nakhova said she went to bed early that night and left her future in the hands of fate. But almost all of them. They had the coveted passes for the sale that had let them in the door of the Mezh and in the door of the saleroom, and they sat interspersed among the wealthy and the powerful, looking a bit nervous, whispering to one another, and, because it was the rage that had suddenly gripped the members of the tour, autographing catalogues. At that moment, this playing at celebrity seemed to them to be a game.

In the back third of the room, there were no chairs. Cordoned off by velvet ropes, as though this were a museum, or perhaps a zoo, was space for all the rest of invited Moscow, people with cards that had been sold and passed around—so the visitors from the West whispered to one another—at amazing prices, cards for which paintings, houses, perhaps lives had been exchanged. Behind the rope were the curators of the Pushkin, and all the friends of the Soviet artists, the other members of the vanguard. Except for Ira, at home asleep, everyone who had touched the world of Moscow art was there. Some artists from Leningrad had come; the first cousin of an artist in the sale had made the trip from Tbilisi. Behind the rope there was no room; it was like the subway at rush hour. No one could see anything much; people pushed and shifted toward the front of the mob, only to be borne back

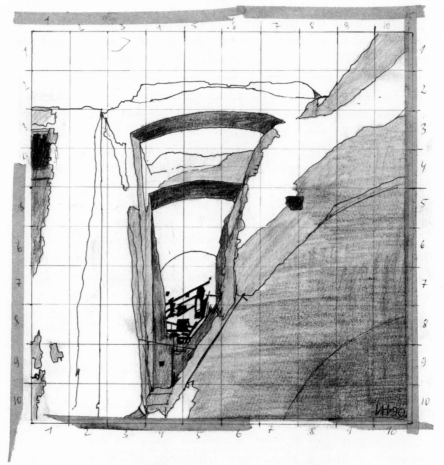

IRINA (IRA) NAKHOVA: *Sketch for a Painting*

again on the waves of people against people, crushed but redeemed by
the blissful air conditioning in mid-July. There were some people
from the West behind the ropes too: the ones who could get in by
waving their German or American passports, but who had no other
connection to the sale and no connection to the local structure of
power.

At seven o'clock, the bidding began. Lord Gowrie and Julian Barran were on either side of the lectern, and Simon de Pury, sweating
despite the air conditioning, was standing behind it. Gowrie, who
had caused a famous scandal in Britain when he resigned the Cabinet
post of Arts Minister on grounds that one couldn't be expected to live
on £33,000 a year, looked calm as a mountain lake. His bearing
throughout had been of unpleasantly unfailing politesse and correct-

ness; by eliminating the predictable awkwardness of any situation, he set everyone very slightly on edge. Julian Barran did the same thing on a smaller scale. They were like little twin kings on their stately platform, and Simon de Pury was like the master of ceremonies at the greatest show on earth.

This is what happened: the sale began with a handful of works from the twenties and thirties, from the old avant-garde. The first lot was by Nadezhda Udaltsova, and it was only a pencil drawing, estimated at £7,000 to £10,000. It sold for £12,000. Some more of her work exceeded its estimates; paintings by Aleksandr Drevin went for two and three times theirs. Then came the Rodchenkos. The first one, an oil estimated at £60,000 to £80,000 sold for £180,000. Some photos and a poster all sold very well, and then came a painting of a line, called, simply, *Line.* It was estimated at £90,000 to £120,000; it sold for £300,000. Eyes were rolling heavenward, but this was not yet the real sale, this was the preliminary, this was the introduction, the sale of this old work; the excitement was yet to come.

So this, then, is what happened: Lot 18, by Mariya Ender, was sold, and with Lot 19 the sale of Soviet Contemporary Art began. The Soviet artists were in alphabetical order, according to the Latin alphabet. So the first artist was Grisha Bruskin, a tiny gnarled man who had been at the periphery of things for years, a crossover artist who had been marginal in the world of officialdom until the danger was over, until Gorbachev had come to power, and had then been marginal in the world of unofficialdom. Grisha Bruskin was the first artist, a man deemed by his friends to be sweet and very technically capable but by no means a great thinker, a man they all liked well enough but to whom no one had ever paid more than a modicum of attention. They had been surprised when one of his paintings had appeared on the cover of the auction catalogue and when people from the West had flocked to his studio. Grisha Bruskin's paintings are beautiful, and the ways in which they are Soviet spring instantly to the eye; there is no question of this work's having come from a disgruntled painter in, say, Antwerp. His work is explicitly political, or else it is explicitly concerned with his Judaism. His images are haunting, like the images of advertising, with a scary slickness that is almost savage. Bruskin's work caught the eyes of the buyers at the sale. All his paintings doubled, tripled, quadrupled their high estimates; then one of them, estimated at £17,000, sold for £220,000.

Inevitably, the artists began to look at one another with new and sharper eyes. They finally had occasion to watch how people from the West spend money. With casual, almost weary gestures, the members of the Sotheby's tour raised paddles of blanched wood into the air, offering one hundred twenty, one hundred forty, one hundred sixty thousand pounds. A difference of a thousand pounds seemed to move them not at all. Fortunes such as many of these artists had never dreamed anyone could have were casually handed over for a painting. A Soviet painting. And at that moment, the artists saw that they might be wealthy beyond anything they had hitherto been able to conceive.

After Bruskin came Ivan Chuykov, one of the most highly esteemed elder statesmen of unofficial art. If someone would pay £220,000 for a painting by Grisha Bruskin (Grisha Bruskin!) then surely the work of Chuykov would be worth millions? But *Fragment of a Fence* failed to reach its low estimate of £8,000, and *Noughts and Crosses* didn't reach its low estimate of £11,000. The paintings sold; they had exceeded their reserve prices. But just barely. And so the sale continued, with high prices that were, in the eyes and minds of the Soviets, altogether inexplicable, and low prices that were embarrassing, but then again represented, even so, so much money. Glances were exchanged when a painting by Sveta Kopystyanskaya came on the block; she was a serious woman, and a good painter, but not a great original, and her painting was going higher and higher. How could it be? If most members of the vanguard had not been sequestered behind their rope, they might have seen that there was a paddle battle going on for the piece. Had they been at the posh official dinner the previous night, they might have heard an elegant woman from Switzerland announce that she would have that painting at any price, and they might have gathered that a rock star had instructed his manager to bid on it. After the sale, the artists would repeat and repeat themselves in a sort of misinformed drone. "That painting realized £40,000," they would say in hurt tones of voice. "Does that mean that people from the West think Sveta Kopystyanskaya is a better painter than Chuykov? Than Kabakov?"

Almost every painting sold. The ones that didn't sell were bad paintings by a Union big wheel whose work had been absurdly highly priced: Ilya Glazunov, virulent anti-Semite and people's hero; Glazunov, at once the most popular and the most hated artist in the U.S.S.R.; Glazunov, whose wife threw herself from their window the day his exhibition opened to tell the world how cruel he was, but whose dramatic gesture failed to keep him from the opening; Gla-zunov, who was presented a Fabergé egg and drilled a hole through its delicate enamel so that he could run the wire to a Japanese stereo microspeaker he had placed in it—Glazunov didn't sell. That was cause for celebration. Except for Glazunov, the sale was a success on a scale no one could have dared to hope for. It brought in £2,085,050, as opposed to the original (and supposedly optimistic) estimate of £796,800 to £1,068,400, and everyone was delighted. Simon de Pury hugged Sergey Popov, and festivity was in the air.

This is what I heard after the sale: a man and a woman leaving the great room at the Mezh, chatting away. "I bought this one," the woman said, pointing at her catalogue. "Or else this one. I don't remember which." "Whichever," said her friend. "As long as you have something to remember tonight by. Wasn't it great?"

Therein lies the tragedy of Sotheby's and its hyper-publicity, but therein too the genius. The prettiest paintings, or sometimes the strangest-looking, sold for the most money, and though some of the best work sold to people who understood it, a lot went to people who were shopping for souvenirs. The consequent imbalance of the infra-structure of the Moscow art scene is still resonating. While the auction house cannot be held responsible for the bidders' ignorance, there is no question that had the sale been staged somewhat less theatrically, some of the souvenir-shoppers would have stayed home. But there is also no question that the paintings would not have brought in such an enormous amount of money. The people who stood around in the lobby after the sale saying, "I'm so glad I bought a painting, which-ever one, just to have something to remember this trip by," under-wrote the success of even the really second-rate work—and if the sale had not been such a huge success, the Ministry of Culture would have been far less likely to allow the subsequent events of like nature that have helped to liberate Soviet artists of every sort. Nor would it have looked with increasing kindness on the artistic community that, once detested, began that day to find easy love as a prime source of hard currency for the U.S.S.R.

I think Sotheby's saw both truths; they knew that they were open-ing up a new source of continuing profit for themselves, but they also contrived to transcend the pedestrian commercialism one has come to associate increasingly with the auction houses. At this sale, even the profit-seeking often seemed to spring from a commitment to the general good. Simon de Pury went to Moscow in 1984 with a vision of communication among worlds that had been strangers to one another for too long, believing, not inaccurately, that his ability to make this art a recognized source of hard currency for the Soviets would ease the plight of the artists struggling there, and that it would at the same time bring something worth knowing to the world of contemporary art in the West. He went because he believed in the Soviets enough to seek out their sagacity, and because he believed in the West enough to offer it the work that sagacity produced.

At the farewell dinner, the day after the sale, even the most cynical of the Sotheby's staff—and the most fearful figures in the Ministry of Culture—were on the brink of tears with the thrill of having created history. Perhaps the Treaty of Versailles is not so inept a metaphor after all. The Sotheby's sale was a miracle of engagement for two sides that had long stood in emblematic opposition to each other, and if one accepts that the function of art is ultimately communication, then this sale was itself a work of art. Whatever the misapprehensions and blunders surrounding it, Sotheby's acted throughout with integrity, and for that they deserve praise.

But the artists themselves could hardly see this; they left the Mezh feeling that their whole world had caved in, and they could not imagine what would arise to replace it. The day after the sale, they organized a steamer trip to protest Western commercialism: partly out of anger, partly out of fear, and partly out of sheer confusion. There is a tradition of boat trips among the members of the vanguard. In 1987, Sven Gundlakh—one of the seven Furmanny artists—founded a rock group called Middle Russian Elevation. Other artists, including Sergey Vorontsov, Sergey Volkov, Dmitriy Prigov, and Nikola Ovchinnikov, played with the group, which reconceived habitual visual ironies in musical terms. They exploited every aspect of official Soviet rock music and of received wisdom about rock performance in the U.S.S.R. and in the West. In their playfulness, they came up with some catchy tunes that made them a popular underground group. Tapes of their performances were passed from hand to hand, and they soon had a devoted following—though, as Sven has said, it is unclear whether any of the followers were fully aware that the purpose of the group was ironical. Soon they began to win prizes at musical festivals. Of course this amused them to no end; it was the culmination of their ironies. But it did not amuse the authorities, and in the spring of 1987 they forbade Sven to appear on any stage in Moscow.

Artists outside the narrow confines of officialdom have always had to seek out places to meet, and they have on various occasions been banned from the public and private spaces of Moscow. Sven took to the water. He and those around him hired a large steamer on which they could perform without sullying the soil of Moscow, and about two hundred fifty friends came along for the ride and the performance. Middle Russian Elevation's big hit song was "Moscow Is the Third Rome," after the cry of the medieval Russian monks, who warned that when Rome had fallen, Constantinople had come to power, and that the fall of Constantinople left Moscow the third, and last, Rome. Sven, of course, was also making a mockery of Stalin's vision of Moscow as the center of the world, a city which must be remade on the grandest scale ever known so that it could lead the communist revolution, which, like the triumph of Christianity, would save the world. So in the spring of 1987 he hired a boat and set off down the Moskva/Volga Channel, the group singing, "Moscow is the third Rome! There won't be a fourth!" They accompanied their singing with a hand gesture with three fingers. Their trip was an act of defiance; in those early days of glasnost, the defiance was tolerated, and the boat became a symbol of freedom and protest. It sailed to a resort area ordinarily used by collective farms for their holiday excursions, and everyone took great delight, on their subversive day out, in strolling past the truest lifeblood of communism; they laughed at the workers, but enjoyed the same views and used the same picnic tables, accomplishing, in this way, the most profound subversion of all.

All that happened almost exactly a year before the sale, and so the boat ride the day after the sale was not without historical resonance. This time there was no music, but there was an enormous crowd, since everyone in the Moscow art world was in touch and in town for Sotheby's; some artists from Leningrad were also in evidence, and all the Western journalists who could be dredged up were eagerly asked along. We assembled at the docks at about noon. The familiar faces were there; a spirit of guarded festivity ruled. On the upper deck, people greeted one another much as the members of the Sotheby's tour had greeted one another the evening of the sale: with the quiet enthusiasm appropriate to people in a protracted series of meetings or reunions. The boat pushed out into the channel that joins the Moskva and Volga rivers; this channel, as wide as the Hudson River, was built by hard labor under Stalin, and the bones of the men who died during its construction are said to line its bottom—so said by Sven Gundlakh, at least, with a good measure of enthusiasm.

The journalists polarized the situation even further than it would have been polarized by circumstance. Nervous little Grisha Bruskin sat on the upper deck trying to look at the view; he had no chance of talking to other Soviets. A journalist from *Vanity Fair* who had cornered him conducted his interview in a suspicious and proprietary way, hoping that he would get the real scoop on this most important artist before anyone else got in on the act. Viktor Miziano, then the curator of contemporary art at the Pushkin, who had invited me along on the boat, made a great effort to introduce people to artists who hadn't been in the sale. His countenance was grave and his carriage was gracious as he tried to orchestrate conversations much as though the people around him were guests at a cocktail party. His status at the Pushkin has always made him a figure between the official and unofficial worlds, and his remarkable fluency in a variety of languages has given him a certain ease in negotiations with the West; that in turn has sometimes made him an object of suspicion to the artists. Here Miziano made every polite effort to negotiate those around him into neutrality.

But he did so with limited success. There was a certain separation among the artists. Those who had done too well stood at a distance from the others. Figures such as Josif Bakshteyn, who had organized many of the intimate exhibitions put on in the years immediately preceding the sale, were busy indicating their importance to the shape of the Moscow art world, but to no avail; in the eyes of the West, at least for the moment, only the painters themselves were important. One of the decisions made by Sotheby's was that they would sell only flat paintings; conceptual work, installations, even sculpture were all excluded from the sale. What was the new status of conceptualism? Josif organized a press conference—I think he liked the importance of the words—and he assembled a panel to sit at the front of the boat. Everyone began asking questions at once, but there were no answers to the real questions: Are you happy about the sale? Was it a good thing? It was hard to hear, and people kept raising their voices. Jamey Gambrell, an American critic who had been writing about Soviet art for years, was acting as translator, but she had a bad cold and was trying to yell over the crowd with only partial success; everyone interrupted her and demanded attention, bellowing in both languages.

As the press conference crescendoed to a fevered pitch, as Vadim Zakharov launched into a complex and theoretical response to someone's question, the boat reached the shore. And the tension broke. Disembarking, we found ourselves on a grassy bank. The celebrating parties from communal farms were scattered about, going through the sort of rituals that are popular in America on the last day of summer camp—giving prizes, eating food cooked outdoors, singing songs in uneven harmony, wearing costumes, dancing bashfully, and then running down to the water to swim. Moscow workers promenaded along the narrow paths, men and women holding hands and breathing the fresh country air. The sun was shining, and the people all looked their best, but they also looked like figures from Socialist Realist paintings.

The effect on the Soviet artists was magical. As sophisticated New Yorkers will groan at the things people wear in once-fashionable nightclubs, so the Soviets exchanged knowing looks of amusement over these festivities. They laughed. They bought *shashlik* (meat on skewers cooked over an open fire) and ate it with their fingers. And then we found the boats, all in neat rows in a bay that lay beyond some pine woods and over a hill. For a few kopecks, we could rent paddleboats or rowboats, and this, with no further discussion, the artists did, while a few more peripheral figures and some of the Western journalists sat on the shore, looking out across the water. I ended up in a rowboat with Viktor Miziano and a young painter called Zhora Litichevskiy. Zhora, wearing a white fur hat and a Russian peasant shirt, white cotton embroidered at the neck, proved a strong oarsman, and soon we were out in the channel, which is in that area so wide one can hardly see the far shore. We rowed, and we called to those who were left on the shore; we called to the artists in other boats.

Fun overtook us. Artists raced with one another up and down and across the water. People beached their boats and clambered up the hill, or collected people standing on the bank who hadn't known where to go for boats. We stole one another's paddles, or tried to capsize one another, or splashed one another. Everyone got wet. Everyone bellowed with enthusiasm, while in the background could be seen the thick-limbed members of some commune or factory putting on a pantomime. Viktor Miziano, in my boat, remained calm throughout. He would point to someone who was shaking the water out of his eyes, about to take revenge on those who had capsized his boat, and say, "That is Oleg Kotelnikov. He is an important Leningrad conceptualist." Or else he would point to a boat that had drawn off at some distance and was about to rush into the fray and say, "That

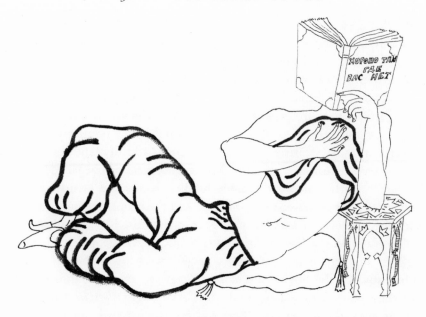

GEORGIY (ZHORA) LITICHEVSKIY: *Self-Portrait as Sheherezade*
(reading a book entitled: *It Is Good Where You Are Not*)

is Yuriy Albert, who is a highly serious post-modernist, in the Soviet
sense of the word."

Eventually, damp and happy, we all congregated again on the
shore. And then the playful jibes began—"If you think that because
your work sold yesterday you can capsize *my* boat, you're certainly
wrong." It was only banter, but it had been enriched with a whole
new series of references. And when we got back on the big boat, there
was a round-table discussion among the leading figures who had gone
out that day, a protracted and serious debate in Russian that went on
a bit relentlessly. Younger artists sat in the sun above, trying to dry
off. A few of the oldest figures went to sleep. And in one seat upstairs,
poor Grisha Bruskin, who had most decidedly not been out in a
paddleboat, continued to talk to the man from *Vanity Fair,* and to
make appointments with the other journalists who were flocking
around him.

Grisha Bruskin's situation was repeated a thousand times at a thousand levels, and though he himself was then and has continued to be
singularly unsubtle in his negotiations with the press and with collectors and curators, proving himself as simple in his conceptions as
many in Moscow had supposed him to be, other artists were able to

locate in these meetings of Soviet and foreign minds an inspiring challenge. Secrecy always remained a priority. With time, the artists became increasingly expert at providing for the West a rhetoric with which to criticize their work; they articulated frames of meaning that were intentional versions of their sometimes-fortuitous surface resemblance to Western art, on the assumption that anything that works on an accessible level will neither be abandoned nor be too wholly penetrated. In the simplest terms, Soviet artists in the spring of 1988 had learned that they could mask the true meaning of their work behind one that the West could easily grasp, and so could achieve popularity without giving up their secrets. With exquisite fluidity, they exchanged the false insignificance of fiction—their old stance, taken for the benefit of the authorities—for an insufficient philosophy —the patter-songs they performed for visitors to their studios. The artists explained the level of the work which amused them the most; it would be as though someone who painted and made jigsaw puzzles were to explain only how the pieces fit together, without reference to the original image or to how it had been taken apart.

Analyzing this situation, of course, placed the Western critic in a deeply problematic position, for these distinctions invited the formulation of a false canon, in which influence itself could be traced along lines of stunning irrelevance. Nadya Burova, wife of the poet and artist Dmitriy Prigov, told me of an occasion in the seventies when a group of artists in Moscow first saw Andy Warhol's Marilyn Monroe prints. Monroe's face meant nothing to them, but they had never before seen photo–silk screens, and they were amazed by Warhol's technical accomplishment. Here, they concluded, lay the merit of this much-discussed Western artist. And just as the Soviet artists took from Warhol something we forget he had, they take from one another meanings even more obscure to us than Marilyn's image was to them. Our traditional canon is based on the issues and events relevant to Western art. It concedes that we can never decisively pin down the full significance of any given work, but it nonetheless seeks to identify, in a consistent manner, historical influences. The critic observing Soviet art from the outside could find valid connections that were, from the Soviet standpoint, tantamount to our confining our examination of Warhol to his connection with all other artists who have used silk screen.

Of course the easiest thing to lose sight of when a work is cut off from its maker is its irony; the Sotheby's buyers and the Western press were almost always blind to that terrifically significant aspect of the work they confronted, and their blindness became an issue for the artists. What could be done with people who came not to decode entangled acts of communication, but to judge the aesthetic and conceptual successes of the work they encountered? For such judgment was more than impossible; it was entirely beside the point. In the eyes of the Soviet artists, Western critics' yen for a canon was closely tied to the buying public's yen for overt politics (Soviet art that deals in obvious ways with issues like oppression seems more authentic to many Western buyers, and did well at the sale), and to the Ministry of Culture's pleasure in satisfying both. After years of consistently suppressing any hints of subversiveness, the Soviet government had begun to take delight in the way subversiveness could capture both the imagination and the hard currency of capitalism. Was the only truly subversive gesture left an unironic return to Socialist Realist painting of the happy-farmers-atop-a-tractor sort, simply because such work would be utterly unmarketable? (Within a year or two, this work too would become marketable for its kitsch value.) Or was it possible to do work in which all the layers of meaning remained undisturbed under cover of total simplicity, and so to be left in peace? It must be remembered that the overtly and explicitly political art produced by some members of the Soviet avant-garde at that time escaped being a simple continuation of the invented mode of Socialist Realism only when the play between the politics "described" by the painting and the politics of painting itself confronted one another. A canon that privileges work of explicit political content over work whose ideology was more intuitively derived and expressed would trivialize grossly the significance of both practices in a nation where the very act of lifting a paintbrush could carry the onus of putative treachery.

This is the dilemma I faced: to rest content with the assertion that Soviet art is by definition incomprehensible to anyone outside the Soviet avant-garde seemed useless; but at the same time, to formulate a canon based on misapprehensions was clearly idiotic. The few critics operating within the Soviet avant-garde had disciplined themselves to speak of the art as though they had come from outside, and were judging only formally. But their canon reflected the infrastructure of the avant-garde in which they had achieved their maturity. Was it reasonable for Western critics to throw out the Soviet canon and formulate one entirely their own? Or should the West simply acknowledge total ignorance and fill up museums on the word of the artists themselves? The Soviets, recognizing the problem, perhaps tried to pave the way toward a third solution: the coexistence of two canons—one Western, one Soviet—with some overlap and many inconsistencies—accepting, as they still do, that it is best not to communicate too much and not to be too well understood.

In the realization of this doppelgänger agenda, the West has made itself ridiculous. Throughout its pursuit of vanguard Soviet art, the West has paid high prices for work without knowing the process as part of which it was made. The Sotheby's sale was only the noisiest version of a general phenomenon. The situation has changed as the artists have changed; but this basic misinformed impulse is intact. And it is absurd. We might as well opt for beauty. To fail to judge a work of art on the basis of how it functions in the world and in the experience of its viewers—independent of the artist's personal claims for it—is to lose its very essence. For Soviet art, an insistence on a multiplicity of truths is as political as the act of painting, while acceptance of a single and easy truth is an old habit of Stalinism. Thus it is the nature of the Soviet artists' elusiveness itself—rather than the thing eluded—that must be the focus of any critical effort, and that is why sociological examination is a highly apposite way to proceed. It is, in short, valid to applaud brilliance of disguise; it is comical to applaud the disguise itself.

This is ultimately the locus not only of meaning, but also of affect. Much of the evasiveness of these artists is founded in what seems to the West to be exaggerated paranoia. Self-indulgent anthems to the courage and "risk-taking" of artistic expression, no matter what the attendant rigors may be in any given time or place, are familiar tunes in Western art. But the fact was that the work of the gifted artists of the U.S.S.R. brought much-needed Western currency into the country when freedom of expression was only another provisional experiment in the continuing quest for food and industrial goods. There was always too much at stake, and too much to lose, for the visionaries in this company to give up their evasions. Bred to believe that what is worth saying cannot be said, these artists learned that what can be said can be reduced, and can cease to be worth saying. When I arrived in Moscow, I encountered artists approaching the turning point, between mistrust as an intuitive response and mistrust as an intentional system. It was good luck that allowed me to sidestep that mistrust, but it has been more than bad luck that has led so many of the people collecting and exhibiting this work to make fools of themselves.

I had had some hints of this by the time I went on the boat ride, and it all gelled the following day, Saturday, the day I was stood up by the Ministry of Culture, the day when I first began to feel that I was in the thick of things, when it dawned on me that what these people did indicated more than how their paintings looked. On Sunday, as I had agreed to do, I went to a train station for Monastyrskiy's Action, about which I knew nothing. At ten-thirty that morning, the thrall of my eighteen hours of discourse had waned, and my insights seemed blurry and insignificant. I had slept four hours, and it was not enough. I had not really understood what was going to be going on at the train station, and I felt very nervous about trying to find it on my own.

The station was enormous. When I arrived there was no sign of any of the artists I was supposed to meet. I had been told that something would happen beneath the station clock, and my understanding was that we were to meet there. I had expected to find dozens of artists milling about at the station, looking purposeful; what I saw instead were the untold thousands who are always milling about in Soviet train stations, looking like a vast herd of unshepherded sheep. I was a few minutes late. Had I missed the train? Were we taking a train? A train where? A few minutes later I spied Andrey Filippov and Kostya Zvezdochetov, and they spied me. "Hello," they said, and handed me a train ticket. They too, I thought, had lost some of the wild excess of enthusiasm of the night before; I felt almost that I might be imposing, and was unsure whether I had been wise to come.

We were to take a train. We got on board, about thirty of us in all. Josif Bakshteyn, whom I had met at Ira Nakhova's house and on the boat, greeted me and motioned me to a seat on the carriage next to a painter I had also met earlier, Igor Kopystyanskiy. "Where are we going?" I asked Igor. "Only Josif knows," he replied. "What exactly are we going to do?" "It's an Action. None of us know yet what will be there. You'll see," said Igor. The train pulled out of the station, and as it left, Josif came and tapped me on the shoulder. He put a finger across his lips to enforce silence, and led me between two cars, where we stood in a strong wind and a terrible din, bouncing somewhat uncomfortably. "Try not to let anyone know you are from the West," he said. "Don't speak English. You are not officially supposed to be on this train, and you have no visa for where we are

going. I don't think there will be a problem, but don't do anything
that might attract attention. Now come and sit down." And he led
me back down the carriage and deposited me again next to Igor, who
began chatting away in English. I simply shook my head and tried to
keep my face low. But I wished that someone had warned me in
advance that I was embarking on something illegal; at that time, I
still thought it was within the bounds of possibility to spend time in
Moscow and stay strictly within the limits of the law. In fact, ordinary
daily life inevitably involves the violation of dozens of laws—if they
want to get you for some reason, there are always enough excuses, and
if they don't, then your trespasses are ignored. Even so, it is best not
to be too obvious about the things you do contrary to the received
standards; if I had known I was to go into a forbidden territory, I
might not have worn a peach-colored polo shirt and espadrilles, and I
might not have carried a camera and a high-tech-looking tape recorder
with me.

We were on that train for nearly two hours. People sat in relative
silence, even though they were Soviet and were not doing anything
illegal; there was a feeling of keen suspense to the whole thing. We
went through miles of industrial suburbs, and then through further
miles of irregular countryside. Each time the train slowed, eyes would
turn toward Josif, who would shake his head and strike a beatifically
calm face, his profile as dignified as one on a Roman coin. Josif is an
organizer, and I have come to think of him as an energizer as well.
He describes himself as a critic, but he has written relatively little; he
has curated various exhibitions in Moscow, and more recently in the
West, some of them very good indeed. He arranges things and sets
things up and finds the space to realize big ideas that have been
collectively conceived. One of the most maddening things about Soviets is that they don't get things done; Josif Baksteyn, by hook or
by crook, does get things done, and his favorite game is to look
modestly at his accomplishments, so long as you are aware that their
simplicity belies none of the contortion involved in their realization
in Moscow, and to say, "It's good, yes?"

As we approached the appointed station, Josif came down the aisle,
tapping us and motioning toward the door. The station itself was as
inexplicable as anything else: it stood in the middle of nowhere like
an installation in the woods. One could not imagine that anyone had
ever had occasion to use it before, or that anyone would have occasion
to use it again. We stepped off the platform into the thickness of a

pine forest; single file, we walked between the trees down a narrow path. This, I was told in a hoarse whisper, was an Action, by the Collective Action Group (K/D), and the mystery was part of it all. As we walked, we talked a bit in low voices, sometimes laughing, waiting to see what would happen. We were waiting to meet Andrey Monastyrskiy, leader of K/D, whom we expected at every turning. After the first bit of wood came great fields of corn, with odd tumble-down houses beyond them; then came a wood of birches, a lake surrounded by reeds newly gone to seed, and then a pine wood with stolid trunks rising from a perfectly smooth floor. All the Moscow vanguard, the many faces of genius and the eager eyes of the hangers-on, walked like a silent parade through a pine wood as still as dawn.

At the end of the wood we came into a field with a river running through it; on the river there were Soviet fishermen in rubber boats, casting their lines and watching with some puzzlement, but not much interest, the procession of artists. Then at last we came to a rise, and there we stopped, stood in a row, and watched the river. Soon we saw an artist, Georgiy Kizevalter, standing by the water. He jumped in, swam across, and disappeared on the other side, and we watched the spot where he had disappeared. Then he returned to the water's edge, carrying a huge flat package, with which he leapt back in, and swam back. He went to a hill opposite our rise, where he was joined by Andrey Monastyrskiy (at last) and another artist. They took the brightly colored outer wrapping off the package to reveal a black-and-white painting. Then, carefully, they took out the nails that held the canvas to the stretcher, and laid the canvas on the ground. They took apart the stretcher, which was of complicated design, until they had only strips of wood; then they wrapped the wood in the canvas, and wrapped that in the outer covering. Monastyrskiy distributed Xerox copies of the painting to the onlookers.

All the while, on a hill behind us, a bell was ringing in a blue box, and no one heard it.

That was it. Two hours there, two hours yet to spend on the journey back (not to mention the time going to and from the train station) and ten minutes of what seemed to be ponderously self-important performance art. But there was more to the Action than that. When the performance was over, all the artists sat down on the hill and took out cucumbers and tomatoes and loaves of bread and pieces of cheese, and we ate. Someone told me about the bell in the box, and then someone else began to explain how every Action related to all the previous Actions. K/D had been founded in 1976, and one of the most important Actions had taken place in the late seventies on the very spot where we found ourselves more than ten years later. In this earlier Action, hundreds of balloons had been collected and put into a single larger sack, like a greater balloon, and the whole thing had been set to float down the river in which Georgiy Kizevalter had just been swimming. The painting that had just been deconstructed—as it were —represented that earlier Action, and the Xeroxes that we had were of the painting itself, in black and white because it was painted from a photograph taken by Kizevalter himself at the earlier Action, an Action that Monastyrskiy had conceived as a pure comment on the status of the Soviet artists. The bell in the box had been present at an even earlier Action, one of the first, and at a few Actions since. In fact each reference to earlier Actions was layered and intercepted by references to later ones, and to ones that encompassed early and late ones.

This explanation was provided to me by several people, usually speaking at once and sometimes interrupting one another. The most coherent description was provided by Sergey Anufriev, an Odessa-born artist and a leader of Medgermenevtika (Medical Hermeneutics), a movement founded on the notion that artists need not create art, but can amply fill their days and realize their ambitions by commenting on the art of those around them. Anufriev is dark and rather good-looking, and he shaves his head halfway up the crown, to create the effect of an abnormally high forehead. He has a tense smoothness of manner, at once swaggering and uncertain. At that time, he was twenty-four years old; when the original Action took place, he was not older than fourteen.

How then could he possibly have remembered, even if he had been at the Action—as, indeed, he was not; at the time that it took place he was living in the Ukraine—all this amazing detail? Some of it had been brought home by other, later Actions, but that was not the full explanation. For these artists, the repetition at one Action of what had happened in the course of another one was almost ritual. I, asking questions at the picnic, was playing a role almost as traditional as that of the bell in the blue box, and for Anufriev, one of the youngest of the acolytes, to be the one appointed to explain everything to me was only appropriate. Of course his version of history was the most coherent and lucid: he was the one who had learned this history as a history, bridging whatever gaps there might have been. His perception, like mine, was synthetic; from the rambling stories he had been told he had put together something solid and palpable.

GEORGIY KIZEVALTER: *The Cat in the Bag Wept* (Author's note: Kizevalter has conflated two common Russian expressions here. To say that someone has bought "the cat in the bag" is to say that he has got something without knowing what it is. To say that "the cat wept" is to say that there is virtually nothing; you might use the expression if, for example, you were to look for bread in your kitchen and find only a single stale crust. The work has been read as a comment on glasnost.)

The repetition of history is a part of any religious ritual, and the Actions are like part of a religion. Each one serves to confirm and justify what has come before, and to pave the way for what will come next. I saw Georgiy Kizevalter swim across a narrow stream on a chilly day, but the other spectators saw the continuation of a narrative that was very much part of their lives. Furthermore, they confirmed their own status as members of the group, not only because they had been invited, but also because they understood the apparently meaningless spectacle that was unfolding before them. Each one understood a different amount and to a different degree, and each of them was aware of understanding references to what they had heard of, and to what they had experienced.

The Actions gave meaning to the community they encompassed, and to which they made constant reference. But they also confirmed community in the most mundane way: there we all were, having a picnic together, way out in the countryside. It could have been a school field trip or a meeting of the Boy Scouts. People shared their bread and their cucumbers and their cheese. People exchanged greetings. Because it was the weekend after the Sotheby's sale, artists who lived in other cities were in Moscow; this was a festive reunion for them, a reunion with a purpose. But it did something else as well. I was not the only visitor from the West who came along to the Action. Some German artists who wanted to work with the Soviets were there. Another American critic was there. An American documentary filmmaker was there with her crew. Moscow was crawling with aficionados and experts from the West.

Our egos were held in check. We were reminded that no matter how engrossed we might have become in Soviet art, no matter how kind and receptive some of the artists might have been, we were still in a place whose strangeness would never be entirely uncloaked for us. Nothing you do, the Action seemed to taunt us, can make you a part of what has happened in this country. You could move here tomorrow, and you would still never be able to say: I was at the early Actions, and so I understand in the dark recesses of my soul what these endless references mean. Sergey Anufriev was not at the center in the way that Georgiy Kizevalter was, but he was closer than the interlopers from the West could ever be. Whether you like us or not, whether we like you or not, is irrelevant, the Action flung at us. You can come so far and no farther.

The train ride back was long and silent. We were all tired, and the artists themselves were looking at one another in a new light, because the sale had finally happened. The Action had been planned before the sale; in a funny way, it was the last event that confirmed the community of artists before the strange events surrounding Sotheby's shattered and shifted the fragile world they had touched. I think the possibility that this would prove to be so sank in while we were going back into Moscow, and everyone sensed the implicit sadness of a belated but eloquent conclusion to what was familiar. As for the new thing beginning, the unfamiliar, it had already proved monstrous— but perhaps it was also good? "Maybe yes," Josif Bakshteyn said to me when I asked, back at the station in Moscow. "Maybe." By nightfall on Sunday, I was tired, but I was also in the thick of this new world, brave since before it was new, and invested with a fervor and intensity of purpose that would, so far as I could see, only grow during the days ahead in Moscow.

So far as I could see was perhaps not so very far. When I came to Moscow, this community's innocence was already past its blossoming; Sotheby's was only the apotheosis of a process that had started years earlier. The days of pure purpose, the days when intensity was on the upswing, were in the late seventies and the very early eighties. Even if one puts that aside, however, sentimentality about these people and their lives, about the community of Soviet artists, is inapposite. It is true that they produced great works by building a brilliantly inviolable world, but it is also true that they were capable of great pettiness before the West came their way, and that there are dozens of stories of nasty or disagreeable things that people did to one another well before the evil powers of commercialism made themselves felt. The West and its values gave a greater weight to unattractive impulses, made it possible to realize those that might otherwise have been held always in abeyance; but it did not create those impulses. They came from the people themselves. It is too easy to allow one's admiration for people whose circumstances are alien to blunt one's insight, and I know that I have often found myself rationalizing my uninformed instincts about people in Moscow with the foreigner's prerogative to abstain from harsh judgment. Easy judgments in this circumstance, as elsewhere, are a mistake; but even extraordinary circumstances are made of and by flawed people. One's own flaws are the most intolerable, and the worst of these can be suffered only when they are referred to outside circumstance. Protesting Western commercialism is part of a system that blames the West both for the problems it has created and for the problems within.

At the same time, whether you have come from the West or not, you are hard-pressed not to involve yourself in some of the internal discord. "You like him?" you are constantly asked: it is a test, a question that requires a correct one-word answer or an exegesis which the auditors will usually deem ignorant. More times than I would care to remember I explained neutrally that a critic must meet everyone and judge for himself only when he knew enough to judge. But the onus of unfortunate associations clings heavily in Moscow. "If you don't like him, why spend time with him?" they ask; you devalue your friendship significantly every time you share it anew. And when, in this black-and-white-and-gray world, you are seen in conference with men of darkest charcoal, you undermine altogether your other friendships, and must set about reconstructing them; in this society, no one talked to the KGB or to the Union bigwigs because they were interesting. Insofar as possible, they talked only to the people who were on their side, and kept everyone else steeped in ignorance. If you come from the outside and refuse to subscribe immediately to this system, you undermine your own position; more subtlely, you undermine the position of those insiders whose judgments you seem to reject, and you stir up trouble by giving people who had preserved a mutual anonymity something in common.

The closed system was not simply a matter of defensiveness. Artists suffered in the days of Brezhnev, and in the days of Khrushchev, and in the days of Stalin. They suffered in a way in which they no longer suffer. I used to be startled constantly by the offhand way in which someone would say, "That was the year I was in Siberia," or, "That happened only after my parents were able to leave the prison camp," or "He was the doctor who kept me in the mental hospital." Such eventualities were constantly present, and though most of the artists managed not to be shipped off anywhere, the possibility transformed their daily lives. The closest metaphor from the West is of disease. We all live in fear of disease; it haunts us in those moments of silence when we search for a reason behind the lingering semiconscious panic that so easily blooms into existential crisis. Until recently, everyone in the U.S.S.R. has lived in similar nagging, essentially irrational, but not wholly groundless fear of the powers that be: they were a horrible thing that could come upon you with no warning and for no reason. To extend the metaphor: people who have had a disease that tends to be recurrent, or who are unusually prone—cancer patients, for example, or people in high-risk AIDS categories—live with a different kind of fear. They are constantly monitoring themselves, constantly being tested, knowing every day how strong a chance there is that the news will be bad. They crowd their minds and think of other things, but when everything else goes, there is fear to revert to, and the suggestion that the fear is groundless falls on deaf ears: this fear is sound. The situation of Soviet artists paralleled this. Their mindset, their opinions, and their work were like the physical situation of such people, and exposed them to greater reason for fear than that experienced by ordinary Soviets. The irony was that their work and their membership in the community of artists were also the distraction that kept that fear at bay. They were like people who smoke to distract themselves from the possibility of lung cancer, and in whose smoking lies all their genius.

All that is, for the moment, over. The change has been ineffable and inestimable. Of course there are still difficulties and inconveniences; there is the possibility that the current liberalization will end in a dramatic clampdown of the Tienanmen Square variety; but for the moment, at least, the fear is diffused. Since the change may be temporary, it reaches only halfway into anyone's self-regard; it is important not to lose the habits of fear, which might one day be useful again. But there is more here than a simple instinct of self-preservation. The artists miss their fear, even if they do not miss its reasons, in both real and associative ways.

It is difficult for a community united in opposition to something to find reason to be united once the object of its opposition is gone; that has been the basis of the great crisis in Soviet art. But more important than that is the love for the past simply because it is the past, the sorrow of finding that what has already taken place cannot take place again in the same way or for the same reasons. In this context, every transformation is a sorrow, and the artists' assuaged fear becomes as great a sorrow as any. Fear fostered a kind of love among these people that tranquillity cannot inspire; it reached into their most deep and distant and truest selves and pulled from the center of each an entirely singular vision, a particular belief in the way the world works. Solipsism inevitably comes into play; if you would keep fear from destroying you, you must persuade yourself that you are more important and stronger than the object of your fear, and a self-obsessed optimism is the easiest way to do that. When the artists eventually came to the West, that solipsism too often translated as arrogance. And of course arrogance is there; but so too is something better than arrogance. It was arrogant to stage a boat ride the day after the sale, to invite all the journalists who had gone to the sale out to see not only that the artists disliked this intrusion more than they liked it, but also that they were quite capable of having a good time in their own way, without engaging with the West at all. An enviably good time: the paddleboats were delightful, and they made the British grandeur of the week's events seem rather imbecile. But beyond the arrogance was grim determination that had at last found its object. Their self-reliance sent chill waves of self-satisfaction through them; they were in no sense dependent on their new circumstances, any more than they had been on their previous ones. They had refused to sell themselves to escape intimidation; neither would they be bought with dollars and pounds sterling. As for fear—they were making their habitual point that they had nothing to be afraid of; the notion that there *was* really nothing for them to fear was too new to cut through their bias of personality. For them, the West was the latest alien force in their lives; they would neither fear nor love it, and it would not change them. Fear is most often about change.

But there is something more. The fear itself was not then and is not now entirely gone, even when the future is not brought into play. Because if you have been afraid enough for long enough, then you cannot stop being afraid. The love these artists feel for the past is in many ways also a love for the present; they have defined themselves as separate from the world beyond them, and they are still separate from it, however much it improves. This is their defense against change. They were separate from the journalists on the boat, separate from the Sotheby's people, separate from the Ministry of Culture, and separate also from the communal farmers and the factory workers who were promenading in the park we visited. Separate lives are lives of fear. These artists are not prone to integration into their own society or into the one beyond. Their powerful self-definition is the subject of their work.

The great bravery of this, and the equally great pettiness that is perhaps the inevitable weakness of any internally defined community, are constantly manifest. There is no point trying to describe all the artists of the Moscow unofficial art world; there are too many of them, too many whom I met and too many whom I did not meet, too many who were introduced to me on my first trip to Moscow and too many who emerged later. Even now, three years later, I am still constantly hearing names in conversation that I have never heard before. "Oh, he's not a bad artist, I think a friend of Nikola's," someone will explain if I ask. Like all groups that appear to be tightly defined, this one has blurred margins that fade into nothingness over a range of increasingly peripheral figures. "Come," someone will say, "and meet two very good artists who live near Kashirskaya." I wonder why I have never heard of them before. "Only recently we have realized that they are very good artists. Also, it was a problem, I thought if you liked Misha's work then perhaps you would not like this work. But now I think you will, maybe." And so, on a note of maybe, yet another vista will open before me.

Some of the elder statesmen of the vanguard were not in Moscow when I first came, and some of them I simply could not reach. Ilya Kabakov had refused to receive anyone on grounds that he was too tired to see people from the West, though I met him many times in the months that followed. Andrey Monastyrskiy I met the day of the Action, but I did not get to talk to him at any length until almost a year later. Ivan Chuykov I met only much later. But I did see Dima Prigov and Erik Bulatov during that first visit to Moscow. Prigov was introduced to me the day of the sale; he was in the milling horde closely packed at the back of the saleroom. His focus and intensity of purpose seemed to separate him from that mob; he was the first person to say to me, "If you come to my house, I will explain our art for you." And so, some days later, I did go to his house.

Prigov has military features animated with his tremendous energy: a closely trimmed beard, large square glasses tinted just slightly yellow, hair cut very short, and a constant look of strain in the muscles of his face and neck. He brings a prodigious, sometimes exhausting fervor to any subject of conversation; it is as though he is in constant brave battle with the complexity of life itself, staying on top of daily routine only by dint of this outpouring of mental activity. For Prigov, art is the exposition of a philosophy of communication; verbal and visual language meet in his work as though no single means could carry the weight of all there is to say. He is a poet; widely acclaimed as one of the best in the U.S.S.R., he finds himself hopelessly hemmed in by the Soviet system—though it provides him with his truest subject—and has written:

In Japan I would have been Catullus
And in Rome I would have been Hokusai
And in Russia I am the one
Who in Japan—Catullus
And in Rome—Hokusai
Would have
Been.

His works on paper are strange and compressed, a concentrate of his ideas. There is a series of drawings of beasts, done with liquid-ink pens—each drawing exhausts three or four of these—in a mystic system as complex as any alchemical chart. These are phenomenally detailed, inverted, covered in writing and decorated with strange figures. Prigov never speaks simply as himself, but is always in an adopted persona. When he does beasts, he is a monk. When he does monumental single words on sheets of newspaper, with the same meticulous edges and the same wondrous variety of shadings, he is a social commentator. When he does installations, usually also with newspaper, he is a politician. When he writes poems, he is in other adopted modes: sometimes a prisoner, sometimes a communist, sometimes a woman. The real Prigov is the sum of these selves. When, more than a year later, I went to his house for dinner on his birthday, he greeted me with the news that he was forty-nine years old and had become a post-cultural self.

Prigov's wife, Nadya, came with me to translate when I went to see Erik Bulatov. Bulatov and Kabakov, Kabakov and Bulatov, Bulatov and Kabakov: they are the names one most often hears in the West as the great names in Soviet art. They were the first to appear in the Venice Biennale (in 1988); they were the first to have one-man shows in Switzerland (Kabakov in 1985 and Bulatov in 1988); they were the first to appear in the Centre Pompidou in Paris. When Nadya and I went to see Bulatov, he was trying to teach himself English, and he had papered the walls of his studio with words in English above and in Russian below, so that behind his paintings there appeared strange fragments of information: "To Go," "The Woman," "Blue," they said.

His paintings appear to be similarly straightforward. One might mistake them for Socialist Realism if not warned to look more deeply; among his best-known works is a portrait of Brezhnev as a cosmonaut, in which the great leader stares blankly from the canvas with the

DMITRIY (DIMA) PRIGOV: *Installation for a Cleaning Woman* (The text at the lower right reads, "Suddenly, she sees a hole in the midst of all that usually surrounds her, and she falls down on her knees and starts to moan, "Oh, oh, oh!"")

portentous look he has in posters made during his years in power. Bulatov's paintings are about space, about the relationship between the two-dimensional and the three-dimensional. They have a rigorous visual formula to which they almost invariably adhere: there is a plane, and there is a domain beyond that plane, usually behind it—though in *Brezhnev as a Cosmonaut* the domain is in front of the plane. Often the plane is articulated by the monumental letters that have become one of Bulatov's most distinctive motifs; Prigov is interested in the tension between language and form, but Bulatov is interested in language as form, in the way that the letters themselves define the space they occupy. Beyond the plane there is a more distant space, whose boundary seems not to be recognized by the figures within it, and it is here that the viewer is both privileged and excluded; he has the superior knowledge that there *is* a boundary, but he is unable to penetrate beyond it and enter into the vivid pictorial space. The variations on this are myriad, but the formula is simplest in Bulatov's earlier work. The painting *Danger,* of 1972–73, shows a group of attractive people having a picnic in a perfect landscape; they are portrayed like the happy mindless figures of Socialist Realism. Painted in front of them, on a foreground picture plane, is the word "danger," written four times to form a square, as it would appear on a road sign. The viewer actually knows that the idyllic scene is a dangerous one, as the dream of Socialist Realism *is* dangerous, and he experiences the frustration of being unable to warn the blithe picnickers. At the same time, however, he experiences another frustration, that of being unable to join their cheery repast, both because of the visual/physical barrier of the words and because of the knowledge that to do so would be folly. Bulatov does not describe for the viewer the frustration of knowing too much in a paralyzing system that precludes any useful response to that knowledge (the typical Soviet situation), but rather re-creates it, so that the viewer actually undergoes the experience to which the painting refers. He finds that his knowledge has lost him the easy pleasures of communality and a belief in his own freedom, but has been inadequate to locate the real freedom for which he searches. He has lost two ways at once.

Bulatov's work is painterly; its philosophies rise out of visual form. Kabakov has the greatest conceptual vision and the truest humanism of any of the Soviet artists. Monastyrskiy has perhaps the clearest intellect; he and Kabakov have each defined a dramatic mysticism, and work from its center. Prigov's work functions on the most mul-

tidimensional level. Younger artists are indebted to these artists in
varying degrees, but the strongest influence in the best new work is
from Kabakov and Monastyrskiy. The behavior that initial contact
with the West made a necessity, keeping the world in abeyance, varied
among the generations; it still differs for older and younger artists,
though the terms of that difference have become somewhat harder to
define. The elder statesmen were trapped between their urgent desire
to clarify the context of their work and their deeply self-conscious
sense of responsibility to the artistic community they had helped to
shape. Their belief in the high seriousness of their project was too
strong to permit them to construct illusory significances for their
work, but their attempts to fill in the gaps for foreign viewers tended
to culminate in works about the frustration of an impossible task. The
younger generation divided itself into groups that were both social
and intellectual—the Furmanny artists, the members of Medgermenevtika (Medical Hermeneutics), the remnants of the Kindergarten,
the Champions of the World. The trope of disguised meaning, though
operative in both generations, was most fully acknowledged by these
younger artists. Their dignity lay in their refusal to make an easy
package for viewers; they would neither programmatically blur the
line between personality and persona, nor draw a single reductive
correspondence between the two.

Loosely included in this generation were painterly, graphicist, ab-
stractionist, theoretical, intellectual, and conceptual artists. I spent
much time during my first visit to Moscow with such sober artists as
Igor Kopystyanskiy and Sveta Kopystyanskaya; she works with random meanings and textuality, and he works with the destruction and
reconstruction of paintings, with the transience of the work of art. He
has also literalized the old communist dictum that works of art should
always be useful by folding his paintings into tables and chairs. Also
serious and painterly was Andrey Royter, who had been a leader in
the movement of carefree exuberance and fun called the Kindergarten,
which had been cut short when the government destroyed the building
in which it had existed. When I met him he was doing rebus paintings
and radio paintings in which the shape of a speaker was cut into the
canvas; the work felt uprooted, as though it were searching for new
definition.

After Royter, I met Gosha Ostretsov, who was at that time causing
a stir in Moscow, wearing absurd outfits and surrealist hats, leaving
his hair so long it fell to his waist, sometimes piling it on top of his

head in a mass of paint. He claimed that his art was the art of pure communism; if you live in a communist country, he said, you must act like a communist. He maintained that his pose was not an ironic one, and took Lenin at his word with a bizarre self-dramatizing seriousness. Gosha designed tablecloths, wall hangings, clothing, and other items that were decorated to remind those who used them of communism in every aspect of daily life. Gosha has since emigrated to Paris, and is designing chalices and other jeweled items for the Catholic Church in France.

Zhora Litichevskiy, with whom I rowed the afternoon of the steamboat journey, worked, like Gosha, in a graphic mode, painting on long stretches of fabric and drawing strange cartoons and sketches. He is a classical scholar, a translator of ancient poems, a lover of Greek and Latin poetry. He had started life as a creator of comic books of blackest humor. Litichevskiy's work unites lyricism and slickness; it is an unlikely combination of the romantic and the glossy.

At the theoretical extreme was the group Medgermenevtika, whose thought was so abstract that they would not stoop to create actual works of art. Instead, they created a series of texts in which they posed as artists posing as critics, until their criticism made them artists again. There were three of them—Sergey Anufriev, Yuriy Leyderman, and Pasha Pivovarov, who calls himself Peppershteyn. They took drugs often, which irritated some of the other artists; they claimed that they were liberated in their thought in this way. Their fluid flights of rhetoric, their high abstract thinking, and their refusal to accept the normative made them the logical heirs to Monastyrskiy, the man who conceived the Actions; but they lacked his exquisite control and precision. Some of their texts were very witty, but others were just wrenchingly dull.

What I came to understand, as I met these various groups, was that the coherence of the community did not rely on a standardization of thought processes or of modes of address. The West has asked insistently what underground Soviet art looks like, and what its concerns are. Its concerns, of course, are to do with its situation, but its ways of considering that situation are as rich and various as what may occur over any several generations in the West. When the artists began to travel, their work came closer together, and some of this lunatic variety was elided. But in 1988, at the time of the Sotheby's sale, there was still an optimistic multiplicity of intentions and of meaning. The artists' knowledge of the West was limited to what they had seen in smuggled magazines. And how much meaning could be derived from that? Yuriy Avvakumov, a Moscow architect, once described the process of studying Western architecture magazines as being tantamount to pornography. "You see the picture, you imagine the building, you imagine yourself with the building, with the building in three dimensions, how you would go in and out of the building, what it would feel like around you. Your mind takes off into space, traveling through the building. And then you remember, suddenly, that you have only a picture in front of you, and that there could be gross deformities at the back, or a strange absence of sensation inside. You remember that all photography is trick photography."

So the variety of work is an extraordinary accomplishment. Most of my own time I spent in Furmanny, and with those artists who were friends of Furmanny, like Nikola Ovchinnikov, who was at that time repainting familiar paintings with new elements—a famous painting of a peasant woman with a hand pointlessly in the air was given new meaning when an oversized matchstick was put in her hand so that she could scratch her ear—and Sergey Volkov, who had not yet discovered the humor that illuminates his work today and was painting emblems designed to objectify our most fundamental values. Within Furmanny also, the artists were working in almost unrelated styles, making independent jokes of one another's meanings. Vadim Zakharov, whom I had visited with the Sotheby's group, was the great intellectual, master of a highly theoretical system. Kostya Zvezdochetov was the master storyteller and the player of games. At that time, he was working on a series of paintings of and artifacts from a mythical kingdom called Perdo, a happy land where the people worshiped rest and the female form, which resided jointly in the form of the watermelon. One day an evil vampire—who resembled a Soviet bureaucrat—came to Perdo and took away all the watermelons. For the people this was a tragedy; their joy was gone, and the color of their lives. Furthermore, they were unable to reproduce. Then a young hero came to the land, and managed to find the pipeline which supplied blood to the vampire's heart. He turned the appropriate valves, and the vampire withered. The people were saved, and their melons were returned to them. Kostya would tell the story very seriously, sometimes adding new twists or episodes to it. He would come into the main room in Furmanny dressed in a long coat of curling sheepskin and a blue hat, and announce that he was the priest of the melon. His life and his art were inextricable. His wife, Larisa, who would in the following months emerge as one of Moscow's best painters, was at that time making little clay models that looked like Mexican folk art —the sculptures I had seen my first day at Furmanny—and cooking.

The Mironenko twins, Sergey and Vladimir, were more explicitly political than the rest. Sergey had caused a big stir by creating a painting that showed him in various poses and bore the caption: "Sergey Mironenko, the first democratic candidate for presidency of the U.S.S.R." and, written below, "Mother-fuckers! What have they done to our country!" Vladimir did perfectly finished paintings: a five-paneled map of the world without the Soviet Union, or a series of paintings of inexplicable military-looking symbols called *Completely Secret: Plan for World Transformation.* While the Mironenkos did political satire as a gesture toward the future, Andrey Filippov employed the "Moscow Is the Third Rome" concept as a complex gesture to the past. On this basis, he reconceived classical scenes in Moscow, showing the burial of Caesar on the Prospekt Marksa, showing imperial processions in Stalin's cultural parks. Andrey Filippov had in one corner of his studio a guillotine with two welcoming crescents cut for two blades to descend at once: it was a guillotine for a double-headed eagle, the crest of the Romanovs. Filippov was big and bearded and a little bearish; he spoke slowly and gently, as if he might break something.

Yuriy Albert made democratic art in series of paintings: paintings for sailors, paintings for stenographers, paintings for the blind, paintings for the deaf. For sailors, he spelled out in semaphore flags "Hold to a leftward course"—the old cry of the revolutionaries. For stenographers, he painted political messages in exquisite shorthand. For the blind, raised black domes on the canvas told their story in braille. For the deaf, human figures gestured in sign language. Of the diptych *Photo-Realism* the first panel is a photograph of a man taking a photograph, the second a painting of a man making the sign for realism.

Sven Gundlakh's art, even more than that of the others, was about his compelling personality. Sven is wonderfully articulate, and was the one who always put the past into perspective by finding metaphors to make it accessible. He would give dinners at which he would assume a fictive role for the evening, or he would read poems aloud, or stories he had written. When I first met him, he had just written a symphony to be performed with his paintings as a backdrop, but because he could not get large enough stretchers to execute those paintings, the symphony was to remain unperformed. And Sven was, of course, the one who founded Middle Russian Elevation (with Nikita

YURIY ALBERT: *Unfinished Painting: Amsterdam*

Alexeev and Nikola Ovchinnikov), the rock group that caricatured every aspect of ordinary Soviet life.

Middle Russian Elevation gave a concert the last night of my first visit to Moscow. Assembled in the hall were all the people who would naturally come to an underground rock concert in Moscow. The event was impromptu, but news had spread by word of mouth in the two days before it took place, and the auditorium was packed. The group's big theme song, of course, is "Moscow Is the Third Rome," but there were others that I liked more. The words to one were: "Gala goes away, Gala goes away, Gala forgets me. Fruit juice, water, beer, tobacco, *pelmeni* [Russian ravioli]. Let me hide my face in your knees." This is "a tragic love song for conceptual artists," which plays on the absurd list of goods available at that time from certain corner kiosks in Moscow. In Russian, the lyrics build to a climax of sound, and the music has the heavy industrial tone associated with Eastern Bloc rock. On the stage, Sven sang while Dima Prigov played the saxophone, Sergey Volkov played drums, Nikola Ovchinnikov played the electric guitar, and Josif Bakshteyn played the triangle. A beautiful woman with hair to her waist played the accordion and tapped percussion on an empty caviar tin of monumental dimensions.

Toward the end of the concert, Sven and Dima Prigov announced that the group was dedicating its next song to me and called me up on the stage, where I stayed while they sang: "I thought you were a common soldier, but now I find you are an American spy, an American spy, an American spy." It was a gesture of acceptance, in the typical mode of the Soviets. They included me in their anti-Americanism, which was itself only the more ironical in this new context, and they accepted their own activity as a negative definition of me, so that I too was part of their history and their structures. The things we did together became points of reference for their relationship with me and for their relationship with one another; that was the real sign I received of their friendship. Had I known when I left Moscow how enmeshed in their world I was to become, I might have listened more closely to the words of their song, and I might have known that the mock disavowal—since, after all, I was *not* an American spy—was an invitation to complicate my own personality, my own status within the group. The gift of a position was the most profound one they could offer. I was to understand their world not by simile but by metaphor, not by explanation but by experience. I was to become a sign for each of them in his own right. It was with that understanding that I left Moscow.

Leningrad, I have come to understand, is always a relief after Moscow. Moscow is a city in which there are many beautiful things hidden, but Leningrad is a beautiful city. Moscow is a city one can learn to negotiate by metro and by taxi, but Leningrad can easily be explored on foot. To be in Leningrad, after being in Moscow, is to feel that a great weight has been lifted. People in the streets are somewhat better dressed, their carriage is somewhat more erect, and they smile somewhat less infrequently. The air is fresher; the sun is brighter; everything is easier: eating, shopping, transport, and the rest of life-support. And the fact that the city is beautiful is like a constant gift. Each corner, each turning, exposes some further wonder. Boats drift along the canals, past domed or neoclassical buildings painted in the colors of a pastel rainbow. Corners boast inexplicable arcades, a colorful church, a baroque sculpture of a glittering bronze horse rearing up into the light. To enjoy Moscow, you must have a reason to be there, seek out your amusements, and pour your energy into the task; to enjoy Leningrad requires no effort at all.

The artistic situation perhaps follows from these circumstances. As in Moscow, there are in Leningrad friends who show their work to one another, but there are no rituals of encoding, no habits of secrecy. It's more like a trendy gang who have formulated a common denominator of mutuality. In Leningrad, it is very, very important to be cool. Whereas most of the Moscow artists look like vagabonds fresh from the streets—even by Soviet standards—the Leningrad artists are beautiful to behold. They have the right haircuts, the right clothes, and also the right faces and bodies. They're into the best and most faddish music, and many of them are performers also. It is true that Middle Russian Elevation was a sort of rock group, but it was also an ironic gesture; the Leningrad artists want to be rock stars the way the Talking Heads have been rock stars, funkily at the cutting edge, perhaps, but still pretty mainstream and easily recognized. In a country in which homosexuality is both illegal and ill-regarded, many of the Leningrad artists are gay; the others are comfortable with this. The drugs are endless. Stoned, beautiful, and totally cool, the Leningrad artists sit in attic rooms holding paintbrushes. Some of them do amazing graphics, and others make simple visual compositions of spare, accessible elegance; others yet practice clumsy neoexpressionism, work in which too much paint has been hastily applied to too little canvas with too much gusto. This work looks, as the artists themselves look, straight out of the East Village; energy here has in most instances outstripped ability, but energy is not to be dismissed lightly in the U.S.S.R., where ordinary life can leave one entirely drained.

On my first trip to Leningrad, Afrika was not in evidence, but his absence became as much of a presence as his presence could have been. Afrika is at the center of what happens in Leningrad. Slender and boyish, with narrow shoulders and a slight stoop, he is nonetheless the dominant figure in town. Some people find him beautiful; he has a strong-boned but small face and deep-set blue eyes. At that time he was just twenty-two years old. Afrika was born Sergey Bugaev in an obscure town called Novorossiysk; when he was fourteen he went to Leningrad, changed his name, and began the dizzying checkered career that has cast him constantly up and down. He emerged as a popular celebrity in a country which has no popular celebrities. He

contrived it without TV appearances and without accomplishing anything concrete at all. He did it by public action and by the projection
of his dramatic persona, which he learned to focus sharply on all
appropriate targets. Almost everyone I met in the U.S.S.R. was at
least aware of Afrika; he was, like an overdivorced film star in the
West, an easy topic of conversation.

I had heard of Afrika before I went to the U.S.S.R., which was a
good thing, since Afrika always assumes that people have heard of
him. He was in Moscow for the boat ride in protest of Western
commercialism, and it was on the boat that I first met him. He
explained that he would not be in Leningrad when I went because he
was going on a "resort holiday" to the Crimea. I think that he was
going back to visit his parents, but I don't know; when I was in
Leningrad, he telephoned regularly to report on the strong sun and on
the progress of his tan. Afrika is clever. In 1985 he sent Andy Warhol
a proposal for an art project in outer space; Warhol apparently was
duly charmed, and sent Afrika six autographed cans of Campbell's
tomato soup. When Afrika learned of Warhol's death, he held a dinner
at which he opened the soup and ate it. A journalist from the West
heard about this and went to see Afrika. "How did you feel about it?"
she asked, hoping for an emotive explanation of the event. "I thought
it was very good soup, but it was just like our tomato paste. Before
Warhol died, I wish I had been able to send him our meat with
tomato paste," Afrika replied.

Such episodes are charming, and they easily outweigh the fact that
the proposal for artists in outer space was for all intents and purposes
a series of jokes, and that Afrika is a grossly uneven painter; the
childlike quality of the paintings he was doing of the first dogs sent
into space was appalling. When I first went to Leningrad, I met the
other artists without Afrika; but I was shown his work, piled in the
homes of his friends, and I was filled in on the exact content of his
telephone calls. Several times I was told that we were going to see an
artist whom Afrika had suggested I meet. It was good to feel that I
was connected to this immeasurably important figure, but there was
something eerie about his presence by absence, something creepy.

Timur Novikov is the one who discovered Afrika. Timur is older
—in his early thirties—but he seems as young as Afrika. Timur has
great visual acumen. He founded the Leningrad movement, the New
Artists, of which Afrika is a key member, and he also originated the
Mayakovsky Club, the trendy organization that unites all these Len-

BETEP   TИMУP   1990

TIMUR NOVIKOV: *Wind*

ingrad figures. These organizations echoed the Moscow infrastructure
with its well-defined groups, but as for internalized communication
—these artists were and are the great simplifiers, deliberately creating
immediately accessible work and immediately accessible public personalities. In the mode of their heroes, Andy Warhol and Keith
Haring, they constructed celebrity images of themselves on the assumption that they would become as prominent as their work. They
thought of themselves as great innovators as they carried out an agenda
in fact pioneered with consummate subtlety by their antiheroes, the
Moscow vanguard. In contrast to such elder statesmen as Kabakov and
Prigov, for example, who always made the distinction between their
"real" personalities and their "constructed" personalities a tense and
difficult one in order to engender complex questions, the Leningrad
artists, in the face of the influx of Western attention and influence,

found it all too easy to present their created voices as reality. They ignored or evaded the notion that the ultimate significance of a work of art emerges not out of willed intention, but out of that often contradictory juncture of the artwork produced, which has a life of its own, and the artist's stated aims.

Being in Leningrad was like attending a surrealist costume party—not so much because the artists wore extraordinary clothes as because one could never be sure who was behind the festive masks presented, could never be quite sure whether they were masks at all. The people were charming, more familiar in type to a Westerner than the people of Furmanny. Timur looks like a high-cubist Braque, a face composed all of strong lines with no apparent bearing on one another. Timur's work is playful, cheery, whimsical, a series of games with graphics and symmetries. In his collages, a few tiny images float at the centers of large sheets of fabric as if suspended: three tiny boats and three tiny clouds, or three tiny houses and three tiny hammers with sickles. He is always working on some semidefined and usually fictive project; when I first met him he was writing his novel, *Nevsky Prospekt II*, "which is to Gogol's *Nevsky Prospekt* as *Rocky II* was to *Rocky*." He projected it as a Tama Janowitz/Jay McInerney story of drug dealers and sex and painters and life on the streets in Leningrad. Timur is chock-full of anecdotes which he volunteers into the occasional silence: how Fernand Léger's widow disguised herself as a grandmother and pinned the badge later adopted by the Mayakovsky Club on the baby carriage in which she smuggled arms for the French underground, or how he grew up without ever going to school, receiving education from crazed and ancient family friends, or how Mikhail Larionov (second only to Mayakovsky in the pantheon) first made it to Paris. Whether or not these things are true is a matter of high irrelevance.

One of Timur's best friends was Georgiy Guryanov, who called himself Gustav, and who was the drummer of Kino, one of the Soviet Union's top bands, an equivalent to Madonna that sounded like Kraftwerk with an overlay of Bananarama. Gustav also wrote a lot of Kino's music. He is very cool and perhaps the best-looking Soviet I have met, and he cut not only Timur's hair, but also his own. His visual sense is keen: his work, which is ultra-slick and super-commercial-looking, shows the same sense of balance as his haircuts. At its best, its riveting smoothness can be deeply erotic.

The Kino people—the coolest of the cool—did not get on so well with Sergey Kurekhin, whose brainchild was the band Pop Mekhanika

(Popular Mechanics). Sergey Kurekhin is actually a gifted musician, and he was also pretty hip, though maybe not quite as broad-market cool as the Kino people. He improvises; at one of his concerts, he managed to improvise a single theme in and out of two concert orchestras, a rock band, a jazz band, and a Georgian folk music troupe, to indescribable and spectacular musical effect. The Leningrad New Artists and the members of the Mayakovsky Club—except the Kino musicians—took part in the concerts of Pop Mekhanika. During several of the Leningrad concerts, the painters attacked one another with giant inflatable figures of snakes and dinosaurs. Many of these people had just been in a film called *ASSA*, directed by Sergey Solovev and starring Afrika, an interminable and incoherent story in which misty cinematography and music by Kino and a similar group called Akvarium gave the impression of an extended music video.

In Leningrad, at four in the morning, I would be in someone's studio, but we would not be debating art theory. We would be watching crazy David Bowie videos from the late sixties, laughing at how creepy and sincere Bowie once was, reveling in retro-chic. Or else we might be dancing. I would be talking to Afrika's wife, Irina Kuksinite, who was stunningly and sensually beautiful with the elegant self-possession one usually associates with wealthy Continental women. I would look at her and wonder. She didn't look like anyone else I had seen in the U.S.S.R. Perhaps she had made her elegant clothes herself, but where did those handbags come from? And those shoes? I never found out.

By the time I went to Moscow, the artists there had made their first contacts with the West, and they had adjusted to the stream of curators who came to see them. But their knowledge stopped there. In Leningrad, I was constantly asked about a different category of Westerner. "Do you know my friend Keith Haring?" someone would ask, or "Have you ever met my friend Brian Eno?" They would look at my clothes and say, "Is that Armani?" or "Do you ever buy things from Comme des Garçons?" They looked at my tape recorder and volunteered that Sony was a less prestigious make than Aiwa but was better than Panasonic. They quoted songs by groups I had never heard of, who they assured me were all the rage in California. They told me stories about Madonna's childhood. And again, one could only wonder —where had all this come from?

As for politics: Timur seemed genuinely offended when I suggested that there might be political underpinnings to artistic activity in the

Soviet Union, and after a long discussion finally volunteered that he could find me artists who had suffered under the political regime if I really wanted to meet them. He seemed to think that politics was boring, or even vulgar, and he clearly thought it was tiresome to carry on about it. The other Leningrad painters seemed to think much the same thing. And that was the profound marker of their paucity of vision. It is unpleasant to dwell on the politics of the Soviet situation, but to ignore them is irresponsible. The Leningrad painters, especially Afrika and Timur, were great friends with an official photographer called Sergey Borisov, who Moscow artists said was with the KGB. Finger-pointing is dangerous; anyone could be in the KGB or otherwise, and I have certainly never seen real evidence that Sergey Borisov is anything more than a photographer, as he professed. But he lived better than other artists, had a big apartment in the center of Moscow, ate well—one had to wonder. When I asked the Leningrad artists whether it might be the case that Borisov was in the KGB, they shrugged; if he was providing them with good food, then his affiliations were a matter of supreme indifference to them.

There is a fashion for being apolitical in the West, and it may have its reasons; but to be apolitical in a country in which the publicly articulated policy of the government has been to define all mundane experience within ideological boundaries is a self-indulgence that cannot easily be excused. The Leningrad artists led lives of leisure; many of the Moscow artists had done petty labor or illustrated children's books or worked in commercial design to get by. The Leningrad artists never bothered with anything of the sort; they had enormous apartments and plenty to eat and unending supplies of hash, and they would not divulge the origins of their money; it came from a mixture of sales of work to the West, black market negotiation, good timing, film appearances, rock concerts, and pawned friendships. There were quite a few visually interesting painters there, including Inal Savchenkov and Oleg Kotelnikov and Vadim Ovchinnikov, but they were all philosophically vacant. Andrey Khlobystin, who was working in the library of The Hermitage during my first visit, and was not living in uninterrupted leisure, was unable for all his intelligence to get the lackadaisical charm of the New Artists into his work; his industry and his self-examination made him an odd duck indeed. In a way, if you weren't resistant to deeper human activity, you couldn't make it in Leningrad. The shallowness of the Leningrad artists was sometimes a pose; sometimes it was a matter of sheer stupidity. At the fringes of the New Artists there were scads of hangers-on; a naive and untalented young man called Igor Smirnov, who painted Smirnoff vodka bottles as a trademark, said frankly, "I paint because it's fashionable. If it stops being fashionable, I'll stop doing it." It was clearly to be a long wait.

And yet—it is an alluring world. When you leave Moscow for Leningrad, you feel as though a great weight has been lifted, not only because it is a beautiful city, but also because there is more direct and actual humor, more energy, more frolic. Everything stops being so impossibly serious; every irony ceases to cry out for interpretation. I have now gone four times to Leningrad after visits to Moscow, and I have always felt by the time I arrived that I too was sick of politics and that I wanted to be where things were easy, accessible, and fun. It was always a relief to watch videos and amusing to talk to rock stars. Afrika's ideas make me laugh. Work by Timur Novikov and by Guryanov can be visually terrific. Why should these people, of great visual talent, be compelled to intellectual accomplishment?

On my last day in Leningrad that first trip, I was made a member of the Mayakovsky Club. Two days before Mayakovsky's birthday, Timur decided there should be an exhibition, and so he phoned or went to see everyone. People stayed up all night for two nights, exhilarated, painting away. On the day of days, the exhibition opened, and Timur stood on the lectern to make a speech. It was like any beautiful-people party, and Timur, who had been the nexus of so much of this, who, though he looked as young as anyone else, was the officiating senior officer, glowed with pride. He reviewed the ideas of the club—it is for people who love Mayakovsky not so much for his poetry as for his clothes and his hair style—and made a long speech about the significance of the day. Some funky people from Sweden were there, and a few Americans, and everyone talked about carrying the exhibition off to glorious climes in the West. At the end of the speech, Timur took out several of the badges that Mayakovsky Club members wear: a white field with a red square, the symbol for the "Revolution in Art" (the black square is the "Revolution in Economics"—both were formulated by the artist Kazimir Malevich, Mayakovsky's older contemporary). With great ceremony, he presented them to various new members, mostly from the West. Being called onto the stage by Middle Russian Elevation was deeply ironic; this was lighthearted but unironic, like any testament to popularity. And like any testament to popularity, it felt transient, partial, a trifle meretricious, and very satisfying.

I was very tired by then. I was glad to leave the U.S.S.R. But I left also with some sorrow. It was only the dawn of glasnost, and I could not imagine that many of these people would enter my life again. We seemed at the time like planets in chance alignment, which leave their brief proximity as rapidly and inevitably as they have moved toward it; and I was only sorry that I could not give them as much of my own life as they had given me of theirs. I had said over and over that I would try to come back to the Soviet Union soon, but how likely was it, really, that I would return? My mouth watered at the sight of the British Airways meal as I took off (I had never before gone so long without an adequate dinner), and I remembered that what I had experienced was too foreign to be part of the real life of anyone complacently installed in the West. Only later on did I realize how, with each such thing I remembered, there was also something I forgot.

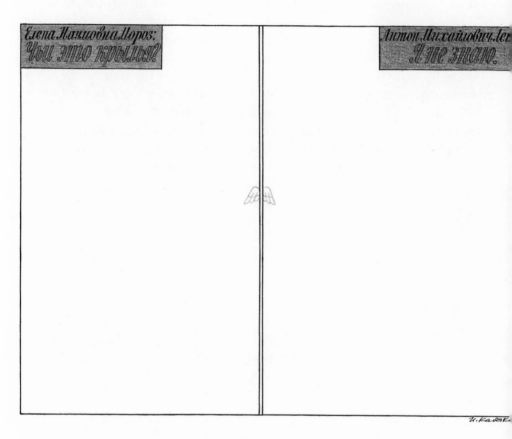

ILYA KABAKOV: *Yelena Naumovna Moroz: Whose wings are these? Anton Mikhailovich Lech: I don't know.* (Author's note: These names are both highly suggestive, and include roots for "na" (on), "the brain" (um), for "frost" (moroz), and for the verb "to cure" (lech) among others. Kabakov, of course, has made no comment on whether such suggestions are meaningful or accidental.)

CHAPTER II

Some History

Few Soviet artists place the beginning of the history of the vanguard at the World Festival of Youth in 1957. One said to me: "I know that, traditionally, we say that our history began with the World Festival of Youth, but of course it actually began in the twenties, with Malevich and Kandinsky." Another said, "Despite everyone's insistence that the origin of everything is the World Festival of Youth, I think that our art, like all avant-garde art, is indebted to things that happened in Russia in the years immediately following the birth of photography." Yet another said, "What happened in 1957 was important, of course, but our history didn't really begin until well into the seventies. What came before that is irrelevant." I also heard, "In one way, our history began with perestroika," and, "Our history, like all history, began in Mesopotamia, and continued right through the pyramids, the Renaissance, and the World Festival of Youth." Another artist told me, "Our history did not begin with Stalin, but the meaning of our work—that did begin with Stalin. Maybe our history began with Stalin's birth."

One might as well begin with the World Festival of Youth. Whereas the avant-garde of the twenties was committed to enforcing the highly abstract dictates of communism on the people, the work of the later vanguard was about retrieving people's humanity from the wreckage of dehumanizing Stalinism, and so their histories, though not unrelated, are not directly linked. What happened in Russia immediately following the birth of photography had little to do with new ideas of representation and its functions; the preoccupation at that time was with genre art, an abundance of solitary and not-so-solitary reapers, sometimes reaping, more often gazing mournfully at their crops. Such work helped to formulate Socialist Realism, though it also, like the later vanguard, gave dignity to the painful and compromised business of everyday life. To begin in the seventies would be to begin too abruptly; things perhaps became really interesting in the seventies, but the seventies don't make sense without at least a breath of the sixties. There is not time to think of Mesopotamia and the pyramids. Stalin's birth, like anyone else's birth, was a matter of a screaming child and a severed umbilical cord, and his years in power are like a black hole, a lacuna in avant-garde artistic history, a terrible blank in which insight itself was subverted. To begin any history after such a blank, after, as it were, the wiping clean of the slate, is painfully appropriate.

That takes us to the Festival of Youth of 1957. It is striking that the artists who were alive and mature in 1957 have constantly said that this *was* the moment of transformation. "It's a fashionable affectation," more than one older artist told me, "to dismiss the Festival." The World Festival of Youth was the first sign in the cultural world that the days of Stalin were giving way to something less horrifying, and it was greeted with delight. It is an oft-stated fallacy that Soviets were unaware of the gulf between their lives and the lives of people in the countries from which they were cut off. "Everyone understood that everything produced in the Soviet system was very bad, that the system of surveillance was very bad, that the KGB was also very bad. There were jokes about this everywhere," Sven Gundlakh has explained.

What does it mean to say that there was no unofficial art in Stalin's times, to speak of this as prehistory or as a black hole? It would be inaccurate to suggest that while a circle of official artists was engaged in the production of agitprop art, no one else in the Soviet Union lifted a paintbrush or carved a piece of wood or sketched a still life on the back of an envelope. But there were no social or personal circles based on the mutual inclination to create art and discuss it. No one unofficial said of his art that it was his lifework. No one did work in which there was a frank or a secret or a partial hint of political reference. You could not go into a shop and buy canvas and paint and brushes without arousing suspicion, without being asked what you were going to do, whether you were working to glorify the state; and so no one bought too much paint or too much canvas. Old men sometimes got away with painting landscapes in the remote country-side, and their work was not part of the official structure of Soviet art. Perhaps a few people scattered here and there tried to remember the tradition of Malevich and Kandinsky in purely visual terms, in sketches they kept under their beds. But this could hardly be called an "unofficial" art movement in the terms that emerged in the sixties and seventies. Everyone understood in Stalin's day that to create work in which you were trying to communicate anything was too danger-ous, too obviously foolish even to consider, and no one did it. Secrets were too hard to keep. "What continued were ideas," Kostya Zvez-dochetov has said, "and they continued not so much secretly as deeply." The great avant-gardist Vladimir Tatlin, having managed to avoid imprisonment or forced emigration, the fate of most of his circle, spent the last twenty years of his life painting flowers.

That doesn't mean that no one thought of art, or that there weren't seeds of aesthetic dissidence waiting to germinate as soon as Stalin died. Vladimir Nemukhin, now in his late sixties, has recalled that in 1944 a teacher took him into a locked room to show him, in secret, reproductions of van Goghs and Renoirs. Others have described hear-ing the stories told by old men about the artists of the Revolution, being told even (because what is spoken, unlike what is written or drawn, can sometimes stay outside the clutches of officialdom) what the work of Chagall looked like, or what a cubist was. This tradition of *speaking* was crucial in shaping the textual orientation of Moscow conceptualism.

The World Festival of Youth took place in a country that had been culturally isolated for almost thirty years, a country that had been cut off not only from developments abroad, but also from what had taken place before its own isolation. Khrushchev's Thaw, clumsy and partial though it seems by Western standards of freedom, was a monumental event in the U.S.S.R., and the World Festival of Youth was its apex. Moscow was cleaned up like Potemkin's village to fulfill Khrushchev's demand that it be the most beautiful city in the world. Monuments were constructed overnight, and, to give them the look of eternity, they were surrounded with plots of grass and trees. It was all done too quickly; within months, the grass had turned yellow, the trees had died, and the monuments themselves, cheaply constructed, had begun to chip or to dissolve in the elements. But by then the Festival was under way. A country that had seen only occasional diplomatic visitors from abroad suddenly found itself overrun with foreign youth, mostly idealist believers in communism who had come to see their utopian dream in reality. The Soviets were mad for contact with these people, besieged them with questions, tried to befriend them; 1958 saw the birth of hundreds of children to unwed mothers, many of them of mixed race, who were known as "the children of the Festival."

It was a time in which there was little rationale to what was allowed and what remained forbidden. It was, for example, forbidden to wear tight trousers in the city, or to embrace in the street. And yet at the same time, the Thaw saw the beginning of a new poetry culture: such unofficial poets as Andrey Voznesenskiy and Yevgeniy Yevtushenko gathered next to the monument to Mayakovsky in Moscow and read their poems openly. People became aware of jazz, and some heard the first hints of rock 'n' roll. Though no one had records, there were studios as discreet as speakeasies in which bootleg tapes were illegally produced; a friend has described seeing Miles Davis music recorded onto the vinyl used for printing x-rays. "In those days," Sven Gundlakh has said, "there were many things one could not see that one saw, many things one could not hear that one heard."

The effect of the Festival on would-be artists cannot be overestimated. In the American pavilion there were paintings by Jackson Pollock that were so far from anything artists in the U.S.S.R. had seen previously as to throw them into a state of shock. In other pavilions were works showing other schools of thought and patterns of influence from the West: France had sent Georges Mathieu, and Germany, Hans Hartung. Though there were a few old people in the U.S.S.R. who remembered the Soviet avant-garde work of the twenties, the new Western art of the fifties seemed discontinuous with this, and the tradition of Malevich and Kandinsky, such as it was, was more or less truncated by the appearance of Pollock and his ilk at a time when radical Soviet work of the twenties was still relegated to the basement storerooms of museums. This disappearance of the old avant-garde was a critical step in the formation of the new vanguard. "In fact," Sven Gundlakh has said, "we hated our old avant-garde because it was tainted with communism and stained with the Revolution. If we sought a tradition in our own country, we looked more to Diaghilev than to the suprematists, though later, when we came to work in the styles of the past, we found that Malevich was easier to do."

Many artists were paralyzed by the Festival, and went into a mode of frantic pastiche from which they never escaped. Such artists as Anatoliy Zverev found styles that year that they continued to imitate for the remainder of their careers. Mikhail Roginskiy and Mikhail Chernyshov, however, exploited the new ideas that had been given to them and came up very quickly with a rich version of Soviet Pop art. Few of the members of the later vanguard produced work immediately after the Festival. "There were too many styles, and they came all at once," Dmitriy Prigov has explained. "In the early period that began in 1958, everyone was trying to learn and to use all the things that had appeared simultaneously before their eyes. Ideas never arrive in our country one by one; in Russia we receive ideas that have developed independently of one another in bundles, and we always suffer under the impression that they have more in common than they have to distinguish them. Much as someone uneducated in Egyptology thinks that work from the fifth dynasty and work from the eighth look the same, artists in the U.S.S.R. thought that all the movements there had been in Western art since the turn of the century were variations on a single idea, and so each artist created a chimera of his own, based on the attempt to work with that one idea he perceived, to absorb too many influences too quickly. Later, when Pop art and hyperrealism and photorealism and conceptual art all came to us together, it was our feeling that they were variations on a single style. It took years to understand that it was useless simply to do these things, so new for us, but so tired for the rest of the world, and only after that did we realize how, in our misguided impression of a single style, we had discovered their unity rather than their difference. Then we understood that their unity also had its important place, when it was perceived as the unity of disparate ideas."

The years following the World Festival of Youth were chaotic ones. There was an ebullient sense of freedom everywhere, and people tried experimental poetry, experimental painting, experiments of every kind. Certain Western authors were translated and became immediately popular, though they were often read without either social or literary context. Hemingway became a national obsession when his complete works were published in four volumes, and many artists even tried to look like Hemingway, growing beards and dressing in big sweaters. Brecht was also translated, and much read. In official art, also, the subjects began to change; people stopped painting factory workers and communal farmers, and began to celebrate figures in other professions. For a while, the geologist was the most fashionable subject, because he was away from the influence of civilization, communing with nature, and, significantly, seemingly free of the constraints of ideology; furthermore, he could plausibly be dressed like Hemingway. Official art became sentimental; such artists as Tair Salakhov, now president of the Union of Artists, came into their own with portraits of women looking wistfully at the open fields, paintings of ordinary and touching scenes.

Unofficial art was everywhere, in its thousand protean forms, and though it was not explicitly political, it was well outside the realm of the official, and for a little while it seemed almost that there was no limit to what one might do. Then in December 1962, the Union staged a big exhibition that included some unofficial artists. The exhibition was carefully calculated; the authorities brought Khrushchev there, having warned him that he would encounter the terrible subversive art that was infecting the country and that needed to be obliterated. Khrushchev himself was, of course, a philistine; he had no judgments of his own about art, and accepted the word of the conservative Union leadership. The artists included in the exhibition understood its not-very-well-hidden agenda before taking part, and exhibited as a courageous suicidal gesture. When Khrushchev arrived at the exhibition hall and saw the work—much of it closer to Jackson Pollock than to Socialist Realism—he became furious, and denounced the artists as homosexuals (his most vicious pejorative, in this instance entirely inaccurate), fools, and traitors. The chief offender was the sculptor Ernst Neizvestny, a member of the Union who had done some expressionist and surrealist pieces that were not part of his official work. Neizvestny stood up to Khrushchev; their battle, captured on film, has become almost iconic within the vanguard.

If what unofficial artists wanted for their art was publicity, they could not have chosen a more effective way to find it; and in its way their scandal did as much for their art as the scandal surrounding the Impressionists did for modern art in the West. "Whereas the Impressionists offended society," Sven Gundlakh has explained, "these artists offended the authority which was hated by everyone, or, at least, by everyone the unofficial artists wanted to reach." These people had waited years to see themselves taken seriously in the official reviews: to be taken seriously, even as enemies of the state, was no small thing.

Though many of them had difficulties, and Neizvestny himself ultimately emigrated to the United States, no one was sent to Siberia or imprisoned. They became celebrities of a sort: they had seen Khrushchev with their own eyes, and spoken to him, and argued with him, and they weren't dead. Though few of them are now remembered individually, their decision to exhibit gave meaning to the idea of unofficial art. If it discouraged many of the carefree Thaw artists, it implanted the idea that nonstate art was a powerful medium in the minds of others.

But this was also the beginning of the suppression of modern art and modern artists in the U.S.S.R., and, after it, unofficial art existed in a relatively small circle under conditions of relative secrecy. The group that most successfully sustained its coherence through and just after the Thaw was the Lianozovo school, named after an unpleasant, inconvenient industrial area at the outskirts of Moscow inhabited primarily by factory workers. The artists, by chance, had been given apartments in this area, and they came to know one another and to work closely together. The colonels of the group were Oskar Rabin, Yevgeniy Kropivnitskiy, Dmitriy Kraspovevtsev, and the poets Genrikh Sapgir and Igor Kholin. Later, younger people joined, including Lidiya Masterkova, Vladimir Nemukhin, and Dmitriy Plavinskiy.

All born around 1925, the Lianozovo artists were culturally and socially at the margins of Soviet society even before they started to work as artists. Yevgeniy Kropivnitskiy (whose sister was the wife of Rabin) was the son of a man who had studied with El Lissitzky, the great avant-gardist of the twenties, and so the group had, by the standards of an era in which almost all radical thinkers had been slaughtered, a direct link to the tradition of the old avant-garde. Their work, however, was always figurative, frequently in a style that was not far from that of the official artists around them, but with subjects implicitly critical of the system: new buildings already decaying, or ordinary tired people reading the fallacious headlines of *Pravda*.

They earned money by doing menial work, and showed their art primarily to friends; but they also sought, and found, a certain amount of notoriety. There were some liberal art critics in the U.S.S.R. who published only essays about official culture, but who watched what was happening unofficially as well. The Lianozovo artists mounted an exhibition in an apartment and invited one of these men, Dmitriy Sarabyanov, to see it. He was very much impressed by the exhibition, and slowly, by word of mouth, the news got out that there was a

serious and interesting movement brewing in Lianozovo. At about
that time, Alexander Glazer, a friend of the Lianozovo artists, began
to collect their work; he subsequently emigrated to Paris with the
most important existing collection of Lianozovo paintings. Though he
was generous to the artists, he was not a collector in the Western
sense. He accumulated and commented on work, but he could not,
and did not, pay each artist for each picture. Shortly thereafter,
George Costakis, the great collector of avant-garde work from the
twenties, began to collect the Lianozovo artists as well, and he established contacts for them with Western journalists. A few paintings
were bought by collectors from the West, and a few others were
purchased by Edmund Stephenson, an American married to a Soviet
woman, who was the Moscow correspondent for an obscure Midwest-
ern newspaper.

By the late sixties, the Lianozovo artists were established in the
circle of the antiestablishment. They were a noisy and energetic lot,
bohemians in the Western sense, fond of drink and full of joie de
vivre, prone to late nights and escapades and incautious acts. In their
heyday, however, a very different group of artists began to emerge,
artists who sought no publicity, who shied away from drunken nights
and free love: a group of educated, intellectual, highly serious men
who were as old as the Lianozovo artists but had waited until later in
their lives to take up unofficial art. If the Lianozovo artists appeared
from the outside to be vagabonds, this second group appeared from
the outside to be solidly conformist, the middle-of-the-road element
in Soviet society. They had clean homes and close marriages, and they
were well-read in classical literature. They were kind and honest.
Whereas the Lianozovo artists were mostly untrained, some of them
dropouts from the official art schools, this new group were all well
trained, meticulously versed in traditional art theory and in the tech-
niques their work required. Though they certainly did not follow in
the footsteps of the Lianozovo artists, they owed that group the curious
debt of their own status; it would not, perhaps, have been possible to
be a quiet radical had not the clamorous radicals gone first.

The primary members of this decorous group were Vladimir Yankilevskiy, Ilya Kabakov, Erik Bulatov, Viktor Pivovarov, Eduard
Shteynberg, and, slightly later, Eduard Gorokhovskiy. Most of these
artists trained as illustrators or book designers and joined the Graphics
Section of the Union of Artists, which was later to become a sort of
club for members of the vanguard. In this way, they were assured of

official positions in Soviet society and were recognized in the world of official applied art, which was unfettered by the politics associated with official painting—the politics not only of communism, but also of the Painting Section of the Union itself. They did not begin to produce unofficial work until they were well settled in official careers; and when they did, it was done clandestinely. Only their friends knew that they were leading double lives; they always fulfilled their obligations as illustrators and designers, even while they became increasingly committed to their work. "In the late sixties," Ira Nakhova has recalled, "they produced art from eight o'clock in the morning until after midnight, sometimes until dawn, like a sort of devotional act. Their official work was a pause in their long days."

Already at that time, the people around Ilya Kabakov were aware of his extraordinary vision; but though he was in some senses the spiritual leader of the group, the actual leader at the beginning was Vladimir Yankilevskiy. It was Yankilevskiy who first decided to make large works of art, who took the discussions with which the group was initially preoccupied and concretized them. Yankilevskiy had, by Moscow standards, a reasonably large studio, and in the late sixties and early seventies, he began to fill it with brutal, abstract, very strong paintings. He went on to make what he called his "coffins," large rectangular wooden boxes, always painted, sometimes containing an object or objects. The scale of his work, and the amount of it, served as a model for the other artists; Yankilevskiy set the standards of productivity. Kabakov at this time occupied himself with found objects, Bulatov and Gorokhovskiy with emblematic painting, Shteynberg with quasi-suprematist painting, and Pivovarov with poetic/imagistic diaries. They were still recovering from the waves of information that had come through during the Festival and immediately afterward. Although there was much impassioned discussion, the solidarity of the artists remained close to the surface; and though some of what they did foreshadowed their lifework, the coherence of the group was really founded only in its opposition to the official. The works bore fleeting resemblance to one another at the level of meaning, because each of them responded to a different level of social or political reality; but they bore no resemblance at all to one another in their appearance.

It was in the early seventies that the figures now hailed as the great minds of the older generation of Soviet art found one another and formed a cohesive unit, at the time when Pivovarov emigrated to Czechoslovakia and Yankilevskiy began to fade to the periphery. The new group had at its core Ilya Kabakov, Erik Bulatov, Ivan Chuykov, and Oleg Vasilyev. Bulatov, Chuykov, and Vasilyev were all painters, all of them trying to define and alter the reality around them. But Kabakov was more than a painter. How to describe Kabakov, how to give some explanation of the power he exercised over the minds around him, of the sheer magnitude of his vision? How to explain why he became enshrined as the source of every idea the younger artists were to have?

Ilya Kabakov is not a warm man, despite certain initial appearances to the contrary. He looks elfin: short, plump, often wreathed in smiles, he is always full of praise for others, and is dismissive of himself with a modesty so extreme that you almost wonder whether it *is* in fact the remarkable Ilya Kabakov to whom you are talking. Kabakov never says what he means. "Not entirely bad," is what he says when he is conferring very high praise indeed. "Genius!" is his favorite word, used to denote what he thinks is entirely without substance. "Genius, sheer genius!" he exclaims, clapping his hands with glee, when he encounters something that is obviously terrible. Ilya Kabakov is always glad to see you, but he is also always glad to see all the other geniuses he knows. He is generous to a fault with everyone. In the end, his kindness and goodness and enthusiasm are an absolutely impenetrable wall. Even the artists who have worked with him intimately gave me cockeyed looks when I asked whether they felt close to Kabakov. "Of course I don't feel close to him. Maybe his wife is close to him, but for us, it is not important to be close. No, close does not enter into it."

Kabakov has always styled himself a coward. He has consistently refused to take part in explicit political activities organized by other artists. He would come to watch and stand in the crowd, but he would always shrug his shoulders if anyone asked him why he didn't join in. "I'm just an ordinary frightened Soviet man," he would say. "I'm afraid even to walk in the streets. Don't ask me to be a hero. Don't make demands of me. I'm not strong enough to meet them." And yet there can be no question that his ideas, in the hands of other

IVAN CHUYKOV: *Untitled*

men, were the basis of a whole unofficial way of life. The coward Kabakov taught everyone around him how to be courageous, and he knew it, and they knew it. It was absurd, this posturing as a coward, as absurd as those cries of "Genius!" of his. But it was Kabakov who believed and who taught that you can say everything if you are fast enough so that no one catches up with you, if you always cover your tracks guiltily whether you are guilty or not. Kabakov is never where you think he is, and by the time you pursue him to where he was, he's somewhere else again. While he tells you that it's not very interesting where he's gone to, you realize it's the most interesting place in the world, and so you pursue him and his image of existence as if he were a dappled mirage on a receding horizon. The effect is not accidental; Kabakov mystifies himself and his work by way of social and personal protection. He once described it as a typical Jewish complex, remarking that the Jews, caught between other nations, have had to keep their history and culture alive and secret, the secrecy being the key to continued life, since ancient times. "Kabakov himself," Nikita Alexeev has said, "was always only partly in the circle of Kabakov."

Kabakov's work is in some ways as difficult to pin down as he is himself. It's easy to describe his drawings, or to talk about installations he has done to accommodate the West, but it's impossible to comprehend the whole of his work. Perhaps the best one can say is that each new image on paper, each idea articulated in conversation, each painting, like each smile, is a hint of some large and synthetic world view in which the things that can most seldom be ordered into sense are made sensible. Kabakov's work is never overtly about politics. It is about establishing a neutral, nonpolitical zone in a world where everything has been politicized. It is about withdrawing from Soviet life into the truth of your own being. In his world, it is braver and also wiser, perhaps, to fight political reality with the absence of politics than to fight it with other politics. Kabakov's work is about retrieving the humanity the Soviet system denied its citizens, not about a new set of superhuman ideals or about a bill of rights.

Kabakov's primary medium until perestroika was the album, though he also paints and has, in recent years, done many installations in the West. These albums are unbound books, sheets of card with illustrations, and sometimes with tiny fragments of text. The medium was, of course, ideal to Kabakov's hermetically sealed Moscow life: the albums could be shown to friends, lent to other people, hidden if anyone came to look for them, burned if necessary. They used the same supplies and mostly the same skills as his illustrations for children's books, and so there were no questions asked of him when he purchased materials. The blank white page or canvas is a matter of tremendous significance for Kabakov. He has said that the world is a great barren field of whiteness, and that we live in tiny spots of color, oases of sanity. So his album pages are often almost entirely white, tiny phrases or images sketched into their corners. In the early seventies, Kabakov composed a series of ten classic albums called *Ten Characters* (on which he would later base his installation *Ten Characters* in New York), each of which ends with the death of the character described; this is signified by several blank pages at the end of the album. The albums grew in part out of Kabakov's need to escape from the single image or the single statement, to approach the continuity of shifting images. Kabakov holds you at a distance even in his works: nothing is the work of Ilya Kabakov. Each one is the work of some adopted persona, some figure of fiction, often the ostensible subject of the work. And yet the most bewildering thing is that the adopted persona is always, at a certain level, the same, that you never find a character whose life does not fit Kabakov's pattern at the most profound level. What has changed is the surface; but Kabakov's work, so spiritual, is not about surfaces. Or, then again, is it only about surfaces? Kabakov creates characters of intricate strangeness and then tells you the most banal things about them, takes a whole album leaf to show you that they poured themselves tea, put on a coat, went outside, or came through the door. His work is about how daily life has also been overrun with ideology. He poses intricate/simple questions. When you pour yourself tea, are you doing something within ideological prisons, or do you escape for that moment from the omnipresence of the dictatorship in which you live, and is that moment, therefore, one of supreme power?

His paintings pose similar questions. They too are often largely blank, with sometimes a simple kitchen object or a coat hanger attached to them. Some have long lists, bits of verbiage pulled from the everyday, the items available at a certain restaurant or shop. More often, they have apparently banal dialogue flattened into a kind of surrealism, like something out of Ionesco. "Nikolay Ivanovich Kovin: This coffee pot is all dirty. Mariya Sergeyevna Yelaginskaya: It's Anna Fyodorovna's." With these paintings, as with Kabakov himself, you feel that you get it all too easily and too quickly, that its simplicity is closing you out, and you almost wonder whether you have come up against another ideology, against something as potent as communism itself. In the albums, there is always a moment of redemption when clear light streams in and the subjects see themselves accurately, but in the paintings you are left waiting for that moment; and even in the albums, it is a moment that passes. Is it a dark or a redemptive view?

It is part of Kabakov's method to deny the complexity of his own works, which are always said to be simple, simple, simple, with nothing about them to explain; but that also is part of his process of mystification. Because Kabakov, modest though his comportment may be, has been most willing to establish himself as a figure of genius, and to play the role of genius to the people who gathered around him. It was part of his pose in the early seventies always to point toward the enigmatic Mikhail Shvartsman as the man to whom all the artists should look, identifying him as his teacher, his guru, the greatest artist of the century. To what extent this was part of the usual distortion of "genius" and to what extent it served a more complex function it is difficult to say. Shvartsman is a restorer of icons, who has said that an angel stands behind him and guides his hand when he paints, that he is a prophet, that his paintings are not paintings but signs of his divine message. Shvartsman's self-mystification was an overt version of Kabakov's, and Kabakov's mysteries take on depth against the baldness of Shvartsman's. Kabakov's work is small and easily hidden; Shvartsman's work is large, and was, until recently, seen by no one. In fact, Shvartsman himself was not seen by members of the circle of Kabakov, and many people thought he was a legend, an eleventh character made up by Kabakov for his own purposes. "It was fashionable," Nikita Alexeev has explained, "to say that we were all shit, but that Shvartsman was great. On the other hand, it was easy to be a sacred genius when you were known only through rumor. Kabakov himself was *more* sacred, and he was known to the people who held him in high regard."

The group around Kabakov began, like all these groups, informally. Kabakov, Bulatov, Vasilyev, and Chuykov were friends, and they would meet in one another's homes to talk and show their work. The meetings would always take place in the kitchen; the kitchen, center of life in a Soviet household, became a great symbol for this group of the nonideological, comfortable atmosphere in which their dialogues unfolded. They began to understand one another's language, and their activity became increasingly morally based. If Kabakov formulated the mysticism with which the Soviet unofficial art community located its own meanings, Erik Bulatov formulated the pure, romantic dedication to human strength and dignity. Kabakov sought to retrieve his subjects from the confines of the ideology by which they were bound, but Bulatov sought to eliminate those confines themselves. Kabakov is a sort of anti-idealist; Bulatov is a high moral idealist. Younger artists are almost embarrassed by Bulatov; his earnest commitment often strikes them as unsubtle. And yet, though they resist the idea of his influence, it is also inescapably a part of their work. In the early seventies, these roles were only beginning to emerge, and the works of art were just entering the realms of seriousness.

While Kabakov and Bulatov were meeting in one another's kitchens, a group of younger artists were beginning to know one another. A young man named Nikita Alexeev, whose parents knew the Lianozovo artists and were especially close to Kraspovevtsev, was beginning to feel uneasy with life in the Institute of Art. He had been a gifted child, selected at the age of eleven to attend a special art-oriented school set up by Stalin to feed into the Union of Artists and into official culture. "Of course I didn't give a damn about art at that time," Alexeev has recalled. "But even there, I found I didn't want to fit in with what we were supposed to be doing." By the time he was an adolescent, the Thaw was over, but he was just old enough to appreciate its ambience; he had tasted liberalism and understood the heterogeneity of the West, and he resisted the closing of communication. He was ultimately expelled from the Institute of Art, and was never, therefore, able to join the Union even as an illustrator, in the mode of Kabakov.

In 1969, Alexeev met a student, a young poet born Andrey Sumnin who called himself Andrey Monastyrskiy, which translates roughly as "Andrey Monastic," a concept that was to have great resonance for him. Monastyrskiy in turn met Ira Nakhova, a beautiful girl with long blond hair who was learning to paint, and whom he was to marry shortly thereafter, when he was twenty-two and she was just sixteen. They remained close to Alexeev, and later befriended the painter Andrey Demykin and the poet Lev Rubinshteyn. Though none of these people knew much about conceptualism, they began on their own to work toward a less sophisticated version of the Kabakovian world picture.

So the second generation began to evolve. "We were young, without money. It was a small circle. Every Western magazine and every thing we learned was precious; every new person was also precious. It was the time of contacts and studies," Alexeev has said. "I was interested in Duchamp and Magritte, and also in some strange artists whom I've now forgotten. I was fascinated by Ivan Albright because an American magazine published an article about him, and I happened to get this article. I had no notion of context, no idea what was important or unimportant in the West. And we looked very much toward the West."

At that time, the Soviet government published every year a book of criticism against abstraction, or surrealism, or modernism, or whatever was then the rage, and these books became primary sources on the art they disparaged. In their zeal to profane, they described the forbidden work in minute detail, and illustrated their invectives with black-and-white illustrations, blurry but not illegible. The favorite of these was a white book called *Modernism,* from which the artists learned that "abstraction is social delirium." The knowledge so gleaned was supplemented by an assortment of strange fragments that came in from the West. Once, for example, someone saw in a second-hand bookshop a coffee-table book on Paul Klee, published by Skira. No one knew how it had come to the U.S.S.R.; perhaps a tourist had forgotten it in a hotel room. Of course at that time Klee was forbidden in the U.S.S.R., but the people running the bookshop either didn't know or didn't care what they had. The book was too expensive for any of the artists to buy, but they went one by one to see it in the store. It was in this way that information crept into the world of the vanguard.

The younger circle inevitably met the older one. When Ira Nakhova was admitted to the Institute of Art to study painting, in 1968, friends of her parents took her, as a sort of treat, to meet a "real" artist. The man in question was Viktor Pivovarov. "I liked his works very much, and I liked him personally, and for me I understood from the first second that this was a new life for me, a new world. I had perhaps heard of the idea of unofficial art but I had never met such persons before," Ira has said. Pivovarov, wishing to be polite, invited this eager girl to come and visit him again, and she came a few days later, and then again, and again, "and so our acquaintance after this grew by dint of my tactlessness," she has said, "and I even spent nights at Pivovarov's house, and became friends with his wife, who was a poet and an actress and very gifted. Their marriage, for me, was like a prototype of the perfect marriage, and they seemed an absolutely lucky couple, in every sense, in their profession, their personality, their whole way of life."

When Ira Nakhova and Andrey Monastyrskiy met, she saw that they might have such a life together, and she introduced him to Viktor Pivovarov, who in turn introduced them into the circle around Kabakov. And so the connection began. Initially the younger artists were like students gathered around a master; the intimacy, the easy sense of equality that later distinguished these relationships, dawned very slowly. Eventually, the connection between Kabakov and Monastyrskiy would become itself a sort of subject for art. "By the late seventies, Monastyrskiy was John the Baptist to Kabakov's Jesus; or perhaps Monastyrskiy was the Son to Kabakov's God the Father," Sven Gundlakh has said. But in the early seventies, things were different. Monastyrskiy was a young man in Kabakov's eyes, and Kabakov himself seemed to be more cunning than brilliant, not a true artist but a sort of art trickster. "For a long time we considered that to be the case," Ira has said. "But we were wrong. We understood only the surface of his ironies, and did not see that he had more of a sense of humor than the others, a hidden sense of humor where the meaning of his work was also hidden. He represented himself as less devoted to art than the others, and we took him at his word."

Nonetheless, Kabakov's influence began to show itself almost immediately. The younger group would go some days to meet the older ones, but more often they would see one another, and their world began to mirror the other world. Demykin lived in the same building as Andrey and Ira, and Nikita Alexeev and Lev Rubinshteyn lived nearby, and so they met every day, later on also with Georgiy Kizevalter (a photographer) and Masha Konstantinova, whose odd drawings of neo-Asian women complemented her official work as a book illustrator. Every evening, the artists would show one another what they had created, and every evening they would create other things. Monastyrskiy would read his sonorous poems, in his strange, exaggerated, theatrical way, so that the reading and the way of reading were as important as the texts themselves. The artists often dressed in strange clothes, and they sang together, and sometimes danced, "but this was not so much like a party as like a performance," though it was not called performance at that time. Kizevalter would take photos, and would also play endless practical jokes; on one memorable occasion, he hid himself in a wardrobe at Andrey's and waited there for two hours before bursting out with a shout and frightening everyone half to death. Everyone who was involved in that circle at that time remembers it with deep nostalgia, as the time when they were a little bit in love with one another, and with their own and one another's work.

During the early seventies, the two groups became steadily closer, and the younger group began to define itself more rigorously. The atmosphere everywhere was one of increasing self-consciousness about mysticism, and of religious enthusiasm, an enthusiasm directed not so much at the doctrines of Russian Orthodox Christianity or of Judaism as at an abstracted metaphysics. It was the shadow of an idea at first, and then it became increasingly important, almost a matter of form, to work in the province of the spiritual. The art itself became steadily more esoteric, more closed, and hence more elitist. Everyone read a book called *East in the West* by a Soviet scientist named Tatyana Zavadskaya, the first chapters of which were about Zen in the East, the later ones about artists in the West who she thought echoed Zen

Этот ковер подчеркивает значимость могил героев.

MARIYA (MASHA) KONSTANTINOVA: *This rug emphasizes the significance of the graves of heros.*

ideas, including John Cage, Karlheinz Stockhausen, Gustav Mahler, Morris Graves, Henry David Thoreau, and Charles Ives. The group's pro-Western orientation manifested itself in their preoccupation with Cage and Marcel Duchamp, but it was balanced by increasing interest also in the writings of Malevich and Kandinsky about spirituality in art, which were circulated in photocopies. The artists read intently all Zen writings then available in the Soviet Union, the novels of Hermann Hesse, and the mystic texts of Carlos Castaneda. "You had to be initiated into it," Nikita Alexeev has recalled. "If not, you couldn't understand anything—not because we used strange words or spoke a foreign language but because we had developed a kind of hermetic conversation."

The artworks produced became at one level almost irrelevant. "We lived in a country in which factories produced not goods, but the rhetoric of a productive proletariat and its triumphs. In retrospect," Sven Gundlakh has said, "one can understand that conceptualism and the Soviet cultural system were the same, producing not things, but the ideas of things." Erik Bulatov once said, "If you look at my painting of Brezhnev in the Crimea, you will see at once that it is a good and accurate portrait of Brezhnev; but it could never be shown in an official expo—not because of what it is, but because it is I who made it." The thing was irrelevant; the idea and the circumstances of creation were everything. Within this context, the work of art itself was devalued, but also became an occult object, at once redemptive and dangerous. One did not speak of art, because art was the tool of Satan and of Stalin; one said only that one made things, and that it was necessary to separate oneself from these things. It was everyone's way to say, "Ah, look at these terrible things that I have produced." The things themselves were no more than a kind of documentation of the continuing hermetic conversation. Later all of this—needing a more rigorous and ancient structure—blossomed into an obsession with Orthodox Christianity, and in the mid- and late seventies, all the artists, Jewish, Christian, or otherwise, became involved with the rituals of Orthodoxy. Though Malevich was an atheist, the artists mixed his spiritual texts and his physical forms with religion. Everyone acknowledged the black square as his great triumph, but became obsessed with a cross he had once designed, and for a number of years the artists all designed crosses and other objects of religious life. Many took up regular religious activities; Nikita Alexeev, for example, was baptized in 1975.

While this circle withdrew further and further into its private world, a concentric circle was growing up, led by the artists Vitaly Komar and Alexander Melamid, who were slightly younger than Kabakov and Bulatov, and including Misha Roshal, Gennadiy Donskoy, Igor Lyuts, and Viktor Skersis. These artists did not wait decorously in the wings and pursue official careers and work in secret; they began to work unofficially while they were still students, and though they were not loud and flashy in the mode of the Lianozovo artists, they were overt in everything they did. Komar and Melamid were concerned with explicit, rather than implicit, politics and were not afraid to declare their views. They had no time for spirituality and arcane definitions of true art; what interested them was political anecdote and a wry playfulness with it. Komar and Melamid created a style of their own, which they called Sots (short for Socialist) Art, after a friend suggested to them that they were working as if they were Soviet Pop artists.

Sots Art depends on the appropriation of the visual language of
socialism and communism for antisocialist and anticommunist activities. Kabakov's work uses the found images of empty space and the
ordinary things of everyday life; Komar and Melamid's work uses the
found images of the self-glorifying state. It may well be that the artists
in these two schools succeeded at a higher artistic level than the
Lianozovo and other unofficial artists precisely because they were not
trying to invent a wholly new language, but were instead taking
existing languages and giving them new meanings. The best Soviet
work, then and now, depends on this process of redefinition rather
than on the mechanism of pure invention. It is always important to
remember how crucial a role Socialist Realism played in the formation
of the visual sensibility of all Soviet artists; one may speak of Malevich
and of Duchamp, but the structure of images in the vanguard is more
frequently indebted to the art of Stalinism than to any other single
source.

With Sots Art, Komar and Melamid exploited the high kitsch of
Soviet official culture, sometimes with great hilarity, but their work
was not really about kitsch per se. Margarita Tupitsyn has written of
the "inescapable tangibility and concrete reality of such abstract concepts as Marxist-Leninist truth, bright historic destiny, or even Lenin,
Stalin, and Marx, who are, according to official sources, always alive
and with you." The Sots Artists "proposed a deconstruction of that
culture's divine claims and utopian assumptions." They accomplished
this by making paintings that literalized the figurative in a mode of
calculated banality, or by creating works that applied the august
language of Socialist Realism to the tedious unpleasantness of life in
the Soviet Union. So in one of their best-known paintings, *The Birth
of Socialist Realism,* we see a mythic figure, a muse in the best classical
tradition, depicted in perfect detail, descending and placing her hand
under Stalin's chin. Erik Bulatov's paintings also depend on the appropriation of images from Socialist Realism—as in the portrait of
Brezhnev that could never be displayed—and there has therefore been
some effort in recent years to tie him into the tradition of Komar and
Melamid, but this is somewhat misleading. Bulatov is not a Sots
Artist. Bulatov's ultimate concerns are moral and romantic, rather
than political and ironic, and so he belongs squarely in the camp of
Kabakov, no matter what systems of images he may use.

In September 1974, Komar and Melamid joined forces with Alexander Glazer, Oskar Rabin, and the other Lianozovo artists, and the group decided that they had been marginal for long enough. They agreed to put together a public unofficial exhibition of the work of various artists in a field outside Moscow. Two days before the exhibition, the KGB found Glazer's list of artists, and tried to intimidate those included into closing the show. Four KGB men went to the home of Ira Nakhova's parents, said that she was going to exhibit, and indicated that there would be reprisals. Her parents, horrified, took Ira and Andrey Monastyrskiy (who were both very young) more or less by force to a dacha in the country to prevent their participation. The older members of the Kabakov/Bulatov circle, still very much set on secrecy and mysticism, did not join in. But a variety of other artists did. Early in the morning they went to their field, set up their work, and prepared for visitors; but just as the first ones arrived, a battalion of militia appeared in bulldozers from the woods beyond, and plowed down the work. The attack was sudden and brutal; some people were injured, and almost all the work was destroyed within minutes. The episode fitted in well with the tradition of antagonism between the unofficial artists and the world of officialdom; the organizers had expected some kind of encounter with the structures of authority, and had counted on its publicity value, in which they were not to be disappointed. Many artists egged on the aggression; which is to say that though there were, of course, bulldozers, it was in some instances the artists who threw their works under the oncoming shovels.

Horrible though it was, the *Bulldozer Show* served a useful function, echoing the exhibition at which Khrushchev attacked the vanguard in 1962. The international press heard about the episode, and reports of the angry militia with their abominable "tanks" spread quickly in the West. The Soviet government was embarrassed into announcing permission for another exhibition two weeks later in Izmaylovo Park, at which anyone who wished to was allowed to exhibit. This event— christened "Soviet Woodstock" by a Western journalist—was a tremendous success, with thousands of visitors and work by more than a hundred artists. Many of the young artists of the vanguard showed their work there, and the atmosphere was one of great festivity. People asked questions and talked to the artists. "It was, of course, more of a demonstration than an exhibition," Nikita Alexeev has said. "Most of the art was terrible. I was twenty-one. I was making massive monochrome Masonite reliefs, which at the time seemed daring and radical."

For the benefit of the angry Western journalists, the *Izmaylovo Show* was conducted with a seeming smile of tolerance. But for the artists, it was otherwise. Some months earlier, Nikita Alexeev had heard of a program of art therapy in a Moscow hospital, and, young and idealistic, had applied to work with the ill. He had been given a white coat and a key to the hospital door, but a few days later was told of delays to the beginning of the art-therapy program, and was asked to do menial work until it got under way. Shortly after the opening of the *Izmaylovo Show,* he was asked to return his coat. Two weeks later he was asked for his key. And he understood that it was a good time to leave, that soon someone would perhaps have come to put him in jail.

Nikita was at that time living in a different apartment from the one where he was officially registered (as often happens in Moscow), and he had therefore not received a series of letters from the military commissariat requiring that he report there. One morning, an officer arrived in the apartment where he actually lived and demanded that he come at once to the commissariat. When he got there, he was put into a car and sent immediately to a mental hospital. "I was selected for this treatment, I think, not because I was so important, but because someone made a list of names from Izmaylovo, and my name starts with 'A,' " Nikita has said. The director of the hospital, who understood immediately why the artist had been sent there, was, fortunately, a kind man and did not subject him to any of the gruesome "treatments" that others have suffered under similar circumstances; this man released him after six weeks. "I lived there, and ate, and slept; and in a way it was a good experience. That place was so sad and gray, and full of maniacs who, like everything Soviet, seemed to have been standardized, all haunted either by communal-apartment paranoias, by the belief that their neighbors were sending poisonous beams to them through the walls, or by terrors left from war. No one believed himself to be Lenin, and no one saw visions of utopia. Even sexual dysfunction was attached to the manias of communal life and of war. I understood then what illness is, and how it occurs in our system."

In the period following the *Bulldozer Show,* the younger generation around Kabakov and Bulatov came into its own, and in 1976, the Collective Action Group (K/D) was born out of the web of mystical obsessions into which these people had thrown themselves. Andrey Monastyrskiy was the head of K/D; Nikolay Panitkov was the heart; Nikita Alexeev provided much of the energy. Lev Rubinshteyn and Georgiy Kizevalter also took part, and later Andrey Abramov, Sergey Romashko, Igor Makarevich, and Yelena Elagina joined them. Kabakov was always at the core of what happened, and he frequently took part in the Actions, but only as an observer. Monastyrskiy and Nakhova had divorced shortly before the beginning of K/D; though she joined the group in the early eighties, she did not take part in any of the early performances.

"I still remember being at Andrey's dacha in 1973, walking and talking about things we didn't realize were scenarios for future performances," Nikita Alexeev has said. "We would say, 'What if you were in a field, and someone approached you from the forest, someone who seemed to be cut off from real life, what would you do?'" If Kabakov and Bulatov came up with the language of mysticism, Collective Actions came up with its rites. Like Kabakov's work (and unlike most of Bulatov's), K/D depends heavily on irony. Its ritual remains serious but self-conscious, ponderous but not clumsy. Though to the uninitiated it appears, as I learned in Moscow in 1988, extremely bombastic, it is in fact very difficult even for K/D's members to tell when Andrey Monastyrskiy is being serious and when he is being ironical. "It's a shamanistic attitude. It is sometimes impossible to say of the shaman whether he is in a real trance or whether he is just striking a pose," Nikita has said.

This way of thinking began with those evenings in Monastyrskiy's apartment in the early- and mid-seventies, when Andrey was still entirely a poet, giving readings, doing what were, in effect, performances but had not been named as such. In 1974, Andrey created his first object. He asked everyone who came to his apartment to leave on a specially appointed table some small item, anything at all, an ashtray or a stone or a pencil. For several weeks, he continued to ask for these items, and he called what he created *Heap*. Then he made a list of everything that was in the heap, and this was the documentation of the object. After that, it was finished, and the items were redistributed.

In the months that followed, Monastyrskiy became increasingly interested in the idea of objects. He produced a black box with a projecting tube that was placed on the wall beside a buzzer. The people who saw it placed an ear to the tube and pressed the buzzer. When the buzzer was pressed, however, it did not create a sound, but rather turned on a light inside the box. Another object was a box with a large hole at the bottom and a smaller one on one side. This came with meticulously detailed typed instructions that required that you put your hand into the box from the bottom and stick your thumb out through the hole in the side. The object, with its fussy directions, its sexual overtones, and its alienation of the viewer from his own body—because the thumb projecting from this box does look like a severed digit in a science museum—all fit in with the tenor of K/D.

In 1976, Collective Actions officially came into being. The first Action was called *Affiance.* A group of perhaps fifteen people were gathered in Moscow, taken to a field at the edge of a forest, and told to wait. Lev Rubinshteyn and Nikita Alexeev appeared from the forest on the far side of the field, walked across the grass, and gave to the public small certificates saying that they had attended the appearance of Collective Actions. The second Action was called *Lieblich,* in reference to the direction given at the start of a Schubert song. Again, the people met in Moscow and went to the countryside and walked to a specified destination; and when they arrived, there was a blue box with an electric bell hidden in the snow. The people heard the faint ringing, but could not find its source. That was all.

Later, the performances of K/D became more theatrical, and involved elaborate manufactured scenarios. Monastyrskiy's obsession with Kabakov blossomed, and, in later days, Kabakov was said to "command" the Actions of K/D. In fact, Monastyrskiy would ask Kabakov to command him, and then he would obey his own orders. The audience for K/D was composed entirely of members of the vanguard, some of whom understood very well what was going on, and for some of whom the shroud of mystery remained impenetrable. Until the eighties, the Actions all took place outside Moscow, partly because their ritual delicacy required escape from the aggression of urban spaces, partly because of genuine concern that the work be hidden from the eyes of authority, and partly because secrecy and concealment had by that time taken on a quasi-religious significance for the artists involved. The actual travel to the country, usually a trip by train of about thirty kilometers and then a walk of perhaps half an hour, provided what the group called the "frame" for the Action. Without a frame, the performance would not have been an Action. An Action could exist only in the context of time and space and emptiness. Actions frequently took place in snow-covered fields, and the whiteness of this space became a reference to Kabakov's white page, the white space of alienation. Only much later, when the frame had become, on the basis of precedence, a mental construct, were the Actions strong enough to take place in Moscow, in an apartment or sometimes in the streets.

One performance from the late seventies was called *Balloon*. Kabakov's work is frequently engaged with the idea of a stratum of freedom that cuts through the currents of air at some height we cannot reach, and so the idea of flight in a balloon, which might drift to this level and be carried by the winds of autonomy into the beyond, was a deeply appealing one. Some members of the circle started a small samizdat, or underground, publication which was called *The Pilot*. Monastyrskiy suggested that, since it was not possible to have a real/metaphoric balloon in which to fly away, it would be interesting to make a balloon to play with and to roll on the hills. The members of K/D spent what was for them quite a lot of money and waited in the necessary queues to buy some two hundred meters of fabric, which they sewed into an enormous envelope, and about five hundred rubber balloons. A day was appointed for the Action. They went to a forest quite far away from Moscow and spent the whole day, despite heavy rain—Actions are ritualized, and do not bow to such forces as the weather—blowing up the balloons. These were then put into the fabric envelope. "I was very happy as I worked on this," Nikita Alexeev has recalled. "It was not possible to make a real balloon, a real sphere, and what we had was an oblong, but it was very beautiful. By the time we made it, we had only a little time to play with it; then we rolled it into the river and it disappeared."

It is impossible to speak of Collective Actions without speaking also of the documentation that Andrey Monastyrskiy prepared and which for him was part of each Action. This documentation, with scales, drawings, charts, copies of certain papers distributed or collected, photographs by Georgiy Kizevalter, and excruciatingly precise texts by Monastyrskiy himself, now fills four large volumes in Monastyrskiy's apartment. These books bear the title *Travels to the Country,* and are at once fascinating and virtually unreadable. Their fetishistic approach to documentation and tables foreshadows Monastyrskiy's later fixation on pathology, on symptoms, on the charting of one's own symptoms, and on similar questions of approaching the human by means of the scientific.

In addition to the Kabakov/Bulatov circle, with its younger Monastyrskiy/Alexeev grouping, and to the Komar and Melamid circle of Sots Artists, there was a third group whose leaders were Dmitriy Prigov, Boris Orlov, and Rostislav Lebedev, and which included Igor

ANDREY MONASTYRSKIY: *Variant of an Element in the Installation:*
"Semantic Forests"

Chelkovski, Alexander Kosolapov, and Leonid Sokov, though these three were also tied into the Komar and Melamid circle and migrated between the two. If Komar and Melamid were interested in exploiting the subversions inherent in the language of socialism, and Kabakov and Bulatov were interested in finding the language of truth and moral victory hidden behind the social constructs of Soviet life, then Prigov, Lebedev, and Orlov were interested in the idea that in every language —socialist, communist, personal, secret, public, official, unofficial— there is a zone of death and a zone of life; their work was about the process of locating that zone of life in every language.

Dima Prigov was at the center of this group. Orlov is a pure sculptor, concerned with the manufacture of beautiful objects; but for Prigov, as for Kabakov, artistic life defines a means of existence. Prigov is the great mediator, himself a poet, a performer, an artist, and a musician; if he is interested in the zone of life in every available language, then he has been perhaps a translator from each of these languages to the others, explaining the work of one artist to another artist, the work of poets to painters, the work of painters to musicians, the work of Sots Artists to figurative realists. He has about him a focus and intensity that seem to drive forward, an energy that is startling and exciting, a purity of intellect and an insistence on rigorous discourse that can be deeply moving. An obsessive worker and performer, Prigov covers pages and pages with tiny marks from his pen, creating a neurotic explosion of ideological dignity. His light poetry has a kind of lapidary elegance, and his great warmth always shines through it:

> No sooner are the dishes done
> Than there's a new lot piled up
> What kind of freedom then is this—
> To spend one's whole life washing up
> One could, it's true, just leave them there
> But what if people then come round
> And make remarks about the plates—
> So where is freedom to be found?

The zone of life exists in the most quotidian experiences:

> A woman in the metro kicked me
> It wasn't just a case of elbowing
> That one could take—but here she went too far
> And so the whole thing *passed into the realms*
> *Of quite uncalled-for personal relations*
> Naturally I kicked her back
> But at that moment begged her pardon—
> Being, quite simply, a superior person.

And the harsh perspective on ideology was also constant:

> The weather in Moscow's close to the ideal
> Before, of course, it wasn't so at all
> Slow, brutal, dull it used to be
> We often quarrelled then, the weather and I
>
> And then my ideals changed
> And the weather at once drew close to them
> You see: it's senseless to torment the weather
> —How cruelly, doing so, we torment ourselves.

But Prigov is also the author of a series of "Screaming Cantatas," in the performance of which he lists the names of men killed by Stalin's government, his voice rising higher and higher until like a dervish at the peak of a whirl he seems almost to lift himself from the stage where he stands. He is the same age as Kabakov, but his energy has allowed him also to be part of each new generation. In later years, it was Prigov who organized things, started them going, injected life into the vanguard whenever it began to flag.

Until the mid-seventies, the three circles—Kabakov/Bulatov and their followers, Komar and Melamid and the Sots Artists, and Dima Prigov and his group—remained essentially separate. They were peripherally acquainted, crossed paths from time to time, and respected one another; but they led separate lives and did their work separately. Then in the late seventies, artists and friends started to emigrate. Viktor and Margarita Tupitsyn were the first to leave, and were soon followed by Komar and Melamid, then by Leonid Sokov and Alexander Kosolapov (who have since become exponents of pure Sots Art in the Komar and Melamid tradition), by Rimma and Valeriy Gerlovin, and by many more peripheral figures. The ones who left were the ones who were most committed to crying their ideas from the rooftops. The members of the closed and secret circle around Kabakov and Bulatov were able to stay because their work lifted them above the *Bulldozer* encounters that frustrated such artists as Komar and Melamid. Most of the artists who left were granted permission to emigrate on grounds of Jewish ancestry.

For those who stayed behind, the others in effect died. It would never be possible to see them again. There could be no further communication with them. One had to hope that they really were going to a better place, and would find happiness there. As the number of artists remaining decreased, the various circles came together, partly for support and partly because they had recognized enough in one another to be drawn together by shared fixations. In 1977, the Seminar was born. At its center were Ilya Kabakov, Erik Bulatov, Ivan Chuykov, Andrey Monastyrskiy, Nikita Alexeev, Lev Rubinshteyn, Dmitriy Prigov, the poet Vsevolod Nekrasov (who was a close friend of Bulatov), the critic Boris Groys, and the conceptual photographer Frantsisko Infante, a man of about the same age as Kabakov who had previously been part of his own tiny circle with Lev Nusberg. Though one of its members might miss any one session, the Seminar was an essentially fixed company that gathered twice a month, setting the date and time and location (someone's kitchen) at the end of each meeting for the next one. Usually the Seminar would open with a reading, a lecture, the showing of an album or some drawings or slides, the proposition of a philosophical idea, or an oral review of a book recently translated or obtained; the second part was discussion. In the Seminar the artists of the vanguard worked out the terms on which they could confront Soviet life, and it was in the Seminar that many of them defined the articulated language that they have used ever since. The Seminar changed their lives permanently; it was a means of coming into their own, and it defined what some artists living in Moscow today call "the official structure and hierarchy of the unofficial movement." Perhaps most significantly, it became the vehicle for the older artists' mythologizing of their own activities and position.

This was the world as it existed when the Mukhomors arrived. If Kabakov and Monastyrskiy formulated the most important events of the seventies, the Mukhomors created the early eighties. They were, of course, the pupils of Kabakov and Monastyrskiy, and it is an oft-heard truism that Monastyrskiy "created" the Mukhomors. But they ultimately went in a very different direction from their teachers. Komar and Melamid had refused the secret world where Kabakov and Bulatov lived, and they remained apart; the Mukhomors were to enter that world and explode it from within, taking its secrets and broadcasting them into the lives of ordinary Soviets. "We were young, and we were therefore very brutal, and we quickly became the underground within the underground, the enfants terribles among the enfants terribles," Kostya Zvezdochetov has explained. The Mukhomors subverted the existing subversions. If Kabakov's circle had preserved truth and humanity by safeguarding it, then the Mukhomors were determined to uphold the truth by giving it to the whole world.

There were five Mukhomors: Sven Gundlakh, Kostya Zvezdochetov, Sergey and Volodya Mironenko, and Aleksey Kamenskiy (who left the group in 1983 to take up a more conventional life). Their interest in one another, and in art, began early. There is a snobbery dating back to the days of Peter the Great according to which Russian aristocrats speak French, and so people with aristocratic antecedents or pretensions frequently educate their children in the language. Sven Gundlakh and the Mironenko brothers met as children at a school selected by their parents because French was taught there as a principal subject. By the time they were of high-school age, they were cutups in class, and they played "typical student jokes, the jokes of a teenager," Sven has said.

Kostya was born in one of Stalin's prison camps to two actors whose work had caused offense to the Soviet government, but his parents were released when he was still quite young, and he grew up in Moscow. When he was fourteen he went with a friend of his mother's to an underground semiabstractionist neo-expressionist exhibition in an apartment far from the center of the city. The work was by an artist of whom no one had heard then and who is now forgotten, but shortly thereafter Kostya read the memoirs of Ilya Ehrenburg, with their rich anecdotes about Lenin and memories of Picasso, Diego Rivera, Mayakovsky, and Modigliani, and he decided that with art he might speak to the world.

As he would later learn modernism from books that countered modernism, so Kostya learned Trotskyism from the books that countered Trotskyism, and with a friend in school led a group that promoted discussion of political topics. "We were not anticommunist; we were very naive and believed that communism needed only a slight structural reform. Our group was, of course, forbidden; we tried to slip through legal loopholes, but it didn't really work." By the end of his schooling, Kostya was a pariah, avoided by his schoolmates and his teachers. In his last months at school, he was called in to see various people from the City Committee of the Party and the City Committee of the Komsomol (the youth organization of the Communist Party); and at his graduation ceremony, despite numerous prizes won for essays in literature and history, he was not given a diploma. Later he understood that the KGB had forbidden the director of the school to give him credit; he was of course not admitted to Moscow University, where he had hoped to study history. He began to organize political activities. Once he went with friends, all in costume and carrying flags and slogans ("Don't ask me what kind of flags and slogans—I was seventeen, and they were very stupid") onto the metro, planning to do a small ironic demonstration; but as the group emerged from the train they were arrested "with the pomp and ceremony appropriate to the confinement of great enemies of the state." They

VLADIMIR (VOLODYA) MIRONENKO: *Vlaldimir Mironenko World Service*
("Self-Portrait as an American Express Card," from the series
"American Express")

were all photographed and asked to sign statements, which the KGB
would later produce during intimidation sessions in the mid-eighties.

Despite these problems, Kostya was able to secure a place in the
Institute of Theater Design. There he met the Mironenko brothers,
who introduced him to Sven Gundlakh. Sven met Aleksey Kamenskiy
at the Polygraphic Institute and introduced him to the Mironenkos
and to Kostya, and the five of them began to spend time together.
They also befriended a fervent Marxist idealist in the Institute of
Theater Design, a young man named Andrey Filippov whose humor
and artistic abilities appealed to the group but whose politics prevented him from joining it. It was Kostya who suggested that they
formalize their group status, "because I wanted my work to be not
only aesthetic and artistic, but also social. But they were a bit snobbish, Sven and the Mironenkos, and they told me they were individ-

ualists." The artists became steadily closer to one another, and spent more and more time together, less and less time doing the work assigned to them. Kostya and the Mironenkos began a series of "poetic mornings" at their Institute. During lectures they wrote parodic or political texts, and at the end of each lecture they would ask the other students to stay; then they would deliver these texts in the "found time" usually dedicated to standing in the corridor and smoking. Shortly thereafter, in 1978, they agreed to form a group. They called it "Mukhomors," which means "toadstools."

At about this time, Sven began to have problems of his own. "My family was always afraid of the KGB, and of Stalin; many of them had been killed or imprisoned during the purges," he has explained. "What I heard in my family was horror. They always told me to imitate the establishment, not to show anyone what I really thought; they said that one had to think of one's parents or one's children and take care not to offend." In the middle of his first year at the Polygraphic Institute, he was approached in the hallway and asked to come to a room downstairs. There he found several men from the KGB, who said to him, "We have been following you since you were at school, and we find your attitudes sympathetic, and we would like to invite you to work with us." And they also said, "Of course, if you are a Soviet man, you *will* work with us." To say no was, horribly, to be other than a true Soviet man, and of course whoever is not a true Soviet man is a true anti-Soviet man.

They gave Sven four hours to think over his decision, and left him by himself in the room. "I all at once understood what my family had been telling me all those years. In that room my whole life was destroyed. I couldn't think of a solution to the problem, and no one could advise me. I was afraid. I didn't know what might happen to me if I said no, or what might happen to my family, and I decided that I had only one real priority at that moment, and it was to get out of that room as quickly as possible, immediately if I could. And so, to escape, I said yes. But when I left that room, I was not made free. For me, that was the beginning of the torments and nightmares."

Sven went home and told his family the whole story, and they were horrified; but they were also horrified that their son could have so mismanaged his life that he became a member of the KGB. Sven couldn't face them, and couldn't face his new employers, and in a blind panic, he left home and headed into the countryside. "I was without clothes and without money, and for six months I never stopped walking. I couldn't think, I couldn't eat, I didn't know whether I wanted to live or die." He was at last picked up by the police and put in prison, but the director of the prison understood that he was a teenager, that he was hungry and tired and wanted to go home. At the end of a month, he called Sven's mother, who came to get him and brought him back to Moscow.

He tried to behave as though this trauma were only a nightmare, something that had never happened. "But for me the dream was still alive. The KGB gives its members code names; mine was Pegasus, and I used to lie awake at night, tossing and turning, thinking: am I Pegasus or am I Sven Gundlakh? Another six months passed this way, full of self-torture, and at last I understood that the only thing I could do was to tell my friends what had happened to me in precise detail. This was the only way to be honest and come to terms with myself. So I told them my story, and soon I was carried away by this business of telling, and I began to tell my story to everyone, to strangers in the bus, people on the streets, old women in the metro. I had to rid myself, purge myself. And that was the beginning of my actual problems with the KGB. Because the one thing that the KGB hated above all was for someone to tell stories like that." All the artists of the vanguard had problems with the KGB, but Sven's were, straight through until glasnost, on a different scale, more deplorable, more relentless. "I was constantly called before them. When I was in the army, I spent at least half my time in front of the military KGB. And at the end, I wasn't afraid any more; I was just angry. They treated me like a foreign spy, and I was not a spy. I understood that when they had said to me, 'Are you a Soviet man?' the answer should have been, 'I am not a Soviet man; I am a decent and faithful citizen of the Soviet Union.' "

These problems were to set Sven Gundlakh on a course from which he could not return. "All my friends were tied in a bit with society: they were students or illustrators or set designers. For me all contact with acceptable society was cut and broken. Most people at that time in the Soviet Union, even if they hated the establishment, dreamed of having good work, and important work, and traveling perhaps to the West. But I knew that was not in the cards for me, that it was completely finished, that I could never have a good job or a passport, that I could never publish an article, that I could never enter the Artists' Union." In fact, he lived at the extreme edge of irregularity; for a long time he would sign on for menial jobs and arrange with the overseer or foreman, for a kickback of half his salary, that he would not work at all. In this way he managed to reserve most of his time for making art.

The others also had encounters with the KGB. During the time of Sven's self-imposed exile in the country, Kostya Zvezdochetov and the Mironenkos were called to the office of the director of their Institute, to be confronted, when they arrived, by KGB men. They were taken away in separate cars and separately asked to be informers on the circle. "I thought I could say clever things to improve my situation, but I imagine that I only made it worse," Kostya has recalled. "With the KGB it's very difficult to judge these things, especially if you're very young. They said terrible things about the Mukhomors, and I explained that we were always drunk and that everything we'd done was a sort of joke. I thought I had really been called in because they had arrested my political friend, from my school days, and so I tried to say things that I thought would ease his situation, to make alibis for him. I spoke negatively about someone else I knew, the man who is now head of the Soviet Christian Democratic Party, not saying anything very important but trying to shift the focus away from my friend. After three days my friend was free, but I've never known what damage I may have done to the other person. It's always a terrible gamble with the KGB."

When Sven returned from his wanderings, the group was full of energy, and the feeling in Moscow was one of chaotic toleration. They did a painting called *Indians Hunting the Eagle* and took it to Malaya Gruzinskaya, an exhibition hall set up by Oskar Rabin and other members of the Lianozovo circle that had subsequently passed into semiofficial hands. Malaya Gruzinskaya was tolerated by the KGB because it brought underground activity to the surface of society; it showed predominately badly executed amateur still lifes, work that was neither official nor part of the unofficial movement. Still, as an unofficial but public space it attracted obsessive interest: every day lines wound around the block to see the exhibitions there, "more people than I have ever seen at an exhibition in the West, like the most crowded opening every day for a month," Kostya Zvezdochetov has recalled. When the Mukhomors went, Malaya Gruzinskaya was doing an open project called *Experiment,* in which submitted work was selected by a jury. *Indians Hunting the Eagle* was rejected, but the Mukhomors went into the exhibition hall the day before the show opened, hung the painting on an unoccupied wall, and posted beneath it a comical manifesto about Cézannism and Surrealism. The jury forgot they had rejected it, and it stayed there for the duration of the exhibit.

It was at this time that Aleksey Kamenskiy's uncle, who had observed the young group, introduced them to Valeriy Gerlovin; just a few days before his departure for the West, Gerlovin introduced them to the Seminar, to Kabakov and Monastyrskiy. To the Mukhomors, the members of the older generation seemed absurd, with their formalities and their mysticism and their rites, and the first time they went to the Seminar they did a parodic performance, musical and poetical, intended to offend the zealous intellectuals to whom they had been introduced with such ceremony. They considered themselves not so much artists as situationists, opponents of the establishment, and for them Kabakov and Monastyrskiy were establishment. Many of the older artists were indeed offended by their bold-faced arrogance, but Kabakov found them interesting, and so they were invited to join the Seminar itself.

"We had been making jokes for years," Sven Gundlakh has recalled. "But suddenly we found that there was a circle of people who did the same things very seriously. Our initial idea was to laugh at them, but step by step, we became involved ourselves. It was a little like *Rosemary's Baby,* where some young people become part of a cult as a sort of joke, and then bit by bit become more involved and more involved until they are no longer able to leave. The first time I met Monastyrskiy, he showed me all his work, and the most impressive thing for me was his Action with the balloons. I thought, 'Wow! There are guys in the U.S.S.R. who do work like this! It's incredible! It's fantastic!' I was impressed that it was so serious, and I saw very clearly and very quickly that this was a pararreligious life, and that the important thing was the discussion that surrounded these activities."

After each Action the Mukhomors attended with K/D, each presentation in the Seminar, there were discussion and analysis; and after a few months the Mukhomors did a presentation of their own, which seemed to them to be much the same as those they had seen. When they finished, the members of the circle told them frankly that it was terrible. According to Sven, "We understood then that we did not understand the criteria of serious art. We had thought that everyone did what they liked and called it art; but we now understood that there was some method, some system that made their activities art." A few weeks later they did a performance for which they taped sentences and, between them, silences, so that by playing the cassette and speaking during the silences they would seem to be in dialogue with the tape recorder. It was badly done, and in the end there were long silences between the conclusions of their live statements and the statements of the tape recorder. They expected another attack; but when they finished, everyone said that the meaningful thing about the performance was its exploitation of these silences. In this way, the Mukhomors became pupils of the older generation.

Their master was always Monastyrskiy, who dominated their lives so much that at one point they took on his deportment and his intonations. Sven Gundlakh and the Mironenkos would spend days and nights at Monastyrskiy's place listening to his stories. He took the role of tutor, which he has occupied ever since; he is most at ease surrounded by his small circle of friends and pupils. The Mukhomors went through a phase of making fun of Monastyrskiy, a phase of mute devotion, a phase of teasing; but their relationship was always obsessively close. Only Kostya Zvezdochetov remained slightly aloof; he was always uncomfortable with what he perceived as the pro-Western dissident orientation of the Seminar. "I thought of myself as left-wing," he has recalled. "I felt I should know about the West, but I didn't want to imitate the West. I tried to find a third way, neither government nor dissident. Also, the tradition of Kabakov and Monastyrskiy was for me a little bit cold and a little bit snobbish. I needed something more open and more democratic."

The Mukhomors achieved the privileged intimacy that Kabakov's generation, and then Monastyrskiy's, had enjoyed in earlier years. "Ours was a very spiritual friendship," Kostya has said. "We were close as a family, and we were very happy just to be talking to one another, to create things together. We could write poetry all night, or sing, or paint, and we laughed a lot. It was the pleasure of communal work. We accepted that we were born in a totalitarian society, and felt that we must live in it; our only option was to try to be free in this not-free life. Kabakov was anti-Soviet and very secret; we tried to play with this. Of course it was a very dangerous game, but we were too young, and we were not afraid. And for Kabakov, we were new and fresh; at the beginning, he thought us too aggressive, but afterward he came to love us, and was very glad that we existed." Perhaps the Mukhomors were the fulfillment of the collective fantasies of the Seminar: the overeager converts every sect attends.

The performances of the Mukhomors were fun and funny, sponta-

neous in their ironies, at one level a pastiche of Monastyrskiy, at
another a parody, and at yet another a continuation. "We were like
monkeys. We made the same movement, as monkeys do, but with
different intention and different meaning," Kostya has said. In an
early piece, they dressed up as Tolstoy and went to visit his estate,
where they coincided with a political demonstration and were almost
arrested. Their first "real" performance was called *Party for the Memory
of Lieutenant Rzhevskiy*. Lieutenant Rzhevskiy is a fictitious character
of Soviet humor, a local equivalent to Kilroy, or Fred and Ethel, said
to be a great womanizer, a great drinker, and a great buffoon. The
Mukhomors wrote Lieutenant Rzhevskiy's biography, compiled a list
of his friends, made or bought his various possessions, wrote stories
about him, and made paintings of him. Later, they did *Underground
Life*, a performance for which they stayed in the metro from the time
it opened at 6:00 A.M. until it closed at 1:00 A.M. They made a
schedule in advance of arrivals at various stations, and distributed it
to friends who met them at certain stops. But the experience became
strained when they found themselves unable to keep all their appointments, and they wrote notes in a collective diary all day about their
frustrations and disappointments.

Their performances, like those of K/D, became more theatrical with
time. For *Treasure*, Kostya Zvezdochetov, Aleksey Kamenskiy, and
the Mironenkos, in the mode of Monastyrskiy, invited members of
the public to travel to a field in the country, and told them, when
they arrived, that there was a treasure buried there which was about
to be excavated. After some digging, they uncovered a box; in the box
was Sven Gundlakh, who had been underground for several hours,
hunched over, writing in a diary with a flashlight. Sven had been
driven to the brink of distraction by a fly who happened to get into
the box at the same time he did. He was partly suffocated; his diary
fades from legible coherence into scrawled nonsense. Stunned by the
light, he ran away across the field, to the surprise of both the public
and the other Mukhomors.

Brash energetic madness excited the members of the Seminar, but
it could be pushed too far. For *Execution*, the Mukhomors once more
invited the public—a broad public, composed of perhaps a hundred
friends from outside the circle—to a wood outside Moscow, and said
to them, "We have invited you to the forest because we want to kill
someone. Who wants to be killed? Whoever wants to be killed, please
step forward." A pregnant woman, a very young Orthodox Jew, and

an artist named Kolya Kozlov stepped forward. The Mukhomors drew lots from a hat, and chose the young Jew. They escorted him behind a bush, made a sound of shooting, and then brought him out on a flat board like a stretcher. Then a friend of the "deceased" read Hebrew prayers for the dead over the body. Kabakov saw the performance, and said that the Mukhomors had irretrievably sullied his vision and had demonstrated a deep vulgarity of imagery, of intention, of aesthetic, and of purpose.

It was at about this time that members of the Seminar went to see an exhibition called *Ideal People* in a Moscow apartment. When the Sots Artists Komar and Melamid emigrated, Melamid's wife, an art teacher called Katya Arnold, stayed in Moscow. Some younger people who had been pupils of Komar and Melamid continued to see her and work with her, including Misha Roshal—Komar and Melamid's truest disciple—Gennadiy Donskoy, and Igor Lyuts. She also found other students with whom she was in sympathy, and in this way Yuriy Albert came to the Komar and Melamid circle, bringing with him Vadim Zakharov and Viktor Skersis. It is still a favorite line of the Mukhomors that although they were brought up by Kabakov, the circle around Komar and Melamid was abandoned by its founders. *Ideal People* was a show of Vadim Zakharov, Yuriy Albert, and Igor Lyuts, organized by Viktor Skersis and Gennadiy Donskoy. It included installations and drawings; Yuriy Albert read a comic poem about Duchamp during the opening.

The exhibition made a profound impression on the members of the Seminar. They met all of Katya Arnold's circle, though they were initially quite distant from them. But Donskoy went mad, Roshal, always a hearty drinker, became less and less productive, and Lyuts decided to try to build an official career in the Union of Artists, and in the end the artists who were left—Yuriy Albert, Viktor Skersis, and Vadim Zakharov—joined the Seminar. They were the new darlings of that world, young, fiercely intellectual, humorous but deeply serious. They did not provoke the nervousness that always surrounded the Mukhomors; they had an agenda of their own, but were prepared to learn from Kabakov and Monastyrskiy. From the first moment, they and the Mukhomors were in competition, and fixed each other as enemies. The Zakharov group were practitioners of something derived from Sots Art, and they were supreme rationalists, whose rationalism generated its own impenetrable rituals. That rationalism appealed to Monastyrskiy and Kabakov; though its mystery was not the mystery associated with the circle, it still depended on hermeticism. Zakharov was at that time working on a series of performances based on the characters of the elephant and the one-eyed man. Zakharov himself played the one-eyed man, the Soviet citizen whose human power has been severely compromised. For several years, he wore an eye-patch all the time. The elephant was the symbol of the Soviet system: you can't fight with elephants. In his performances, Zakharov wore the eye-patch and arranged model elephants around him and then photographed and captioned himself: "When my wife put elephants on my spine, I was unable to move"; or "When the elephants came out of my mouth, I decided that they were preventing me from living." Everything in this work was encoded and referential.

"For us it was too dispassionate," Kostya Zvezdochetov has said. There were tensions creeping in on other fronts. Though the respect of the young generation for the older remained strong, a very real coolness also set in. Nikita Alexeev moved closer and closer to the Mukhomors, and in 1979 he broke with K/D; he remained faithful to Monastyrskiy, but he ceased to participate in the Actions. "I felt that the Actions had become a kind of elitist cabaret for Kabakov and Chuykov and the rest of them," he has said. "At the beginning, ideas were approved or taken by everyone in the group together, and we did only what everyone in the group wished to do. Then Andrey became more authoritarian, and he began to push for his own ideas. Sometimes I felt like I was in a hall of mirrors. I didn't have to listen to Andrey for five minutes, because after his first three words I already understood what he was saying; and before I understood the message, I understood the structure of his speech."

In this period of transition, the Seminar was held together by the journal *MANI. MANI* was the Moscow Archive of New Art, and it was a sort of substitute for the exhibitions that were not taking place and the magazines that were not being published, a formal means of communication among artists. It was organized by Nikita Alexeev, Dima Prigov, Andrey Monastyrskiy, Lev Rubinshteyn, and Vadim Zakharov. The artists had no access to photocopiers, so they used carbon paper and made just five copies of *MANI,* which was supposed to come out quarterly. Four of these stayed in Moscow studios, to be studied by whoever wanted to look at them, and the fifth was sent, when possible, to Margarita and Viktor Tupitsyn in New York. *MANI* was a compendium of materials given by artists, writers, and critics: copies of works, texts, manifestos, all put together into volumes often of five or six hundred pages. For example: Kostya Zvezdochetov and the Mironenkos asked Sven to sign a piece of blank paper. They wrote above his signature, "On this date, I will not go to work," and then invited him to be photographed with them in a photo studio; the photo and the document went into *MANI*.

MANI ended badly. Once again, some of the older artists were offended by the behavior of some of the younger ones. Vadim Zakharov published a series of photos under the title *I Acquired Enemies*, which showed him with his hand outstretched and, written on it, sentences addressed to older artists. One said, "Shteynberg, you are Malevich with makeup." Another said, "Bulatov, you are clearly bluffing. It's dangerous now." Vadim Zakharov thought that this work would energize the deteriorating camaraderie of the Seminar, that it would start a discussion, but he miscalculated. Though most of the artists, even if they were offended, said nothing, Yankilevskiy and Shteynberg said that Zakharov was a hooligan, and started a campaign against the younger artists.

Shortly after *MANI* was started, a group of émigrés based in Paris, under the leadership of Igor Chelkovski, who had previously been in the Prigov/Orlov/Lebedev circle that existed parallel to the Kabakov circle, started a magazine called *A-Ya*, published in Russian and English with an unillustrated pull-out translation in French. *A-Ya* included work by artists and critics in Moscow, by critics who had left, and by Westerners interested in the Soviet underground. Among the primary writers were Kabakov, Monastyrskiy, Boris Groys, Viktor and Margarita Tupitsyn, Rimma and Valeriy Gerlovin, and Vitaliy Patsukov. Though the circulation of *A-Ya* was not vast, it attracted some notice in the West, and short articles about it appeared in various Western newspapers in 1980 and 1981. There was always trouble getting funds, and it was later said—not only by the state, but also by some artists—that *A-Ya* was sponsored in part by the CIA. Ultimately, Chelkovski ruined the magazine when he turned it from an art review into a political journal, but even in its purest art days, the magazine filled a strangely political role in the lives of the artists. For them, it became insurance, a way of getting their names well enough circulated in the West so that they acquired a certain immunity to the KGB. The idea was that they would become sufficiently prominent that their disappearance would cause a stir. To some extent this agenda was successful; the KGB was daunted. Its bureaucrats were also extremely angry, however, and that anger was not in the best interests of any of the artists. *A-Ya* functioned for the KGB as a guide to the "enemy," and anyone whose name appeared in it was guaranteed close surveillance. It was another step in the breaking down of the hermetic world, another challenge thrown at officialdom.

Boris Groys, a formative member of the Seminar, perhaps the preeminent Soviet critic, suffered the most dramatic consequences of *A-Ya*. Groys had published articles in the magazine on various subjects, usually written in what has been characterized as an abstracted post-existentialist vein. In one, he concluded that "the existence and the work of the contemporary artist [are] groundless." His work was not well received by officialdom, and in 1980, men from the KGB arrived in his office to arrest him. He asked them not to embarrass him during a meeting with a student, and they agreed to give him ten minutes. Groys, knowing that his home would be searched and that he might be imprisoned, quickly called his wife and instructed her to take any suspect literature or belongings in their house to the home of a friend. He told her what had happened, and hung up.

Then he came out of his office, and went obediently downstairs with the KGB men. The KGB is not as slick as they would have one believe; their driver had disappeared, leaving them to discuss at some length the merits of taking a taxi to KGB headquarters. It was difficult, however, to get a taxi that day; and just as one arrived, the KGB car also arrived, its driver, who had decided to earn a quick ruble by giving a ride to a paying passenger, extremely apologetic. Groys was brought in for questioning and intimidation, but he was not treated as harshly as he might have been, perhaps because *A-Ya,* source of these difficulties, really was functioning as a kind of armor. He was asked to sign documents saying that he had lied and deceived in everything he had published. When he refused, he was told that he might find another country more congenial to him. Most unwillingly, he and his wife and their son emigrated to West Germany a year and a half later, after numerous unpleasant confrontations of the sort endured at that time by any enemy of the Soviet state.

The Mukhomors of course appeared in *A-Ya*. While others continued to cling to the remains of their secret and sectarian world, the Mukhomors pushed themselves farther and farther into the public arena. They boosted their fame substantially through the auspices of the artists Yevgeniy Matusov and Dmitriy Vrubel, who had formed a group called the Council of the Sacral Miracles, devoted to the construction of work that commented on conceptual work. Since most Moscow conceptual work was already tied into a structure within which it was a comment on other conceptual work, the efforts of the Council of the Sacral Miracles were noteworthy for the self-consciousness they imposed on a process of meta-removal from the original idea of conceptualism itself. Matusov and Vrubel took to the Mukhomors, and Matusov invited them to come to his studio and declaim their literary works, recite poems, and sing songs. He released the session, on copied cassettes, as the Golden Disc of the Mukhomors. Matusov had connections within the Soviet underground, and was able to arrange distribution through secret channels. The tape became popular across the country, and was sold for what seemed at the time to be a lot of money; the Mukhomors were given a thousand rubles. It was the first time they, or anyone they knew, had made money with their real work and without help from the West. Later, they sold the broadcasting rights to a woman from the BBC World Service in exchange for a Laurie Anderson record, an item previously unknown in the U.S.S.R.

The mannerism of the younger artists' arrogance, the final full flush of their inspired energy, came with Aptart. It was with Aptart that fear met reason, and it was with Aptart that the members of the younger generation articulated most clearly their break from the tradition of mysteries that had formed them. In principle, it was quite simple: in 1982, Nikita Alexeev declared that his apartment was a gallery, and invited artists to plan exhibitions to take place there. He announced that it would be open to the public, that anyone who wished to come and visit would be allowed in. "The idea of the open gallery depended on rumors," he has recalled. Since there was no way to advertise, "it was a matter of starting rumors about yourself."

Of course the idea of an apartment exhibition was not new. The underground had always thrived on apartment exhibitions, but these had taken place by invitation. It is true that invitations were freely given, and that almost anyone who had heard about the exhibitions and had expressed an interest in going would have been allowed to visit; but admitting all interested visitors is not the same thing as stating that your home is a public place, open to any and all. If the whole structure of the vanguard depended on circles of relative initiation, then Aptart was about the deconstruction of those circles. Like the *Bulldozer Show*, it went unabashedly in the face of officialdom; there was nothing discreet about Aptart.

Aptart was a public success, on one occasion attracting more than a thousand people in a single day. All the younger artists took part: Alexeev, the Mukhomors, Zakharov, Skersis, Roshal, Kizevalter, and later on Andrey Filippov, who had studied at the Theater Design Institute with Zvezdochetov and the Mironenkos but who had not until then been a member of the circle. There were seven exhibitions, each with a theme, before the KGB finally closed down Aptart, though there were raids on Nikita's place—the "Aptart pogroms"— throughout. The work remained in many ways very private, full of in-jokes and in-references, but it was a privacy directed toward the public, manifestly political but elusive about the nature of its politics. One exhibition was called *Socialism in Wonderland*. At another, the Mukhomors presented their refrigerator, *The Story of a Life of Adventure,* which later became a symbol of the period. The idea was not dissimilar to that of the *Party for the Memory of Lieutenant Rzhevskiy.* In the refrigerator they placed the manuscript of a novel. They decorated the refrigerator with scenes from the novel, and with pieces of its text. They made up packages with the possessions of various characters and placed them on the shelves inside. They wrote additional anecdotes and tied these in bundles and placed them there as well. When the KGB came to the exhibition at which this work was first shown, with an air of great mystery and a manner of powerful discernment they confiscated several of the packages from the refrigerator, demonstrating a total inability to understand that it functioned as a whole and was not substantially impaired by the removal of some of its contents. Later, it became a game to add things to or take things away from the refrigerator, and the meaningful solemnity with which this was done became a metaphor for the meaningless solemnity of the KGB's approach. In this way the refrigerator functioned like a bait or a hidden camera, tempting the KGB to make fools of themselves and then remaining as a permanent testimony to their folly.

The KGB did not like Aptart, and they took their disapprobation out on the artists. Sven Gundlakh was still having Pegasus problems, so the KGB's attentions were most terrible for him, and it was also a very difficult time for Nikita Alexeev. Others felt the pressure as well; in fact the collector Leonid Talochkin, who had volunteered his apartment for Aptart while it was still just an idea, withdrew the offer when he was telephoned by the KGB and warned that there would be trouble. After an exhibition of Vadim Zakharov and Viktor Skersis, the "pogroms" began to be more serious. The artists followed the model of *A-Ya* and arranged for an article to be published in a Russian newspaper in Paris about the attacks, which was meant to offer insurance against further violence, but the newspaper was obscure, and the KGB was merely incensed.

Everyone became nervous about the publicity that surrounded Nikita Alexeev's apartment, and *Aptart En Plein Air* was held in large part to shift the focus away from that particular space. It was a sort of cross between Aptart, the *Bulldozer Show,* and K/D; it took place in a field outside Moscow, and included a broad range of artists from within the circle. Those who wished to visit the exhibition were conducted to it by train. It was in part a memorial to the *Bulldozer Show,* which, though only ten years earlier, was "like ancient history" to many of the young artists.

At the height of Aptart, the Odessa circle came on the scene. Whereas the Leningrad and Moscow artists have always known and distrusted one another, the Odessa artists eventually emigrated to Moscow and became central to the Moscow art world; they were formed by it, and later they were in some ways to form it. These artists have many of the characteristics traditionally associated with the South: they are emotional, passionate, and terribly clever, but also crafty, melodramatic, and scandalmongering. Odessa is an international city. Though it is part of the Ukraine, its seething masses include Jews, Moldavians, Romanians, Bulgarians, Georgians, Turks, Russians, Gypsies, and many others, and they all live in argumentative mutuality among the rich tastes and smells of their various trades. The Odessa artists came out of a world of alcohol and drugs and free love and rich music and dancing.

At the center of the artistic movement was a spoiled young man with smooth dark skin, long black hair, and white teeth; charming, jaded, cavalier, brilliant, and utterly irresponsible. This was Sergey Anufriev, the gifted child of devoted parents who never fully appreciated either his gifts or his flaws. His stepfather was a professor of philosophy, his mother a glamorous intellectual who held a salon on Tuesday evenings to which came all the brightest men and women in Odessa. It was through her web of connections that Sergey would come to know the Moscow artists, and would enter their circle. As a young man, he was a voracious reader, and his intellect was sharpened by his home life; but he was entirely without discipline, and by the time he was sixteen he had been thrown out of school. To be denied a diploma for political reasons in the U.S.S.R. is not uncommon, but to be thrown out of school for academic or behavioral reasons takes some doing.

Apparently out of sheer boredom, Anufriev found friends and brought them to his mother's salon. Many of these were hippielike would-be artists such as Aleksey Muzichenko, Andrey Marinyuk, and Dmitriy Nuzhin, whose lives of excess ultimately made them almost nonfunctional. Others were more capable: Pertsy (Oleg Petrenko and Lyudmila Skripkina), bitter, argumentative, tense people who were forever choosing friends and then antagonizing them into enemies; Yuriy Leyderman, fiercely intellectual and dryly playful; the mad but charming Leonid Voytsekhov; the gifted but often drunk Igor Chatskin, and the wry, clever Larisa Rezun (who would later marry and become Larisa Zvezdochetova). Larisa was at that time working in a crafts center, teaching amateurs traditional folk crafts, and it was in response to their unspeakable taste that she began to do her own work, which comments at the most profound level on the nature of kitsch. One of her amateurs was a friend of Sergey Anufriev, and took her to the salon. She was charmed by Anufriev, and shortly afterward they began to live together; the circle formed itself around them. "We were not such an intellectual circle; we were more involved with emotion and expression, with protesting against our life in Odessa, which was very ugly and very boring," Larisa has recalled.

By this time, problems had started to cluster around Anufriev. He had no job and refused to take one, which in Soviet terms means that he was a parasite on the state. He took money from his mother and squandered it. He had problems with drugs, and he was being sought for his military service. But Anufriev is as slippery as a fish in a cold stream, and he managed to slide past all these difficulties. In Moscow, through his mother's connections, he met the members of the Seminar. "Nobody in Moscow took him very seriously," Kostya Zvezdochetov has said. "He talked a lot and made everyone very sleepy and he tried to be very fashionable and, because he was in fact very provincial, he was very funny. But we were glad that somebody new had come to our circle from the outside."

Anufriev decided that life in Odessa was tedious without the "true" contemporary art he had seen in Moscow. When he returned to Odessa, he took with him copies of *A-Ya,* and tried to explain to his salon, which included about twenty people at that time, the life of the vanguard. "None of us understood anything the first time we saw *A-Ya,*" Larisa has recalled. "We were like a herd of terrible and wild monkeys, and all this seemed so dry and so tedious to us. I remember I hated the texts of Monastyrskiy and the commentaries of Kabakov. Then afterward I saw some work by the Mukhomors. That appealed to me, but the people—I thought they must all be snobs, and probably also drug addicts, and I was sure I would hate them."

In September 1983, Anufriev and Larisa went to Moscow with Pertsy and Leonid Voytsekhov to take part in an exhibition Anufriev had arranged through friends; Yuriy Leyderman, who was at that time studying in the Moscow Chemical Institute, was also invited. This was *Aptart Beyond the Fence,* the exhibition immediately after *Aptart En Plein Air.* *Aptart Beyond the Fence* took place in the Mironenkos' dacha. At that point the danger surrounding Aptart seemed, if anything, stronger than before, and there was no question of returning to Nikita Alexeev's apartment. "In fact, it seemed idiotic to do the exhibition altogether," Kostya Zvezdochetov has said. "I would have preferred not to take part, not because I was afraid, but because it seemed like a stupid challenge to throw at the KGB. But I felt that I had come so far, and that I could not turn my back on what my friends clearly wished to do."

Aptart Beyond the Fence was a revelation for the Odessa artists. They met Nikita Alexeev and the Mukhomors, and Kabakov and Monastyrskiy, and Prigov. They stayed in Sven Gundlakh's apartment for five days. "And I decided that I liked these people, and I had a new aim in my life," Larisa has said. When they returned to Odessa, Moscow was always on their minds. In May 1984, Larisa went to Moscow without Anufriev, with whom she had by that time broken, and she called Sven and took him her new work. It was a quiet month, in which some of the Aptart furor seemed to have died down, and there was a solo exhibition of Kostya Zvezdochetov's work going on at Nikita's apartment. Larisa stayed on in Moscow through that exhibition, and through an erotically humorous collaborative one by Kostya and Nikita called *For Soul and Body,* which consisted primarily of nude sketches, including a nude calendar designed by Nikita. Sven and Nikita decided to do a show called *Moscow-Odessa,* with work by the Mukhomors, Filippov, Nikita, and the Odessa artists. But by the

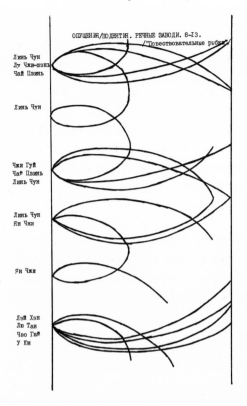

ОПУЩЕНИИ/ПОДНЯТИИ. РЕЧНЫЕ ЗАВОДИ. 8–13.
/"Повествовательные рыбки"/

Линь Чун
Лу Чжи-шэнь
Чай Цзинь

Линь Чун

Чжи Гуй
Чай Цзинь
Линь Чун

Линь Чун
Ян Чжи

Ян Чжи

Лэй Хэн
Лю Тан
Чжо Гай
У Юн

YURIY LEYDERMAN: *Lowerings/Raisings. Word Factories 8–13.*
/"*Narrative Little Fishes*"/ (Author's note: The words along the side of
the graph are "fake Chinese"; the first line, for example, says,
Lin chun lu chzhi-shen chay tszin. . . .")

time the exhibition opened, on Sven's birthday, the destruction of the
Mukhomors had begun.

Though there is mandatory military service in the U.S.S.R., very
few people from Moscow serve in the Soviet army. The easiest way to
be excused is to prove yourself insane and present a doctor's certificate
to this effect to the military commissariat. This is a common proce-
dure, and in artistic circles it is referred to in the most offhand way.
"Oh yes," someone will say. "That was the month I was in the mental
hospital, proving that I was schizophrenic." You have to be careful
not to prove yourself too insane when you go lest you be detained, but
in fact the doctors know which people have come to avoid military
service, and so long as these men do not have any problematical
political history, they are routinely discharged with their certificates.

The system works well for the army; Moscow citizens are usually frail and self-indulgent, snobbish and difficult, and they do not take orders well. It is better not to have them.

All of the Mukhomors had been excused from the army in this routine way. When they incurred the wrath of the KGB, they were to some extent protected by their high public profile and by the fact that they had been mentioned in the Western press. It was a time when the Soviet government was trying to improve its image abroad, and it was obvious that imprisoning the Mukhomors would run contrary to that purpose. At the same time, Moscow was being prepared for another Festival of Youth. Konstantin Chernenko, who was at that time the Secretary of the Communist Party, had said that he wanted the city to be spotless. Dissident or disagreeable youth was to be banished, so that the streets would be filled only with bright young Komsomol types, valiant champions of the Soviet way.

The Mukhomors had to be broken. They were making too much noise and causing too much trouble. With this agenda in mind, the KGB decided to dismiss their pleas of insanity and call them for punitive military service. They sent Kostya north; Sven they sent east; and Volodya Mironenko they sent south. Sergey Mironenko they spared, but he read the writing on the wall and went to an obscure village to work as a set designer. "It is by virtue of a triumph of modern Soviet medicine," Volodya was told, "that we are able to say to you today that you are not schizophrenic, that your own Soviet life has cured you of this terrible disease."

In some very profound way, the Mukhomors *were* broken by the army; and for some time after they left, the whole of the Moscow underground seemed to die. The older artists, who had admired but feared what the Mukhomors did, learned dread itself, and they closed their lives tighter and tighter against the world. Vadim Zakharov and Yuriy Albert became isolated. The Odessa artists went home. Fear dominated as it had not done since Stalin; everyone knew his name was on lists, and each artist waited with perpetual bated breath for trouble to visit. Nikita Alexeev could not be called to the army because he was too old, just past the maximum draft age, but he was called in twice by the KGB. "I was treated as an enemy of the State, like a foreign spy. By the time they got to me, the KGB had eliminated all the real opposition, and so they had to waste their energy on the next best thing." The government tried to meddle in his personal life; visas were repeatedly denied to a French woman whom he had planned to marry, and whom he was therefore unable to see for several years.

The fates of those who were drafted were terrible. Volodya Mironenko was stationed in the desert near the Volga delta at the Second Cosmodrome, where he was subjected to constant KGB questioning —though after his mother formed an attachment to an important person in the military service, he was transferred to a regiment near Moscow, from which he was sometimes permitted leave to visit his family. Sven Gundlakh was sent to a province near Japan, and "spent more time being grilled by the military KGB than I did in service. I was on duty every night. I was asked to sign papers, to tell stories. I was tortured and tortured with my Pegasus problem. I was made to clean everything all the time. I went months without being allowed any time to sleep, being forced to stand at attention with a gun for hours on end, then scrubbing some more, and then being brutalized by the KGB."

It is not possible to tell everyone's army stories; there is not enough space in this book about art to write a collection of military histories. But it is important to understand what life in the army was actually like. Kostya Zvezdochetov has said, "You must understand this to understand how I am different from Western artists. You must understand each joke, each game, each punishment, each day. Without this you cannot understand Soviet art, and you cannot understand the lives of artists." The ability of these artists to make the agonies of military life into an occasion for triumph, to use their subtlety and intelligence to get the upper hand against an organization as powerful and terrible as the Red Army—this is what makes them good artists. The army honed these abilities and so made the Mukhomors better artists. Kostya's introduction to the army was singularly brutal. In the last days of Aptart, his grandmother was very ill, and he divided his time between the exhibitions and her bedside. Shortly after *Aptart Beyond the Fence,* she became paralyzed. It was at this time that Kostya was called by the military commissariat to report for service; they had reconsidered his plea of insanity and found it groundless.

It was necessary to prove that it was not groundless at all, that he was indeed mad and ill. He gave up eating and became fearfully emaciated. There were several meetings with the military. At the first, Kostya was asked to strip, and refused, saying that he was afraid to be seen without trousers, which made the examiners very angry. Later, Kostya asked his doctor to provide evidence of his continuing mental maladies, which the doctor did; but the KGB brought pressure to bear, and shortly thereafter he backed down. Finally, Kostya called Andrey Filippov, whose girlfriend at that time was an ambulance paramedic, and she came and gave Kostya a large injection of insulin, which caused him to have fits and then go into a coma. Their original plan had been to undertake this in some provincial town, but there was no time; pressure was mounting, and so it was in Moscow, in this condition, that Kostya was rushed to a hospital barely alive. The KGB had overheard some months earlier a telephone conversation in which Kostya had agreed with Filippov that if the military situation got out of hand they would proceed in this way; when he came out of his coma, he found a doctor preparing for surgery, but before he could be anesthetized, men came from the KGB and took him, in his pajamas, to the military commissariat.

Though he had emerged from his coma, he was starved and still half delirious. In the commissariat, a major yelled and pounded a table with his revolver. Kostya asked whether he might see his grand-mother one last time to say goodbye, and they said no. Then he asked whether he could at least call his mother to tell her where he was going, and that request also was denied. He was put on a plane and sent to a processing point to be readied for his military career. "I had prepared for such an experience all my life, seeing the experience of my parents. All the time I would ask people who had been in prison, 'How is it there; what do you have to do there; how do you survive there?' But when we arrived at this processing point, and they opened the door, I saw forty young men without hair and with terrible, terrible faces. All these people had previously been in prison. And they looked at me from their terrible eyes, and I felt still very ill from the insulin and the trauma, and I thought to myself, this is the end."

He was pushed out of his plane and introduced to the battalion. The man who had brought him from the commissariat said, "This man is dirt. Keep an eye on him or he will try to run away. Abuse him as much as you can, and kick him whenever you like." That was a great mistake; because whereas the battalion had looked at this overrefined Muscovite with hatred when he toppled into their midst, they now realized that Kostya was, like them, a fugitive from society and from life, as criminal as they, and so they welcomed him almost as a brother. He was so thin—he weighed less than a hundred pounds at the time—and so sick and weak that they all felt instantly sorry for him. They gave him food to eat from their plates, and assisted him through the exercises that were put to him. Someone helped him send a letter to his mother explaining what had happened to him. She received it ten days later, and went at once to the processing point; but by the time she arrived, Kostya was far away, and no one there would tell her where he had gone. When she arrived back in Moscow, her mother had died.

Kostya was sent to Kamchatka, at the northeastern corner of Siberia. There his battalion was mixed with uneducated Soviet Asians, who had their own system of life and of justice. "If you were suddenly drafted straight from Cambridge into Hezbollah," Kostya once said to me, "it could not have been more shocking or alien than this was for me. There were an infinity of these terrible and criminal faces everywhere." The lot of small or weak men in the Soviet army is not usually a happy one. Younger soldiers are treated as slaves of older soldiers; in Kamchatka, weaker soldiers were the slaves of stronger ones. They were forced to polish the shoes of the strong soldiers, to sing them to sleep, to clean the toilets for them. And they were beaten all the time. The real terror is always of rape. According to the terms of the Soviet army, the man who commits a rape is not a homosexual, but the object of his rape is called a pederast. Pederasts are entirely cut out of society: they live in separate barracks; they have their own plates from which to eat; no one speaks with them. They are untouchables. Rape was frequently undertaken as a kind of execution. A group of soldiers would conceive a hatred for another soldier, and would say: to kill this man is not enough; it's better to rape him, because then he will be truly lower than the low. "I saw this a lot," Kostya has recalled. "It's terrible, you cannot imagine how awful. It happens often to people from Moscow who end up in the army. An old friend of mine, a very intelligent computer engineer, with whom I used to talk about art and literature—he was called to the army, and when I saw him, some years later, he was unrecognizable. He smelled disgusting because he was always making shit in his trousers, and he looked like an animal at the end of the hunt, and he could only think about getting enough to eat. It was far worse than to see him dead."

Kostya was so frail when he arrived that he was helped by the strong rather than abused by them. His first day, he was stripped of his clothing, as is usual in the army. "In this I was lucky; I could have lost my favorite shirt or my best shoes or my wallet, but I had come to the army in pajamas, and all I lost were those, fifteen kopecks, and three cigarettes." Then he was marched nude through the ranks, so pinched and so skeletal as to arouse the humanity of those around him. "Even among thieves, there is honor. And all the time, I was very clever, and very jolly. You can preserve yourself as well through spiritual strength as through physical strength. You must say and do the right things, and you must never show fear. If you are afraid, and you show it, it's the end. Also I was lucky because though I was with criminals from Moscow, I was, still, with a battalion of Muscovites among the Asians, and in this context, what we had in common was greater than our differences, and we all defended one another." Kostya was moved between physical labor, during which he often broke down, and art work, making propaganda paintings for the officers. He became popular among the soldiers by doing tattoos for them, and they would give him bread, jam, and tea. There were many Azerbay-dzhantsy people stationed at the same point in Kamchatka, who spoke very little Russian. Though they were Islamic, none of them had read the Koran; but Kostya had read it in the days of the Seminar, and "I told them about the Koran, and I smoked hash with them, and they called me 'artist,' and they asked me to draw an icon of a Shiite holy man, and there also I was all right."

Kamchatka was painfully cold. It was autumn when Kostya arrived; it was dark all day, and everything was covered by ice. His battalion was assigned to excavate the foundations of a military building that had been built on the ice, and so they were underground and under water, among icebergs and the sewage from the building, trying to dig through the ice—which the heat of the building was melting—to more solid rock below. "We all had our own shovels. And we would wedge the shovels into the ice, and we sat on the shovels in the water, and one man stood at the door. Periodically he would say, 'Officer coming!' And then we would show the officer that we were working. When the officer went away, we sat again on our shovels. It was a very cinematographical situation: very dark, a lot of shovels, and all of us always cold and hungry."

Other military tortures were more banal. Every frigid morning, the battalion did gymnastics in the nude. "Then the toilet. The stench of excrement was terrible. There were many people together, and they were all shitting together. At the beginning I could not shit there, but then I managed, and now I could shit in front of the Royal Palace. I think Western people cannot imagine this. We really were like animals. But there was a good library at our base, and it was in the army that I first read Evelyn Waugh. I think it's often this way in the

Konstantin (Kostya) Zvezdochetov: *Drama! In Kaffe! Drama!*
(Author's note: Almost all the words in this sketch are jokes of some
kind, many of them seminonsensical. The big sign at the upper left edge
of the image says, "to Perdo"; the small letters under the man with
glasses say, "And how was your work today?"; the word on the
projecting canopy is a sort of fake bureaucratic nonsense word, a
compound of several roots with a pointless "1" appended to it.)

U.S.S.R.: where you find the worst toilets, you find also the best books."

All the time, Kostya was denied knowledge about why he had been drafted, and he was never told how long he would have to stay, whether this was a standard military service or a matter of a lifetime. Every week a car from the military KGB came to the battalion to bring him to the local KGB headquarters, and even the colonel commanding his battalion did not know why; he told everyone, and believed himself, that Kostya was doing artwork for the KGB. Every week, for eight hours at a time, the KGB would ask questions and intimidate him. "I thought maybe I would die there, because it's very easy to die in the army. They told me, 'If you don't listen to us and work with us and if you're not good with us, it will be very terrible for you.' It really was very hard. Eight hours of this talking, and then they leave you in an empty room with dark gray walls with a table and a paper. And they ask you to write such absurd things."

On one memorable occasion, Kostya was asked to write an article about his work. He refused. Then he was told that if he were to write such an article, it would make Sven's life easier, because he was "a man who makes no compromises with us." So Kostya spent several days working on an article; but in the end the KGB brought him a text that they had written and asked him to sign it, a text which said that the Mukhomors had never made art, that they were traitors of the motherland, and that they had collaborated with the enemies of the motherland. When Kostya refused to sign it, they asked him to correct its inaccuracies. He spent several days making corrections, and then returned the article. They published it; but they published it with only half of the changes incorporated. The article appeared in the regional military newspaper, read by no one, but it was a miserable experience, and whether it was helpful, either to Kostya or to Sven, it is impossible to say.

Kostya's only real friend in the army was an architect who was carrying out routine military service. This man was called in by the KGB and asked to spy on the artist, promised a lighter time if he would provide information. He went immediately to Kostya, and explained that he could not say no—since this would have shown dangerous anti-Soviet sentiment—but that he must ask Kostya to keep his distance, not to betray whatever his secrets were. Kostya had a better way. "Tell them that you can win me only with coffee and chocolates," he said. "Tell them that this is the way to my heart."

And every week they would sit together, drinking coffee and eating chocolate and planning the next report to give to the KGB, as full of false signifiers and meaningless stories as the most contentious Aptart exhibition.

"It was very bad for Sven, because he doesn't play, and whereas I was in the military building corps, Sven was in the real military. The people in the building corps are more criminal and less disciplined, more chaotic, but also more free. We wrote a lot of letters. Everyone from the KGB read all these letters, and so they had to be carefully constructed; but we wrote them constantly. I corresponded also with Nikita and Larisa, and Sven wrote often to Dima Prigov, and we wrote a lot of theory of art, and about what we hoped would happen in the next years. We were a little bit like prophets: much of what we wrote *has* happened. Someday, I hope, this correspondence will be published, maybe after our deaths."

While the Mukhomors were in the army, the members of the Seminar remained essentially silent. But there was activity brewing in another quarter. Three men who had seen all the Aptart exhibitions, who had been faithful members of the visiting public, began to do art work of their own. German Vinogradov, Nikolay Filatov, and Andrey Royter found that they needed a center for their activities, a place to work, exhibit, and meet with friends, and in 1984 they founded the Kindergarten. Each took one of the eight-hour watchman shifts guarding an abandoned children's school; they made the place into the center of a new semipublic Moscow artistic life. By this time, the West had started to sniff at the edges of Soviet art, and the people in the Kindergarten knew how to exploit this interest. Aptart was public, the Kindergarten was blithely commodity-producing. The artists tried to sell work on the basis of the interest they established. They wanted to be chic and popular; they recognized the benefit to them of being obviously at the forefront. The Kindergarten was the beginning of Soviet Western-style art.

Around the three central artists, others joined. Sergey Anufriev, with his fine feel for the cutting edge, immediately became involved, and Nikita Alexeev did an exhibition at the Kindergarten. Gosha Ostretsov and Zhora Litichevskiy joined this circle as well. A photographer named Sergey Volkov, who had come to various parties at the place, decided one afternoon in 1986 to try his hand at painting, and found that he was really rather good at it. The Kindergarten was the center of a new life of fun; and like Aptart it was a thorn in the side of authority. In 1986, the artists associated with it were individually threatened by the KGB, who came with increasing frequency to disrupt the festivities. In 1987, it was torn down; the artists were given just twenty-four hours to remove all their worldly goods from it.

The Mukhomors were released from the army at about this time. Sven Gundlakh, who had not finished his course at the Institute of Art, was obliged to serve two years on grounds of "minimal education"; Kostya Zvezdochetov and Volodya Mironenko were given their freedom at the end of eighteen months, and Kostya married Larisa shortly thereafter. Sergey Mironenko returned from the north. They found themselves in the unfamiliar world of the Kindergarten. Sven founded his rock band, Middle Russian Elevation, as a sort of joke, a continuation of the tradition of the Golden Disc of the Mukhomors. The name itself is a joke; it is a geological term referring to the hills around Moscow, but it is also the state of mind of a Russian who has been only partially uplifted. Everything Sven wrote for the group was ironic, but only a very small part of his audience understood that it was ironic. It mocked the Soviet rock tradition, the old Russian folk music tradition, the tradition of the vanguard: it was encyclopedic in its mockery. The group's popularity was immediate and enormous, and it became an object of fascination, its members authentic pop stars. Sergey Anufriev immediately joined, praising Sven as a new genius. Sergey Vorontsov, a friend of Sven's, wrote the music with him. Dima Prigov also joined, and Ira Nakhova's new husband, Josif Bakshteyn, played the triangle because he had "always thought it would be fun to be a rock star." Nikita Alexeev's next-door neighbor also came, a young man called Nikola Ovchinnikov, who slowly befriended the members of the circle, and became a member of the vanguard.

By this time, glasnost was in the wind, and people feared the KGB less than they had before. But the problems were not over. Dima Prigov wrote a series of ecological and moral appeals, which he printed on small sheets of paper and posted on lampposts and trees. These said such things as, "Citizens! If you have flattened the grass and destroyed the nests of birds, how can you look at your mother's face?" They were signed Dmitriy Aleksandrovich. "One day as I was walking along in the street," Prigov has recalled, "a man came up to me, and I supposed that he wanted a light for a cigarette, and so I explained to him that I don't smoke. He said, 'No no no,' and showed me his papers, and took me to the KGB, and they called for a car, and they put me immediately into a mental hospital. This was in 1986. It was under Gorbachev. I was the last mental prisoner in the Soviet Union." Prigov's wife, Nadya Burova, received a telephone call that night from an old school friend who was working as a nurse at the hospital where Prigov had been sent. "Your husband is here," she said, and then hung up. Nadya organized a protest; he was released two days later.

Most of the time, in Gorbachev's early days, the KGB showed its pleasant face. Many of the artists had KGB men assigned to them, who called them by their first names, tried to befriend them, dropped in casually to visit them. They would propose in the most agreeable way that the artists visit the KGB building, but the artists were not receptive to such invitations, and they paid no attention to them. The friendly front was only a front. "One time, when they were pressuring me to come to the KGB, I said, 'I will meet you, but only in neutral territory,' " Kostya has recalled. "So we decided to meet one another in the street, and I also invited Bakshteyn and Vrubel. I took with me a big wooden wheel from an old horse cart, and I decided that if they tried to put me in a car, I would block the way with this and start to shout. I knew that the man on my case from the KGB was supposed to be proceeding subtly, and wouldn't like a scandal in the street. I stood near a wall, and when this man came I arranged it so that he had his back to the wall, and I had my back to the street. And I said: 'You want to talk about art? I have invited some great experts for you, for a consultation.' Bakshteyn came from the left, and Dima Vrubel from the right. The KGB man looked very nervous, and he said: 'You know, Kostya, I came here only to tell you that I cannot speak with you today because I am very busy, and I couldn't reach you by phone, but I'll call you later.' And he ran away, and didn't bother me after that."

At this time, decrees issued by the new liberal government made it possible to register officially all sorts of clubs and organizations that had previously been underground and secret, and Gundlakh and Anufriev, with Prigov and Bakshteyn, organized the Club of the Avant-Gardists, composed of the members of the Seminar, Aptart, and *MANI;* they registered it officially and got a space in which to hold, for the first time, exhibitions under official sanction. Many very good exhibitions took place there in 1987 and 1988. Such older artists as Kabakov did not join, though they were honorary members of the club; they articulated increasing discomfort with the noisy commercial bias they saw among their friends.

Two interesting movements emerged at about that time: Medger-menevtika and the Champions of the World. The first was founded by Sergey Anufriev with Yuriy Leyderman and Pasha Peppershteyn, the son of Viktor Pivovarov. The members fashioned themselves the pure students of Monastyrskiy, and like the Mukhomors before them they took on his intonations and mannerisms. Their work is very dry, very self-conscious, very complex. Medgermenevtika began, like the Council of the Sacral Miracles, by commenting explicitly on the conceptual work around them. They were inspectors of all the other artists. They rated them on a numerical scale. They submitted proposals to them telling them what they ought or ought not to do. Their work was shot through with Eastern mysticism, and it employed a language so complex and ritualized as to be almost meaningless. The group's efforts included conversations on tapes, long texts of inspired obscurity, and occasional installations. Pasha Peppershteyn, who had been a child prodigy, modeled himself increasingly on the grave Monastyrskiy; the very name of the group reflected two of Monastyrskiy's great obsessions: medicine, with its scientific import, its charts and scales, its complex pathology; and hermeneutics, which are his camouflage and his raison d'être.

The Champions of the World were very different. When Kostya returned from the army, he felt "full of anger, because first they didn't let me say goodbye to my grandmother, and then they made me feel that I was shit. I knew I had to imagine every way to fight them for the rest of my life." His old friend Yevgeniy Matusov, who was teaching physics in Moscow, introduced Kostya to one of his students, Giya Abramishvili, and Giya introduced him to two school friends, Boris Matrosov and Kostya Latyshev. Together they founded the Champions of the World, which was a shadow of the Mukhomors. Once more, serious jokes allowed a group of artists to define themselves in liberation from the establishment, making music, literature, poetry, and performances. "I had again the feeling that we might create something together, be friends for work and for pleasure," Kostya has recalled.

Each day the Champions met and saluted the flag together and did exercises, and then one would deliver directives to the others, which might say, for example: "Today, you must do a painting. In it there must be a red horse, a nude woman, and a blue sky. In this sky you must use two grams of blue and one gram of white. For the horse you must use three grams of red." The paintings would be executed according to the day's instructions, and presented to whoever had formulated the directive for approval. Once the pictures had been approved and discussed, they were destroyed. "For us," Kostya Zvezdochetov has said, "the production of the work of art was not a goal; it was only an exercise or experience. We wanted to redefine authority; we usurped the power of others to destroy our work. We took reality only from art, only from aesthetics, or questions about aesthetics, much as the Green Party takes reality only from questions of the environment." Both Medgermenevtika and the Champions were obsessed with judgment, with what qualified someone to judge, with the way in which their judgment might be delivered. Such groups found their relevance when the West was encroaching with its aggressively alien standards, which had been given weight by hard currency.

Organized activities became public and spectacular; in 1987, the famous *Steam Baths* exhibition took place. It was a group idea for which many have seen fit to take responsibility: I have heard that it was staged by Josif Bakshteyn; that it was organized by Giya Abramishvili, Boris Matrosov, and Kostya Latyshev to establish their independence from Kostya Zvezdochetov, whose role in the Champions had become too autocratic; and that it was put on by the Club of the Avant-Gardists. It was a multi-media event, more of a happening than a performance or an exhibition, a hodgepodge of Kindergarten-style glamour and Monastyrskiy-type Action. With permission from local government and from the administrative authorities responsible for the space, the organizers invited artists to install work in Stalin's favorite sauna, a grotesque example of the dictator's most extravagant architecture. It was part of their intention that the work hung around the room would decay as a result of the steam, and in this they were not disappointed; it was their first gesture of resistance to the West's "commodification" of Soviet art, then in its earliest stages. For the opening, the men of the vanguard read poetry, sang, performed, and danced. They wore Third Rome togas (though many of them shed these to go swimming). The older artists desisted, but all the younger ones were there, and a feeling of manic fervor reigned.

In what was to become a tradition at all exhibitions in Moscow, and especially at those mounted by the Club of the Avant-Gardists, the organizers placed a large notebook, in which all visitors were asked to record their names and comments, at the entrance. Though in more traditional venues this book is to be found simply lying on a chair at the door, at the *Steam Baths* it was positioned in a glass-domed display case in which various kinds of soap and towels available to bathers were also on view. The usual frequenters of the baths and Muscovites who had come especially for the exhibition all wrote comments over the following months; it is interesting that the only negative remark recorded came from an American tourist who had stumbled on the show. The exhibition was inaccessible to women—Stalin's baths are for men only—and so a few weeks after the opening, a group of angry female artists stormed the place, overwhelmed the desk attendant, startled the old men padding naked through the steam, and examined the works of art. The very idea of feminism in the U.S.S.R. was a novel one; this was its first real manifestation within the vanguard.

While so many people were appearing on the scene, Nikita Alexeev left the Soviet Union in 1987. "I went in the days when nobody left, and when there were no reasons to leave, in the days when there were reasons to stay. So many of my friends left in the seventies, and that was like a slow poison for me. In one year you bid good-bye to twenty people, saying, 'We shall meet again,' and it's important for the rest of your life, that promise, even if by the time you get to the West you don't want to see these people. You dream of going where they have gone. I married a friend of the girl I loved, just to get out, because circumstances had separated me from my first love. I had planned to marry and leave for France, and I was too exhausted to change my mind."

Nikita's disappearance left a vacuum. Friends became more sentimental about one another and, as young artists sprouted up at every corner, they held onto one another more tightly. At about this time, Sergey Mironenko undertook the impossible task of finding a real studio. He befriended a figure in what Soviets call the "mafia"—the underworld of men with illicit connections through whom, since Khrushchev, unofficial people have negotiated anything unusual or urgent—a man who didn't want to work officially but who needed a place from which to carry on his activities. He had good connections throughout officialdom, and could arrange anything, but needed to acquire official status in society to rent rooms. Sergey Mironenko organized his brother, Sven Gundlakh, Kostya Zvezdochetov, Andrey Filippov, Vadim Zakharov, and Yuriy Albert to do drawings for this man, which they signed with his name, so that he could become a member of the Union of Artists; and in exchange, he arranged to rent four studios and sublet two of them at a very low price. These were the famous studios in Furmanny Lane, usually called, simply, Furmanny. "Then we were afflicted with him," Sven Gundlakh has recalled. "We had to live through the discussion of whether he should divorce his infertile wife, because he wanted a child, or whether, since he loved her very much, they should stay together. It was a great day when he married another woman and they conceived a child and he stopped coming in to discuss this problem, and we celebrated as much as he did." In Gorbachev's new U.S.S.R., this man has become the director of a cooperative.

In Furmanny, the Mukhomors were reunited as friends, but not with any real concurrence of artistic spirit. Everywhere in Moscow new artists were springing up, new groups demanding attention. Kabakov and Bulatov were being exhibited in Switzerland. Turmoil was brewing. And then came the men from Sotheby's, who wanted to organize an auction, to sell work for Western money. That, of course, was the beginning of the end.

There are two versions of the history of Leningrad art. There is a proud history that starts in the dim reaches of the past, and then there is the history that begins with Timur Novikov. It is perhaps useful to know what the world was like when Timur broke in on it, but whereas the Moscow artists cherish and recite their history, few of the Leningrad artists know what happened as far back as 1980, and few of them care. In fact, Leningrad was, at the end of Stalinism, the seat of a stronger artistic—but not reflective/intellectual—tradition than Moscow. Unofficial artists working there had been less closely scrutinized during the purges than their Muscovite counterparts, and many students of the great avant-gardists Kazimir Malevich, Pavel Filonov, and Mikhail Matyushin were still alive in the late fifties, ready to take advantage of the emerging liberal atmosphere. So it was that artists then in early middle age—the circle of Vladimir Sterligov, which included his wife, Tatyana Lobova, Filonov's most important pupil, and Pavel Kondratyev—were able to surface.

For all their radical antecedents, these artists were deeply conservative, and when the word "avant-garde" was used by official critics to describe their work, they considered it a disparagement. No one in Leningrad was interested in conceptualism or performances or installations or objects; they made paintings, and though they made them to be meaningful, they also intended them to be beautiful. These early members of the Leningrad vanguard believed in the idea of the masterpiece, in the single work of art, in nature, life, and natural truth. Though the Leningrad artists of this period resembled the Lianozovo artists in character, they were more serious, more earnestly engaged with a neo-Stalinist search for the utopia of the perfect artwork.

In the sixties, a parallel group developed around Aleksandr Arefyev, which included Vladimir Shagin, Shalom Shvarts, and Richard Veysman. These artists had all been expelled from their Art Institute in the late forties when they were found looking at reproductions of Impressionist pictures. They developed an artistic life based on the romance of the criminal mentality, and their art seems to reflect an obsession with drugs, drink, and imprisonment; their work is about the escape as much from boredom as from totalitarianism. Many Jewish unofficial artists were working in Leningrad at this time; they organized a group called Alef, in which Arefyev also participated, though he was Jewish neither by birth nor by faith. Alef was a group of friends, more social than artistic, people united against the official language, for whom method and style were secondary concerns. Another large and largely nonfunctional organization called T.I.E., the Fellowship for Experimental Art, ran beside it.

Whereas the Moscow unofficial art world had tried to mimic the whole scope of the Western art world, to include artists, critics, exhibition visitors, and collectors, the Leningrad scene was composed only of painters working in vague communication with one another in a variety of styles. In the early seventies, Leningrad art became even more conservative, and while conceptualism was blossoming in Moscow, Leningrad art became increasingly provincial, a kind of unofficial salon art. Such artists as Mikhail Shemyakin and Vladimir Vysotskiy did work which was full of extravagant personal images, but which did nothing interesting with those images. Artists in Leningrad were permitted to organize two semiofficial exhibitions, one in the Gaza House of Culture in 1974 and the other in the Nevsky House of Culture in 1976. These exhibitions fascinated; people waited all night to see them, and then were permitted only twenty minutes in the exhibition halls so that the vast crowds might flow through. Official circles were discomfitted by the work and by the interest it had generated, and the later seventies were "a time of bureaucratic papers and documents, of prisons, of a lot of death, of hospitals," as Andrey Khlobystin has recalled.

In those years, at the same time that Komar and Melamid, the

Tupitsyns, the Gerlovins, Leonid Sokov, and Alexander Kosolapov were leaving Moscow, artists began to leave Leningrad, and by 1979, more than half the city's unofficial world was gone: most emigrated under Jewish amnesty, but some, including Arefyev, were asked to leave by the KGB. The artists who remained tended to band together by dint of circumstance, but there was little coherence to be found, and the exhibitions staged through the loose structures of T.I.E. were uneven at best. Boris Koshelokhov—an abstract-expressionist painter who had studied philosophy, become a truck driver, and started to paint when he was thirty—organized the Letopis group. Something of a mystic, a hippie, he was fanatic about African art and primitive culture. His group did work that was very emotional, very Germanic, but that nonetheless purported to carry on the traditions of Mikhail Larionov and Natalya Goncharova. Timur Novikov joined this group when he was nineteen.

Timur was the most gifted of Koshelokhov's pupils, and carried his ideas into an entirely new realm, embarking on a way of life previously unknown in Leningrad. If the Mukhomors were radical, they were radical in the language of the artists who had gone before them; but Timur separated himself from tradition. He reached for and found a single style, expressed by his work, clothes, appearance, and mode of living. He developed his own cuisine, and invented musical instruments—including the *utyugon,* which plays itself—with which to perform new music. It was a movement toward high style, a kind of elegant exuberance, and it was, above all, a movement toward youth and the glorification of youth. Leningrad is a city of façades, an artificial city, built by Peter the Great where by nature there were swamps; how fitting that its art should be concerned with façades, with appearances, and with making those façades into a reality. By the early eighties, Timur had joined with another pupil of Koshelokhov, Oleg Kotelnikov, and founded the New Artists. Novikov's magnetic personality, charm, and élan drew people to him, and the New Artists were united by a kind of love for Timur that was given freely and freely returned. Kabakov and Monastyrskiy found followers by being aloof, and, however generous they may be, they remain aloof. Timur founded the New Artists by virtue of great personal warmth, by sharing his energy and enthusiasm with those around him.

Timur Novikov lived in a large communal apartment, and in 1981 and 1982 the other occupants, all of whom had been waiting years for private apartments, were relocated. As the housing crisis in Leningrad was not too bad at that time, no one was moved in, so Timur invited his friends to occupy the abandoned quarters. This twenty-room apartment was the center of the Leningrad art scene until Timur was forced to leave it four years later. It was in a large building just opposite the KGB headquarters. "There is an old Chinese saying," Afrika has remarked, "that if you want to be truly invisible, you must go to the center of a crowded city and stand under a lamp." So the New Artists blossomed under the eye of the KGB, untroubled by the world of officialdom. Three rooms remained unoccupied, and two of these they converted into a gallery, using it to hang their finished work, and inviting friends in for the exhibitions.

Shortly after the New Artists acquired this apartment, a boy of fourteen came from the small town of Novorossiysk on the Black Sea, strange-looking, quick-witted, and full of ambition. This boy was Sergey Bugaev, called Afrika. He had a friend in Leningrad, Georgiy Guryanov, who moved in the circle of the New Artists, and they visited various studios together. Timur was charmed by Afrika, and went one day to call on him. They spent an afternoon doing works on paper. Timur helped to organize a party for Afrika's fifteenth birthday a few days later, and soon this young boy was installed in the apartment, where he became a part of Leningrad artistic life. In 1983, Afrika went to Moscow, where he tried to make himself conspicuous with outrageous behavior, frequently going to parties in drag. Moscow didn't bite; it was the time of the Aptart pogroms, and no one had much time for him. In late 1983, he returned to Leningrad.

The Leningrad artists of the early eighties, including Timur, Afrika, Oleg Kotelnikov, Ivan Sotnikov, and Yevgeniy Kozlov, put together exhibitions that more and more people came to see. Timur also curated shows of the work of artists from the earlier Leningrad vanguard; one month he mounted a retrospective of the depressive Valeriy Cherkasov. In the mid-seventies, this artist had made a museum in his communal apartment from ready-made objects found on the streets, including ten nonfunctional TV sets with texts saying what they would show if they were working. After Cherkasov killed himself, Timur obtained his work from the communal apartment, saving it from being thrown away. So this man, whom few of the New Artists had known, became an important influence on their work. In the early- to mid-eighties, after Aptart had been closed down and before the Kindergarten had begun, Timur's apartment was the only one in the U.S.S.R. in which exhibitions of this kind were taking place, and some Moscow artists—including Nikita Alexeev, Nikola Ovchinnikov, and, of course, Sergey Anufriev—feeling that Timur's apartment was the place to be, came to see work there.

The Moscow vanguard is full of immigrants, people who came there to find glory and intellectual companionship. Ilya Kabakov, Ivan Chuykov, Sergey Volkov, Kostya Zvezdochetov, Vadim Zakharov, Sergey Anufriev, and many others came to Moscow. The Leningrad artists, with the exception of Afrika, came from Leningrad. "I like Moscow more than Leningrad," Afrika has said. "But I prefer to live in Leningrad. I like the kind of destructive energy of Leningrad, and I like it that everything is falling apart. I live in a city that's dying before my eyes. Of course Moscow is also not burgeoning; but it's a progressive city, full of ministers and official organizations that try to look like they're doing something. In Leningrad you know, absolutely, that nothing has changed in years. Leningrad's decadence comes from the absence of fresh blood; the artists are like the mad and hemophiliac children of hundreds of years of incest."

In 1982, Sergey Kurekhin, a friend of Timur's, created the rock group Pop Mekhanika. Originally, Pop Mekhanika was hardly musical at all; it was more like performance, and depended on the manufacture and exploitation of a variety of bizarre sounds. The artists in Leningrad are almost all musicians, the musicians artists, all of them poets, all of them actors, some of them filmmakers. So it was only fitting that Kurekhin should work with Timur and his circle when he created his group, and that they should be much involved in its metamorphosis into something theatrical and visual. It was also at about this time that Viktor Tsoy founded the group Kino, with Georgiy Guryanov, who at that time called himself Gustav, as drummer. Tsoy was also a painter, and Guryanov was one of the most skilled of the New Artists, one of the few who had gone through the rigors of an academic training; later he was to emerge as a major figure on the Leningrad scene. Kino played experimental music with Pop Mekhanika, and Kurekhin commented on the popular music of Kino.

Much of the work was done in a spirit of great lightness. In 1984, while the Mukhomors were serving army terms, Timur and Afrika did *The Idiot, Ballet for Three Friends, The Shooting Skier,* and a version of *Anna Karenina* in which the train is delayed, and Anna marries the stationmaster. These semiabsurdist ballets, each done with an all-male cast, were presented at Club 81, an organization left over from the sixties in which unofficial poets and writers were permitted to gather officially because they could be more easily watched when they were not meeting in secret. The KGB had lost interest in Club 81 over the years, but the place had remained standing, and was still the location for occasional meetings. "It was gray, with a ceiling that was falling down, and old ladies making tea in the corner," Afrika has said. *Anna Karenina* received a visit from a minor foreign diplomat, who filmed part of it; as the ballet was drawing to a close, the doors swung open, and men from the KGB came running in, demanding that the performance stop at once. They took some members of the audience, including the diplomat, out of the theater. "It was a very good and fitting ending for the performance," Afrika has said. "It was not a big problem for us, or for this diplomat; I think it was a problem only for these KGB men, whose throats became sore and hoarse from yelling in this way."

Timur several times invited an unofficial filmmaker, Yevgeniy Yufit, to show his work in the apartment, and the screenings of many of his films took place there. In the mid-eighties, Yufit founded his own artistic group in Leningrad, the Necrorealists. Andrey Khlobystin has observed that Timur plays the optimistic hippie to Afrika's cynical punk. But though Afrika may be cynical, his work is more inventive and more ambitious than punk. The Necrorealists, on the other hand, are as punk as they come. Their works, all in black and white, portray morgues, undertakers, decomposing corpses, cemeteries, and other subjects associated with death; and the artists, when possible, work not in studios but in these choice locations. Their art defines a way of life as lucidly as Timur's; they carry in their pockets dead animals, birds, and snakes in advanced stages of decomposition. It is one of their rituals to drink their own urine and then sing songs. One of the marginal figures in the Necrorealist group, a musician, managed to get the notice of the painters when, on his birthday, he ate an entire plate of his own excrement. Such behavior is, obviously, tiresome and repulsive, but the Necrorealists stand at some distance from Western punks because they do these things in a tone of high seriousness, with references to Buñuel and Dada and Surrealism, to the nature of life after death, and to the mannerist ornaments of mortality. And of course the New Artists themselves are capable of a certain amount of good-humored grotesquerie. Once someone put chickens in an empty room in Timur's communal apartment, where they lived for some time; after a few months one of the artists declared that the weight of living under the eye of the KGB was heavy upon him, and that he needed to make a painting with blood. "It's lucky," he said afterward, "that there was a chicken on hand."

At the other extreme were the Mitkis, who all dressed in high boots and sailor shirts and wore long beards; they declared that it was their intention to be altruistic and positive at all times, and they made more-concerted efforts in that direction than the staff at a Hyatt hotel.

When regulations governing unofficial organizations were relaxed in the late eighties, at about the same time that the Club of the Avant-Gardists was founded in Moscow, the Leningrad artists founded the Club of the Friends of Mayakovsky—the Mayakovsky Club to most of its members—and registered it officially. Mayakovsky was chosen because he is a figure between Revolution and the status quo, who (like Andy Warhol, but at a quite different level of seriousness) fuses the rhetoric of the avant-garde with the language of mass culture. Officialdom celebrated him as a hero of the Revolution, but also rejected him as a misguided idealist. The Mayakovsky Club, like the Club of the Avant-Gardists, was given an exhibition space by the government in 1986, and over the following two years, the artists most exhibited were Timur Novikov and Afrika, of course; Georgiy Guryanov, who strives for perfect beauty in his work and in himself; Oleg Kotelnikov, whose contribution tailed off as he became more dissolute; Yevgeniy Yufit, the Necrorealist; Vadim Ovchinnikov, who works with redefined and distorted myths; Inal, whose works show robots, hunters, and dogs; Yevgeniy Kozlov, a dandy and virtuoso; Aleksey Kozin, Oleg Maslov, and Oleg Zayka, who worked together in a neo-graffiti style; and Andrey Khlobystin, the only intellectual in the lot, the sage critic, the conceptualist, the Muscovite spiritualist in Leningrad.

The first officially sanctioned exhibition these artists held outside the club, called *New Year,* opened on December 31, 1987, in the House of Culture of the Workers of Art. Afrika returned to Leningrad that day from the mental hospital where he had gone to register his schizophrenia and avoid military service, the mental hospital where he had wrought such havoc—persuading the truly insane to eat flowers from windowboxes while reciting solemn oaths—that he had been released early. Relatively few people came to the opening of *New Year,* and it might have passed unnoticed had not official critics written ostentatiously disparaging reviews. Then in the first week of January, the artists took part in a Pop Mekhanika concert with Nikita Alexeev, Nikola Ovchinnikov, and Sergey Anufriev. Sergey Volkov came along for the spectacle and was arrested for videotaping it. Further official disapprobation brought the public running.

It was not unusual for men who came from the provinces to marry women in the cities where they wished to live in order to get residence in those cities. Several Moscow artists, including Sergey Volkov, had done this. Afrika had paid an acquaintance of Timur's fifteen hundred rubles to marry him so that he might live in Leningrad. She was threatened by the KGB, asked to inform on Afrika, and eventually put in jail. In 1988, Afrika was in trouble with the KGB on several fronts, and after a performance with Pop Mekhanika he was called in for interrogation. They had discovered that though he was registered for a job, he had in fact paid someone else to sign in for him every day, and that he had done no work. They had discovered that this was not a matter of negligence at a single job; Afrika had, in fact, not worked a day since his arrival in Leningrad. The KGB told him that his time was up, that he was going to jail, and they showed him the papers for his imprisonment, all drawn up and ready.

But by that time, ASSA was happening. The artists had decided years earlier that they needed to have a connection to some tradition, and so they manufactured a connection not to the Soviet past, but to a time before time. According to the legends of the Leningrad artists, "ASSA" was the one word Noah carried from the world before the flood to the time of the rainbow. They tell the story of the ark's coming to rest on Mount Ararat, of the dove's flying three times from the ship, and of her returning the third time with an olive branch. When this olive branch was presented, so the Leningrad artists say, Noah fell on his knees before the glory of God and said, "ASSA." The word is in fact used today by mystics in the area around Mount Ararat as a sort of mantra. The Leningrad underground adopted it as a password in 1983, and made up the quasi-biblical story to explain its origins. When they found themselves suddenly the center of attention in Leningrad, they decided to bring their word to the people as if it were a message of salvation.

An official filmmaker, Sergey Solovev, approached the artists with plans to make a film in early 1988, and they agreed that they would do it if the film were called ASSA. On the date Afrika was arrested, "They took me to a room downstairs in the House of Culture, where we had been performing," he has recalled. "A policeman said, 'You don't work. People in our country must work. Where are you getting money for living?' Then he said, 'We know that your marriage is not

AFRIKA (SERGEY BUGAEV): *Blockade Again!* (Author's note: This is one
of a series of works for which Afrika made prints from existing 1940s
plates and then signed them. It has been suggested that history is
currently repeating itself in the U.S.S.R.)

a real marriage, and that you do these weird things all the time, and your art is very strange, and your friends are very strange people, and we think that you have to change the style of your life, but you don't want to change the style of your life. So now we are going to change the style for you.' And so I said, 'No, I'm sorry to disappoint you, but I have a very good paper for you.' It was really a nice moment." Afrika had in his pocket the letter of invitation from the director who would make *ASSA*, signed by the Secretary of the Union of Filmmakers, saying that he was to travel to the Crimea in ten days' time to work on this extraordinary movie. The KGB men were extremely uncomfortable. Afrika was held while they made telephone calls and read the letter over and over again to senior officials. Afrika produced plane tickets for the Crimea, official tickets, issued by official authority. The arguments continued for two hours, and at the end of that time, Afrika was released.

ASSA was a typical phenomenon of the early days of glasnost, founded on the hope that official and unofficial people could work together and produce great art. It was a misty, sappy detective story, with a cloudy romance, at the edges of which images from the vanguard were tacked on like lace trim. There were problems surrounding *ASSA* from the beginning, but in the end it became one of the most popular films in the U.S.S.R. and made the Leningrad artists famous in every town from Riga to Sredne-Kolymsk. For the opening, a big exhibition was staged in Moscow that included work by Sergey Shutov, a Moscow artist closely tied to the Leningrad school, by the Champions of the World, by the conceptualist architect Yuriy Avvakumov, and by many of the New Artists.

After its release in the spring of 1988, *ASSA* brought the eyes of the Soviet Union to the vanguard. And it laid the way for Sotheby's, which was, a few months later, to bring in the eyes of the world.

CHAPTER III

They Came West

This is the letter that Sven Gundlakh sent me in August 1988:

Hello buddy!

We were very glad to get a letter from you. It was an un-looked-for surprise, in the midst of the nightmarish confusion with which Moscow has been possessed.

I believe that modern civilization gives birth to a phenomenon which could be described as metanationality, a diaspora one's membership in which is a matter not of nationality, but of outlook, language, and behavior within culture. It is for this reason that we look upon you as a relative of ours rather even than a friend. It seems to me that there are very few people in the world who are interested in the sphere of culture where we are engaged, and that we should therefore keep together. It is necessary, in the wild, that a species maintain a vital minimum of its members; if it falls short by just one, the whole species dies. It is the same for our metanationality; we belong to the same tribe, and we must not fall out of touch. For us, there is not art-industry where artists-manufacturers produce pictures-goods and critics-pushers help sell them or destroy rivals, but rather an ideal form of existence, a version of what in Orthodox iconography is called sacred conversation. It is centripetal, a matter of sitting around the void, the transcendental, the unlearnable. It is not a trade but rather an existential activity.

I may be wrong. Maybe all this doesn't bother you at all. But you must understand that our works are not the goal in themselves; they have no intrinsic value. It's as if you were trying to explain to a friend who doesn't know your area how to find your house. You would draw a scheme for him and your only concern would be that the scheme be right and understandable. You wouldn't have to be a cartographer to make the scheme perform its function. But the clearer your scheme, the more aesthetic value (in the traditional sense of the word) it would inevitably acquire. Still the aesthetic qualities of it would only be by-products, the side-effects of a nonaesthetic function.

Unfortunately, I feel compelled to wind up here, restraining my inexhaustible talkativeness, because I don't want my friend Ira, who is going to translate this, to go mad over the rhetoric of metaphysics.

I would like to tell you a lot more, or better, to sit down and talk over a cup of tea. In late September we'll all go to West Berlin, where we'll stay until the end of October; it would be just great if you could join us there, at least for a while. You can find us via Lisa Schmitz.

So goodbye for now and best wishes and hellos from all our team at Furmanny.

This is from Sven.

I had not expected to keep up with the Soviet artists after my original visit to Moscow and Leningrad. It was not that I did not want to keep up; it simply never crossed my mind that it would be feasible to do so. My trip to the U.S.S.R. had been expensive, and though I had liked the artists I had met, been fascinated by their work, even felt a deep kinship with them, a return seemed a matter for the rather distant future. It was true that Moscow was riveting, but it was also true that, at twenty-five, I had much of the world left to see. The U.S.S.R. was alien territory; I could not imagine going there on any sort of regular basis, even to see the people I had met and liked. It was all too foreign, too entirely outside the parameters of my life at the time.

And yet I wanted to know what would happen, in perhaps the way that one wants to know how a book about compelling and appealing characters will end—for our intimacy, which had seemed so real when I was in the U.S.S.R., seemed fictive now. My adventures were too quickly turning into anecdotes, the artists, in my mind's eye, into sketches of themselves. My impulse was to watch the tremendous consequences of the heroic deeds I had gone to chronicle, as a historian charts the ramifications of events that passed in his childhood, events whose vanished immediacy, in long-gone radio broadcasts or shots overhead, continues to haunt him. I thought I would keep an eye out for familiar names in the news and in the art press.

But then in the months following my travels, an old friend landed a job leading tour groups of retired Methodists from Ohio to Moscow and Leningrad; and when she volunteered to take some books with her for the people I had met, it seemed only right to take up the offer. It was difficult to decide what to send; I wanted to be aesthetic, but I also appreciated the difficulties the artists were having in their negotiations with the West, and I felt obliged to be practical. In the end, I sent to various people the *Whitney Biennial* catalogue, by way of providing a sketchy, mainstream-but-not-banal picture of new art; the *Art Diary,* the *Art in America Annual Guide,* and the *National Art Museum and Gallery Guide,* which I thought would be helpful in locating galleries and getting some indication of their prominence and their biases; and a sort of self-help book that gave crucial information about negotiating contracts with galleries and listed guidelines for prices, reproduction rights, import/export arrangements, and so on. I wrote a long letter to Furmanny, in which I said that it seemed absurd to speak of making friends in the course of three weeks, that under ordinary circumstances I would laugh at anyone who suggested that such a thing could be done, but that something about the need to explain everything so fast had given the weeks we had spent together a vividness I would be sorry to lose. "If one cannot say that we became friends so fast," I wrote, "I hope one can at least say that we sowed the seeds of what might someday become friendship."

It was in response to this that I received Sven's letter. I could not go to Berlin: that seemed obvious. It was too expensive an expedition to undertake, too complicated, too unconnected to my work. But I could write to the artists there, or talk to them, perhaps; and sooner or later, since they were at last receiving permission to travel, they were bound to come to London or to New York, the places where I live. The fact that they were actually leaving the U.S.S.R. seemed astonishing to me; though people had mentioned when I first went to the Soviet Union that travel might soon be possible, they spoke of it as we speak of the imminence of certain vaccines: with a fond procliv- ity for positive fantasy, a meaningless but good-natured optimism that may not, in the end, be unfounded. That it was actually happen- ing seemed incredible, and also rather exciting. I wondered what these people would be like out of context.

I was in the midst of such wondering when Galina Main entered my life, with a manner of engrossing earnestness and the utterly compelling lunacy of a latter-day Joan of Arc. If it had not been for Galina, I very much doubt that I would have pursued the subject of Soviet art, let alone written this book. In many instances she made things more difficult, but she also made the inconceivable possible. Though some of the artists who form the principal subject of this book mistrust her, others are very fond of her. I understand why the ones who mistrust her prefer to have no truck with her, but I also feel a bit sorry for them; Galina is joy itself.

Perhaps five weeks after my return from the U.S.S.R., I was dragged from my heavy slumbers at six one morning by the ringing of my telephone, which I grabbed upside down, turned back, and answered with the sudden delusion of clarity that abrupt awakenings tend to provoke. A voice said in a thick accent, "Hello. It is Galina Main who telephones. I telephone to speak with Andrew Solomon. I telephone urgently." I indicated that I was Andrew Solomon. "I have messages for you from Soviet artists," she said. "Greetings from Erik Bulatov, from the artists in Furmanny, from many others. I want very much to talk to you about very many things. But we cannot talk by telephone. Meet me in a small café in Paris, two months, Tuesday."

I explained as calmly as I could that I had never heard of anyone called Galina Main and that I had no intention of going to Paris in two months. I added that even if I were going to Paris in two months, I could not very well arrange to meet someone of whom I had never heard who called at six in the morning with a totally inexplicable message. "This is very disappointing," she said, and told me to think about it, and hung up. For a month I heard nothing. And then one day the phone rang, at perhaps nine o'clock. "It is Gala Main who calls again," said the voice, identifying itself with the nickname that would come to seem so very apposite. "Will you be meeting me in five weeks?" I asked her who she was and why she had called me. "I call from Darmstadt, in West Germany," she replied impatiently. "I want to speak to you about Soviet art. I have told you that we cannot speak on the telephone, but in five weeks it will be the opening of an exhibition of Erik Bulatov's paintings, Centre Pompidou. Come and be my escort to the opening of this exhibition."

The emergence of an exhibition, especially one at the Centre Pompidou, seemed to bode well. But I was very much back in the mode of the West, and I still hesitated to escort to a public function a woman I had never met whose manner on the telephone left only doubts of her identity and intentions. Who was she? It seemed more than likely that she was a madwoman who had taken my address from one of the dozens of people in Moscow to whom I had given it, or, worse yet, a spy from the KGB who was going to abduct me in Paris. Nothing I had written had been published yet, but I had submitted to magazines two articles about my trip to the U.S.S.R. Could they have fallen into the wrong hands? They did not, so far as I was aware, make mention of secrets of state. I was not in the habit of making quick trips to Paris for no reason at all, but as I did need to go on other business, I thought I might schedule the trip to coincide with the opening. I made some equivocal remarks, and Gala rang off.

Two days later she rang again, and this time, in a spirit of adventure, I agreed to meet her. We fixed the time and the date, and so on October 11, 1988, I found myself waiting outside the Centre Pompidou for a mysterious figure about whom I knew nothing at all. When I reached the museum there was a crowd outside, and there were perhaps thirty people standing and waiting for those they were meeting. I approached several heavyset elderly women, and said delicately, "Vous êtes Galina?" and received suspicious looks. I realized that it had been imbecile to make this arrangement without discussing some identifying characteristic in advance—I'll wear a red scarf and you carry a bunch of violets—or at least giving some indication of mutual appearance—I'm tallish with blue eyes and short fairish hair, and you're—whatever she was. I suddenly felt ridiculous. What was I doing, standing outside this museum hundreds of miles from home waiting for a woman who had called me three times on the telephone? I felt heartily sick of Soviets, not for the last time. I wanted to go home.

Suddenly a figure in a floor-length Persian lamb coat and a red velvet cap embroidered in gold came sweeping across the square beyond the museum, walked up to me, and without a moment's hesitation said, "You must be Andrew. I am Gala." And she gathered me up and led me through the door to the museum. "I have forgotten my invitation," she announced to the guard at the door. "But I am Galina," she said, and we sailed past, Galina not deigning to take note of his confused stare.

The exhibition was like a small reunion. I saw Bulatov. I finally met Ilya Kabakov, who had come for his friend's opening. I saw the French wife of Gosha Ostretsov, who had returned to France and was expecting Gosha to join her at any moment. When I had gone to Bulatov's studio, three months earlier, I had seen only one of his paintings; he had made sure, over the years, that as much of his work as he could possibly get out of the Soviet Union was taken elsewhere, so that there was almost nothing by him in Moscow when I visited. Still, I had had the experience of going to his studio and seeing one painting, *Brezhnev As a Cosmonaut,* leaning in a corner. Now it hung in state in one of the world's great museums of contemporary art; and I felt a funny pang at seeing it there, on a pure white wall, with a tiny typed label indicating its title, size, and medium. I felt a similar pang at seeing Erik Bulatov himself, whom I had last seen in a dilapidated room crowded with inexplicable objects; he and his work seemed somehow distorted by all this formulaic art-world elegance.

Neither seemed shoddy. It was not that Bulatov was clueless or badly dressed or ill at ease, and it was not that the paintings seemed unsophisticated or derivative or clumsily executed. No: the situation's oddity came from something far more difficult to identify than that. The paintings seemed more like ordinary art, and Bulatov himself more like an ordinary person. He stood in the middle of the room, gravely and graciously thanking the people who complimented him, chatting with influential curators and dealers, autographing catalogues for Frenchwomen who wore shoes from Roger Vivier. He could not have been more dignified; but clinging to him was the anonymity of decontextualization, which I was to see during the next ten months, often accompanied by less self-assurance, in almost all of the artists I had met in Moscow. Many people in the West are conditioned by the possibility of travel; ours is a mobile society. We do not allow ourselves to be defined by way of a single geography: what is German about a German is only made more clear when that German goes to France, and what is American about an American is thrown into sharp relief when the American goes to England. We behave in characteristic ways, evincing national identity in our culinary bias, our manner of speech, our clothes, our demands, and our expectations. Soviets coming to the West are in a disadvantaged position. They cannot make sense of this system of self-definition; they have no instincts for defining themselves outside their own context. They have no culinary bias because they have never been able to choose their food; their clothes are badly made and nondescript, and are usually rapidly shed for Western clothing anyway; their manner of speech is immaterial since no one speaks their language; they make no demands on public services or people they don't know because they are unaccustomed to having demands met; and their expectations are invariably so far from the reality of life in the West that they are almost an irrelevancy. Soviets in the West tend to undergo a sort of loss of personality, or a loss of immediacy. Of course part of their problem is also that in the U.S.S.R. it is not advisable to project too much personality; the more contentious your views, the more they need to be encoded, and the more likely you are to make every external effort to seem ordinary to the ordinary view. With time, the Soviet artists have learned to express themselves fluently in a world where none of the accessories of their accustomed communication exist; by mid-1989, most of them had travel personas, portable selves they could wheel out for their sojourns abroad. But in the autumn of 1988, when they first began to come to the West, they seemed like people viewed through the wrong end of a telescope. As for their work—stripped of context, it was stripped of its immediacy and much of its meaning. Seeing their work was like seeing the artifacts of a lost or distant civilization. Standing in the Pompidou on October 11, I felt the nostalgia someone who had visited dynastic Egypt might feel in the Egyptian wing of an ethnographic museum.

Despite that, the Bulatov exhibition was a great success; Bulatov does paintings on canvas, paintings that are fully accessible at the primary level of painterly exercise. Some of his work has an explicit political message which can be easily grasped; one painting, for example, shows the Soviet state symbol of quality stamped on the open sky. The Pompidou is beautiful, and the paintings were well displayed and well lit. Only later was I to learn the long history behind this exhibition, and understand how Kabakov and then Bulatov had been the first of the unofficial artists to travel from the U.S.S.R. to the West. Only with time would I come to see that their voyages had set the precedent for what was to become, for the entire vanguard, a way of life.

The saga began in the mid-seventies, when a Swiss student of Slavic studies brought a handful of drawings by Kabakov, Bulatov, Vladimir Yankilevskiy, and a few other artists of the older generation of the Moscow vanguard home from a term abroad. A small gallery in Zurich mounted an exhibition of these drawings, which passed quietly, largely unnoticed and unconsidered. But the work caught the eye of Paul Jolles, the Swiss Minister for Foreign Economic Affairs and the chairman of Nestlé. It was his habit, in the various countries to which his work carried him, to stay with the local Swiss ambassador. The ambassadors usually tried to devise diplomatic entertainments for Jolles, but he preferred to understand new countries by seeing how artists lived in them, and he would always ask to be taken on a tour of studios. In the U.S.S.R., of course, this was extremely difficult, but Jolles went in the late seventies armed with names from the Zurich show, and the embassy managed to locate the artists he hoped to meet. "So it was that I went to Kabakov's studio, where I was warmly received. And Kabakov immediately took me to meet the other artists. They were not competitive; they all wanted to introduce me to one another, and I bought some small works, drawings mostly, from the people I met." The following week, Kabakov was called in by the KGB and cross-examined for entertaining a stranger. "I didn't invite him, and I didn't solicit his visit," said Kabakov. "What should I have done when I saw him standing at my door? Refused him a cup of tea?"

Ten years passed before Paul Jolles's daughter, Claudia, went on a trip to the U.S.S.R. with her university class. Hoping for some interesting diversion, she asked her father for the addresses of the artists he had met so long before. She and the other students called on Kabakov and Bulatov at the beginning of their trip, and were very kindly treated. Later that year, her father was once more obliged to visit Moscow on affairs of state; while he was there he went to visit the artists and took photos of their work. Ideas were beginning to hatch. He took the photos to Jean-Hubert Martin, then director of the Kunsthalle in Berne, and suggested that a show be organized. Martin had heard the names Kabakov and Bulatov before, when he had worked on a show of Soviet avant-garde work from the twenties for the Pompidou; several Soviet curators had mentioned the artists, but he had barely met them or seen their work because he was afraid that such unofficial contacts might jeopardize the loans of Malevich and Kandinsky on which his exhibition was based.

Now Martin was free of these shackles, and he expressed great enthusiasm at the prospect of doing this show. He and Jolles agreed that Kabakov would be a good starting point—but none of Kabakov's paintings were outside the U.S.S.R., and there was no obvious way to bring them out. There was no question of getting official approbation for the exhibition; and since Paul Jolles had an important government post, he could not be seen to behave in a dishonest or underhanded way. Smuggling was out of the question. In the end, he applied for permission to take out individual paintings, and encouraged friends to do the same thing. The authorities did not check paintings that were being exported by individuals for private collections in the way that they checked those that were being taken out for exhibition, and though the delays were terrible, the paintings eventually began to arrive in the West. Each one had stamped export documents, across which the authorities had written: "Of No Artistic Value." Kabakov himself began to find people to bring out more contentious work. He persuaded someone who worked in an official packing firm to pack his paintings in such a way that a careless border official might imagine, from the quality of the boxing and bubble wrap, that they had received export approval. He gave his albums to schoolteachers who declared them as teaching aids.

By Christmas of 1984, there was enough work out so that the exhibition could be mounted. Claudia Jolles and Jean-Hubert Martin went to Moscow and presented Kabakov with a list of work and a floor plan of the gallery, and he designed the exhibition. In the summer of 1985, it opened in Berne. No one knew whether it would strengthen Kabakov's position in the U.S.S.R. or lead to more trouble for him. The organizers took great care to say that it was not a dissident exhibition, because they wanted to avoid causing Kabakov serious difficulties; the press lost interest, since at that time the Soviet Union was seen solely in political terms.

In the years that followed, paintings continued to drift out. Finally, in 1987, Kabakov began to plan his own exodus from Moscow. A childhood friend, whom he hadn't seen since his school days, was working in the Ministry of Culture. Kabakov spent some weeks searching for his home telephone number—there is no phone book, no information line in Moscow, and this was not a question to pose on the Ministry phones—and called him. "I have an exhibition in the West," he said. "I want to go to see it. Can you help me to get a visa?" "Call back in two days. I'll think about it," came the reply. So two days later, Kabakov phoned again. "I have thought about it. I will help you. Together we will do this." There then began nine months—"my visa was like a child in more ways than one," Kabakov was to say—of negotiating with the swirling circles of bureaucracy. The ministry friend told Kabakov that he would never be given a visa if he had been seen to apply for it. "I will assign you a mission, to go abroad and make artistic contacts for the Union of Artists," he said. "You will be sent by us on a business trip." The assignment was argued and delayed and considered and stamped and passed on and passed over. As much delay was caused by the envy of untraveled bureaucrats, many of whom fancied themselves artists, as by the strictures of the law. But at last, late in 1987, Kabakov was given permission to travel; and two weeks later, Bulatov, who had been going through much the same routine, was allowed to come West. By that time Claudia Jolles had organized an exhibition of Bulatov's work, and he made it to Zurich in time for the opening, at the Kunsthalle Zurich. Each artist was solemnly paid for his mission of goodwill, undertaken for the Union's glory: they received twenty Swiss francs each. It was at the end of that trip that Kabakov went to New York to install *Ten Characters* at Ronald Feldman Fine Arts.

The second exit was comparatively easy, and the Pompidou exhibition of Bulatov was the first stop on the second trip. This time, Bulatov's wife was with him, and travel seemed habitual. Nonetheless, it must have been extraordinary for him to see almost his complete work of the previous twenty years gathered in two large rooms, including paintings that had been smuggled out of the U.S.S.R. a decade earlier and that he had never expected to see again. It had been extraordinary in Zurich, but there had been so much that was novel on that first sojourn that the reality of the exhibition almost sailed past him. At the Pompidou, it was extraordinary with a new life and vividness. If Bulatov is the great romantic of the older generation of Moscow artists, then these first pleasures of exhibition and travel were like a romance realized.

Immediately after the opening at the Pompidou came a dinner of celebration, which took place in the Musée Grevin, the waxworks museum of Paris. It was the final touch of surrealism. We filed in past artificial versions of all the greatest figures of French history, and descended through a series of hallways and stairwells to a basement room in which stood a buffet table of immense proportions, surmounted by a superhuman quantity of food, all elaborately prepared and presented. There were wax figures at certain tables, and an orchestra of waxworks. Dozens of curators, dealers, critics, patrons of the arts, cultural attachés, and figures from the governments of France and neighboring nations congregated in the room. A wax figure of Rudolf Nureyev was poised by my table, but remained stationary; the guests, however, danced and ate and then danced some more. Bulatov was modest, touched by the tributes paid him, entirely congenial.

Later in the week I had lunch with him, and we talked about his work. We were on the terrace of the Closerie des Lilas, because Bulatov was staying near Montparnasse, and because he had always wanted to eat oysters. His New York dealer, Phyllis Kind, was there, and so was Galina. "There is nothing wrong with the criticism of my work that has been published," Bulatov explained. "But it all seems to be about my status as a Soviet artist, without analyzing even my place within Soviet art. There has been no straightforward analysis of my work as work. My work is about specific questions, specific problems. It is about arresting a moment in time, about the significance of the visual signs in the world around us, about the way in which to name some thing or some moment is to make it real. Do you think that people simply fail to understand that?"

Bulatov didn't feel he had been deliberately shortchanged, or that he had been shabbily treated. That was not the issue. But he was afraid of enthusiasm that seemed to be beside the point of his work. "Of course I *am* a Soviet artist. But my work is not only about being Soviet, not generically about being Soviet, anyway." Phyllis Kind nodded agreement; but she also confessed that most of the people buying his work in New York were buying it at least in part because they liked the idea that it was Soviet. "There are just a lot of people buying in the craze," she said. "Some of them want to understand the work and some of them don't; that's the art business." Bulatov explained his work to me, and touched on the points to which he had expected critics to respond. Much of what he said seemed very wise, and made his work genuinely more interesting to me than it had been previously. But some of what he said seemed obvious, and some of what he said he was doing in his work seemed to me not to be done by his paintings. How much should an artist be able to define the terms in which his work is criticized? Even for a Soviet, born to a system of controlled explanations, the work must be able to speak beyond its creator. Phyllis Kind once compared the Soviet artists to members of an orchestra: "If you hear only the oboe part of a symphony, without the rest, it doesn't make much sense, and what is effective about it is lost. But if you have a really good oboist, he can interest you and make you wonder about the rest of the symphony, and he can astonish you with how beautifully he plays; whereas if you have a bad oboist, you're bored in an instant and all you can think about is escape." Bulatov is a great romantic, a moral artist, a spokesman not for political truths so much as for the workings of goodness in the world. To separate his honesty and kindness from the clarity and generosity of his work is impossible; his work is founded on the optimism of love. The beauty of his work is always subservient to that; but his love speaks in that beauty as strongly as in his personal warmth. And like the oboist, he can delight you with his own performance, sometimes enough so that you imagine you don't need to hear the orchestra.

In the great open marketplace of the West, then, his amazing technical ability can work against him. When the Pompidou exhibition was remounted in London in February 1989, the thing most frequently noted in Bulatov's work was its almost photographic realism. "Is that really a street in Moscow?" people would ask as they looked at his painting *Krasikov Street,* which shows the backs of an anonymous crowd trudging past a billboard from which Lenin seems to be striding forward, animated and alive. "It looks just like the view overhead, like a photo," people would say when they saw *I Am Going,* a painting in which the letters that spell out the title seem to rush back into an infinite sky. Phyllis Kind has shown his work in conjunction with paintings by the technically careful Igor Kopystyanskiy and Sveta Kopystyanskaya, and also in conjunction with the work of his great friend Simon Faybisovich, a man who looks like Santa Claus and paints almost photorealist paintings of such sentimentality as is ordinarily seen only in greeting cards. Artists like Bulatov and the Kopystyanskiys do work which operates at theoretical levels, but its beauty often distracts people from its intentions; and since part of what they have in common is beauty, the conjunction of their work only furthers the misreadings.

"Beautiful?" asked Bulatov over lunch. "The oysters are beautiful. Paris is beautiful. But my paintings? Are my paintings beautiful?" He seemed genuinely struck by the idea, as though it had never been suggested to him. Later on, he was to say, "The picture is the only reality I trust and believe. The world around us is too active, too unstable for us to maintain any true belief in it; everything is in a state of flux, everything is changing. Only the picture is immutable."

Erik Bulatov: *Happy Ending* (from the series "War and Peace")

The beauty of Bulatov's paintings is marginal to an understanding of them. In the narrow confines of the world of Moscow unofficial art, that had been obvious; it was the new language of the West that obscured his intentions. Surely a critic, even without taking Bulatov entirely at his word, could try to articulate that.

I saw Bulatov only once again that week; he had been happily touring the museums of the City of Lights in rapid succession. I saw more of Galina. "What do you want from Soviet art?" she asked me. "Everyone wants something from Soviet art," she said. My last day in Paris, we had tea at the Ritz. We walked in, and proceeded down the long hallway of the hotel until we reached the sofas at which tea is so demurely served. Gala shrugged off her long fur coat, gestured at some men with short haircuts and ill-fitting dark suits who were seating themselves on a neighboring banquette, and said in a complacent tone, "I love that you bring me here. I love that you bring me here, because when there are no menus"—and here disparagement darted from her eyes—"when there are no menus, KGB men are so embarrassed and confused." I believed at the time, and I still believe, that the people at the next banquette were simply businessmen, perhaps German, having a pleasant tea; they must have been even more surprised than I at the sinister character imputed to them, and their looks of confusion surely had more to do with Gala than with the menus.

But the comment brought something home to me. Though it was odd to be told not to speak too loudly on the train going to the Action I had attended in Moscow, it was part of the exoticism of travel to a very foreign land. In the Soviet Union, I was willing and able to accept, in the enthusiastic spirit of paranoia that Westerners tend to carry to the Second and Third worlds, that I might be under observation. In Paris, this seemed inconceivable. In the full bloom of glasnost and perestroika, it may also be unlikely; but many of the émigrés had been watched for years, and they had carried their habits of caution with them to the cities of Europe and America. It was difficult, in the months that followed, to grow accustomed to the trappings of secrecy that the artists maintained. It was more difficult, but necessary, for me to accept that they have had—and might still have—some cause.

Over tea, Gala explained to me, in terms sufficiently dramatic for grand opera, how she had left the U.S.S.R. in her early twenties by marrying an American businessman, how she had subsequently felt that she needed to do something more than be a simple housewife, and how, after various adventures, she had started to work for a financier who collected Soviet art. I had heard of this man several times, his name always pronounced like that of an evil spirit by the Soviets; he had gone to the Soviet Union early on, met various artists, and promised to sell their work in the West. He had managed to negotiate to export the work, and for a few years, from 1985 to 1987, he had taken paintings regularly to the West. "He was charming, so charming," Gala told me. "He made everything sound so simple, so easy. He said he would place the work in the best collections, that he would pay the artists in hard currency, he said all sorts of things. Then he took the paintings, and they disappeared. No one got any money. People would see him and they would ask him, 'Where are our paintings?' and he wouldn't tell them." Gala shook her head. Later on, other people who had worked with this man would explain that the demands made on him by the artists were impossible, that everyone wanted specific and obscure things that were so expensive that it was impossible to get them past customs. I was told that he had given money to various agencies of the Soviet government and that they had failed to get it to the artists themselves, that the fault lay with bureaucracy rather than with him. All that may be so, but the fact remains that he did not get to the artists what he had promised them. Many of them were stripped of years of work, their best work from the seventies and early eighties, and never saw a cent. Even now, it is difficult to trace much of that work; pieces that artists claim they gave to this man he claims never to have seen. It was their first contact with the Western art world, and it was an unfortunate one. "He was a crook, a common thief," said Gala. An uncommon thief, perhaps— no explanation was given when, a year later, important Soviet paintings appeared at his stand in the Los Angeles Art Fair. "Where did these come from?" a visitor asked. "From Moscow," was all anyone would say.

Gala had been seduced by this man's magnetism, and she had in turn helped to draw some of the Soviet artists into his lair. "I gave him the glory of the Soviet Union," she said; later I understood her to mean that she had given him *Glory to the CPSU*, a painting by Bulatov from 1975; but in a sense she *had* given him just what I at first took her to have said. "I hatched a scheme," she explained to me. "I knew that many of the works he bought were in turn sold by Phyllis Kind, and so I stopped working for him and went to work for Phyllis. For months I worked in her gallery, waiting always for the moment when I would be left alone there and could find the records of what paintings she had bought and of what she had paid for them. I wanted to catch her in the criminal act, so I could go back to Moscow and unveil the whole conspiracy. Finally, one day, I was left alone in the gallery. I rushed downstairs to the basement, where everything was stored, and began thumbing through the books, searching everywhere for the missing information. But I could find no mention of Soviet art at all; and besides, I was interrupted in the middle of my search by the sound of a door slamming upstairs." Gala paused. The men next to us, KGB or otherwise, were entranced by the story.

"Quickly I put away the notebooks I had been investigating and ran upstairs. I waited three days, so that there could be no suspicion. Then one day, in the most casual possible way, I said, 'Phyllis, do you keep records of the paintings you buy and sell? Of the Soviet paintings for example?' And do you know what Phyllis did? She said, 'Of course I do. Do you want to see them?' And she opened a drawer, and there were all of her records in perfect order. I spent hours perusing them, and only slowly did I realize that Phyllis was perfectly honest, that she had no idea what was going on with this evil man, or at least had no role in his machinations. And so since then I have worked with Phyllis."

There are so many versions of this story in circulation that the truths and the fictions of the situation have become tangled. There is no question, however, that dealing with this man left a bitter flavor in the mouths of the Soviets. They were already suspicious when Sotheby's came; some of them were suspicious of Phyllis Kind (though after her name was cleared they became more accepting); and many of them didn't want to talk to dealers from the West. They understood, eventually, that the business of negotiating with the Soviet government required a wheeler-dealer mentality, a slickness, an ability to be at least marginally dishonest, a gift for getting what was needed at all cost—and that that was not what they wanted from their dealers. Now that they produce most of their work in the West, things are easier. But anxiety remains about dealing with the Soviets, over whom the threat of bureaucracies and a reputation for unpredictability seem to linger, of which the most disreputable dealers make good use.

By the end of my Paris trip, I felt well and truly that I might keep up with Soviet art, and I decided to go to Berlin to see the younger artists, the ones I knew best. Their exhibition was called *Isskunstvo,* a pun; the Russian word for art is *isskustvo,* and the German word for art is *kunst.* The marriage of the two words provided the name for the exhibition; the marriage of the two ideas was the exhibition itself. I did not at that time know the genesis of *Isskunstvo;* nor did I know Lisa Schmitz. Later, I would understand that she had single-handedly, sometimes high-handedly, transformed communication between artists in the U.S.S.R. and artists in the West, and I would appreciate how by dint of a singleness of mind, a singularity of focus, and an unfailing energy she had made possible what had not previously been possible.

Lisa Schmitz is a German artist in her mid-thirties, tall, with long wavy hair in which blond and gray and bits of red and brown constantly shift toward and away from one another. She has big, clear eyes and a long, craggy nose like one of the foothills of the Pyrénées. When I stayed with Lisa and some other German artists, later, in a dacha outside Moscow, we would find ourselves running at breakneck speed for the bus on mornings when everyone had overslept; once we were on board and had flopped breathlessly back in our seats, Lisa would run a brush once through her hair, put on mascara and bright red lipstick without a mirror, shake back her head, and look—in, perhaps, a pair of tights and a silk shirt and nothing else, or in a man's suit and a silver necklace shaped like a snake—as glamorous as the day. Her work is always highly serious: some performance, some installations, some texts. Like her life, it is usually conceived on a superhuman scale of complexity.

I was later to learn that Lisa's interest in Soviet art had begun with a two-month trip to China in 1986 that she had been obliged to organize because she was assistant to a professor at the Academy of Arts of Berlin who wanted to take his students to the East. She had no real interest in the East at the beginning; but in China she found that the distance with which she had treated the prospective journey, and the frustration of trying to organize it, disappeared into the deep emotion of looking closely at an unknown world. The grand finale was to be the return to Berlin from Beijing on the trans-Siberian express; but a few days before her group's departure someone bought the *Herald Tribune* and saw the headlines: Chernobyl had happened. Everyone was terrified, and the train journey was nearly canceled, since the Moscow-Berlin leg went through the contaminated areas. But the students went to the German embassy, and after some negotiation arranged that the group would take the train to Moscow, and that their further transit would be arranged by the German embassy there.

"We came across from Mongolia to the Russian front," she has recalled. "It was the middle of May, and there was still snow lying on the waterfront, and sometimes also in the woods, but all in all it was an infinity of light green, the color of the meadows and the trees. It was such a soft and light atmosphere through which we continued very slowly, and it was never-ending, birch trees going on for thousands of kilometers. You would wake up in the morning and see this all the day through until night, and the next morning it would be the same, and you began to have the impression that it never ends; it was like being in a slow and never-ending film. We had the most beautiful weather, and we became so comfortable in the train that when we came to Moscow we really didn't want to leave. That one week had impressed me more than I can tell you, and I knew that I had to return to the U.S.S.R." Ordinary travelers from Beijing to Berlin on the trans-Siberian are given only a few hours in Moscow, but Lisa and her group spent two days there, waiting for a flight. And Lisa, primed by the birches, fell in love with a Russian, and knew at that moment that she would have to return to Moscow however she could.

During the following year, she made several short visits to see her love. Just before she left for a trip in the spring of 1987, she went for breakfast with the members of the Atelier Bomba Colori, six artists who lived together in an enormous studio in a Bauhaus building in Kreuzberg. The artists—Werner Zein, Andrea Sunder-Plassmann, Désirée Baumeister, Enzo Enzel, Gaby Rets, and Mario Radina— suggested to Lisa that they might all collaborate on a project with some Soviet artists, perhaps a two-part project for which the Soviets would come to Berlin and the Germans go to Moscow, and she said: "It will no doubt be very difficult, but give me photos of your work, give me your résumés, and when I get to Moscow, I will try my best."

So *Isskunstvo* began its birth-throes. The organization was a task beyond all reckoning. "If I had understood," Lisa has said, as so many have said of such undertakings, "if I had had any idea, I would never have considered it." In Moscow, she approached the cultural attaché at the German embassy, who said that the project sounded very interesting but that it was most certainly impossible. Only people in positions of great power in the U.S.S.R. were given permission to travel at that point. And so many artists, the people Lisa might meet —no doubt they had had trouble with the KGB. He suggested, however, that it might be worth calling a woman in the Union of Artists who was officially in charge of exchange exhibitions between West Germany and the U.S.S.R. Lisa called this woman, who point-blank refused to negotiate directly with a nongovernment agent and added that in any case the exchange programs were fully scheduled through the early nineties. Prospects looked grim. Some weeks later, in the apartment of the Moscow correspondent for a German paper, Lisa made the acquaintance of a scholar who mentioned to her an archive about Soviet artists in a library in Bremen. She made little progress during her remaining days in the U.S.S.R., but on her departure went to Bremen, and found the library and the archive. "It was a very, very big library," she has said. "And it was a very, very small archive. There were two cardboard boxes with perhaps fifty papers in each, mostly photocopies of handwritten texts, interviews by artists of other artists, and photocopies of photos of artwork, and a few original photos of artists. How this material came to be in Bremen I have never been able to discover."

Lisa decided that to penetrate the U.S.S.R. she would need to get a scholarship and live in Moscow and work there as an artist. She went to Bonn to apply to the DAAD (German Academic Exchange Service), and someone processing papers there told her about a book called *Kulturpalast,* an anthology of poems and essays by Soviet artists and their friends, compiled by two Germans who had studied in Moscow in the early eighties. Someone else gave her the name of a German professor who had met some artists in Moscow a few years earlier. "It was like a puzzle. Everything seemed to be linked in a ring of mysteries that was beginning to align itself into sense." Despite having no reason to imagine that the project might reach fruition, Lisa returned to the Atelier Bomba Colori with photocopies of the Bremen archive and with *Kulturpalast,* and she and the other six artists set about reading the material and trying to assess the Soviets, to make a preliminary list of those they wished to include in their project. From the materials at hand they extracted about sixty names.

They first eliminated the artists who seemed too old; the Berlin artists were all in their late twenties and early thirties, and wanted to work with people their own age. Lisa was learning Russian, but a friend spoke it fluently, and came to each meeting to translate and interpret the Bremen material; they tried to assess the artistic priorities manifested in the interviews, and found that a few artists, Sven Gundlakh, Andrey Monastyrskiy, Dmitriy Prigov, and Vadim Zakharov among them, instantly grabbed the imagination. Others were harder to judge. After weeks of debate, they made a primary list of twenty-five artists. Lisa called Sabine Hänsgen, the co-author of *Kul-*

turpalast, to find out how she might find them; Sabine Hänsgen said that one, Nikita Alexeev, had moved to Paris six months earlier.

Lisa telephoned him immediately, and later that week she went to Paris to meet him and talk to him. Nikita is tall and reserved and decorous, capable of the most extravagant of practical jokes or the most extraordinary behavior behind a face of total passivity and calm. If Lisa is like the proverbial storm at sea, Nikita is like the proverbial rock in the stream, quietly and austerely determining the direction of whatever drifts by him. Nikita advised her that her project was really not feasible, but he gave her the telephone numbers of the people on her primary list, and wished her the best of luck. He promised to write to his friends to give advance notice of her imminent arrival.

So in mid-July of 1987, Lisa and two of the Bomba Colori artists went to Moscow for a week. They met everybody: Sven Gundlakh, Vadim Zakharov, Yuriy Albert, the brothers Mironenko, Andrey Filippov, and Kostya Zvezdochetov—all the artists working together in Furmanny at that time. The work was even more interesting than had been hoped. "We had seen only black-and-white photos," Lisa has said. "Suddenly there was color everywhere, and energy, and love for the work. We were at that moment completely happy, and we knew that we had to realize our project." It was difficult to choose artists, since they knew they could take only eight or ten at the outside. But this was before the onset of the Western rush, a year before Sotheby's, and there was no glint of competitiveness among the Soviets. In the end, they tried to talk their way through to a list that everyone liked, to make the decisions without sacrificing mutual good feeling. "We needed to take people who knew they could work together," Lisa has said.

For seven days they saw only art from dawn to dusk. Nikola Ovchinnikov served as a guide for much of the time, taking them to meet Dima Prigov and Andrey Monastyrskiy; and as Nikola had not been in the Bremen archive, they talked to him without discovering that he was himself an artist until the day before they left, when they went down to a cellar in which he had some paintings. "But it's wonderful!" they said. "You too must work with us." Each day there were new artists and new ideas. Monastyrskiy announced that he had no wish to come to the West, that he didn't want to be part of Lisa's scheme. They met Josif Bakshteyn because he was at that time married to Ira Nakhova; they decided that they liked his ideas, and wanted him also to join them. Sergey Volkov and Sergey Anufriev they met

NIKOLAY (NIKOLA) OVCHINNIKOV:
Lenin Confronts the Black Square of Malevich

in passing and found intriguing. Everyone took them to see everyone else. That none of the artists in Moscow had had any idea of such a project before the beginning of the week posed no problem at all; they were quite content that it had come on them out of the sky, as all interesting things in Moscow do. They also thought that the whole undertaking was so far outside the bounds of possibility that the making of these decisions was little more than a rhetorical exercise, an amusement in the warm weather of July. For Lisa, it was inspiration: "Here was the community of the intellect that I had sought for so many years, an echo of my student days. I felt instantly at home with the seriousness and playfulness of the conversation, with the deep engagement with art and with life."

When Lisa returned to Germany, in August 1987, she was told that her scholarship had come through, that she would live in Moscow from March to August 1988. Concerned about funding, she called Tina Bauermeister at the Berliner-Festspiele, organizers of many important international festivals. Tina Bauermeister said that Lisa's plans sounded interesting, and suggested that she send some information to her office. Lisa insisted that she needed a meeting, to explain things in person before her departure, and was told quite firmly that this was not the way things were done; she could not have an appointment. Lisa immediately got on the U-Bahn, went to the Berliner-Festspiele office, quietly pushed past the secretaries there, and walked in the door. "Hello," she said. "I am Lisa Schmitz." Tina Bauermeister looked a little blank. "I told you I don't have time to discuss this with you," she said, and Lisa said simply, "Yes, I know. That's why I'm here." Tina Bauermeister stared for a moment, and then laughed, and agreed to come the following day to see all Lisa's notes and photos; and when she came, she said within ten minutes, "Lisa, it's exactly the project we need."

Some days later, the director of the Academy of Arts mentioned to Lisa that a disused train station was being restored as an artistic display space, and he promised to recommend her project for the Bahnhof Westend if she applied to use it. Lisa telephoned the appropriate administrators, the Karl-Hofer-Gesellschaft, and found that there were six hours left before all applications had to be mailed. She was in the north of Germany, and she wrote her letter of application on an old manual typewriter, doing part of it in the taxi on the way to the town's only postbox, lying barefoot in the street to type the last few sentences. The postman came a paragraph before she finished, but delayed the collection of the mail for five minutes and won his place in the history of German-Soviet relations. When the letter, on frayed sheets of paper, was received in Berlin, a slot in August/September 1988 was immediately granted to the project. Lisa had not, of course, mentioned that she had no idea how she would get permission for the Soviet artists to leave the U.S.S.R.

By that time, her romance from the trans-Siberian was long over, and six months seemed a very long time to spend in Moscow. "I was afraid. I had no idea how to organize this project, and I didn't know whether these people, who seemed so wonderful for a week, would be wonderful for the length of those cold months." She needed to go back for a preliminary visit, to think and decide. In late September 1987, she returned for two weeks, her German backing behind her. Remembering the frosty attitude of the Union of Artists, Lisa went to the newly formed Cultural Foundation to seek help with exit visas. The people there were pleasant and amiable and said that they liked the idea of the project, but indicated that such matters were difficult and had to be taken slowly. "We'll be in touch," they assured her. When after two months she had heard nothing from them, she returned to Moscow, and in November she was told that the Cultural Foundation could not help, but had written a letter of recommendation to be presented to the Union of Artists. Sven Gundlakh read the letter and laughed. "It's just a matter of form, so you'll leave them alone," he said; but Lisa took the letter to the Union nonetheless.

This time, Lisa met a delightful man who said in tones of great respect that he would be honored to work with the Karl-Hofer-Gesellschaft and the Berliner-Festspiele, that he admired the level of seriousness that had been shown in the search for backing so far, and that he was pleased to see that people of some importance in the West were at last in a position to appreciate the cultural significance of the U.S.S.R. He agreed to accept her proposal and make all necessary arrangements and provide substantial funds as well, on the condition that he could choose the Soviet artists to be included in the project. Lisa explained patiently that the selection of the Soviet artists had already taken place, that it was too late for him to make such choices. "This is not a functionary's project," she said. "It is an artists' project, and it must be done by artists who have found one another. The money is not so important, and if you do not want to fund the project with the artists we have selected, I will understand. But we need visas, and I know that you can help." The man from the Union of

Artists smiled at her. "I'm afraid," he said, still politely, "that we cannot work together on this level. If you are determined to stick with your current plan, then I must bid you goodbye. Whenever you want to have a cup of coffee in the cafeteria of the Union of Artists, please call me."

So Lisa got in touch with Pavel Khoroshilov, an important figure in the Ministry of Culture who oversaw the export of works of contemporary art from the U.S.S.R. They had several meetings and much enthusiastic conversation. He thought the idea was splendid, and accepted in principle Lisa's decision to choose her own artists. But when, weeks into their negotiations, he read the list of artists, he became purple with fury. "Two or three of these are all right," he said. "But the rest are simply out of the question. These people, Sven Gundlakh and Dmitriy Prigov—they will never leave the U.S.S.R." Khoroshilov let fly a stream of invective, and Lisa drew herself up to her full height and denounced his intolerance of "my friends and colleagues." Then she turned to his sympathies. "You know that these people can travel only with your help. How can you be so grudging with them?" He declined to apply for the visas, but he said, at last, that he would write a recommendation—"if you want one for this project of yours that will never take place." Lisa left without the recommendation. "Excuse me," she said, pausing at the door, "but the project *will* take place."

Lisa went back to Berlin. Her last hope was the Society of Friendship, a Soviet organization for international understanding with offices throughout the world. She went to the Berlin office and once more met two polite men, who said that they were very enthusiastic about the project, that they respected Tina Bauermeister and the Karl-Hofer-Gesellschaft very much indeed, and that they would send the plans for the project with their seal of approval to Moscow, where a final decision would be made. A few weeks later, Lisa went to Moscow for her six-month scholarship. Every week during those months she visited the House of the Society of Friendship in Moscow, and every week they told her that the matter was under consideration. Every week she sent a letter to the Karl-Hofer-Gesellschaft saying that everything was under control. And in May, she made another scene. "I felt that for them it was just more bureaucracy, that no one was interested in helping us, that this series of recommendations from the Cultural Foundation to the Union, from the Union to the Ministry, from the Ministry to the Society of Friendship was all like a Kafkaesque corridor in which every door just takes you to another door. I told them that I wouldn't work with these gluey Soviet institutions, that we would do it all ourselves if we had to carry the artists out in our luggage." They told her to wait a few days more; then they said that they couldn't help but would give her a recommendation to the Ministry of Culture. It was the last straw.

But fortune sometimes smiles in unexpected quarters. While the bureaucrats had been shuffling Lisa's papers, perestroika had begun to happen. New laws had been put into effect, and it had been announced that anyone from the West who wanted to could issue private invitations to individual Soviets to visit as friends. In May, Ira Nakhova had obtained such a private invitation, and had gone to Italy. Her trip was a new beacon of hope.

Lisa organized it all. She called the Bomba Colori artists and asked them to send invitations at once; Werner Zein attended to these bureaucratic matters. She wrote to the Karl-Hofer-Gesellschaft and asked to delay her exhibition, and asked them also to issue a set of invitations. They wrote back, giving her the month of October, and issued invitations that were shortly thereafter and rather mysteriously lost in the Soviet consulate in Calcutta, not to arrive in Moscow until six weeks later. She met with another director of the Union of Artists, someone who had not previously been in a position to help and who still could not arrange the visas through the official channels of the Union, but who could and did issue more recommendations, papers the artists could present at the police stations where they would have to file for passports. The Bomba Colori invitations came through but were held in a central office; then the Karl-Hofer-Gesellschaft invitations arrived from India and were disqualified on grounds that they were not official enough to be official but were too official to be private; and when at last the papers were in place, the artists themselves were afraid to go to register at the police stations they had so assiduously avoided for decades. "We had all indulged Lisa in her crazy fantasy that we would travel to the West," Sven Gundlakh has explained. "But suddenly she expected us to become involved in this lunatic dream of hers, and since we knew it would never happen, we wanted to avoid getting ourselves into trouble for no reason at all."

By this time, Lisa and the artists knew one another very well. She had been living on her scholarship in Moscow for half a year, in one of the rooms for the ill and insane in a Soviet dormitory. Marked in large letters "Room 10: Isolation Chamber," it was gray-green, perhaps eight square meters, with bars on the windows. It was crawling with roaches and rats. The artists downstairs from her, also from abroad, were working in welded steel, and they hammered without stopping from two in the morning until dawn. There was one telephone for six hundred students. Wishing to record her surroundings, Lisa photographed a notice in the bathroom saying that students were not to put their shoes on the toilet seat, and she photographed the "Isolation Chamber" sign outside her room. Another student saw her; Lisa was called in to the Komsomol office in her building, told that spies were not welcome in the dormitory, and put through several long sessions of questioning.

In the meantime, she met with the artists and joined in their activities, went to their homes and became a part of their lives. Some evenings, she stayed with Sven Gundlakh and his wife, Emma, in their one room of less than ten square meters, which they shared with Emma's mother, her grandmother, and a dog. To accommodate Lisa, Sven had to pile all the furniture (including a piano) in one corner, in a miniature Tower of Pisa; this provided just enough space so that she could lie down. Some days she stayed with Nikola Ovchinnikov and his wife Carina in the southern part of Moscow. Everywhere she felt at home.

Toward the end of her stay, she did a performance in the Club of the Avant-Gardists which has since become the stuff of legend. Lisa was naked, painted red. (Some months later, Sergey Volkov and I went together to an international art expo in London. "I'm very disappointed," he said. "I had been hoping for a sea of naked women painted in the colors of the rainbow.") She had painted on her hands two sentences in Russian. On the back of her left hand was written "soon" and on the palm of that hand, "I will be dead": on the back of her right hand was "Everything is" and on the palm of that hand, "in a way all right." As she sat stationary and naked, turning her hands over, the sentences slowly emerged: "Soon I will be dead" and "Everything is in a way all right." There also emerged the conjunctive sentences: "Everything is soon," and "I will be dead in a way all right," and "Soon in a way all right" and "Everything I will be dead." These lines were even less coherent in Russian than they are in English. Lisa's Russian is a running joke among the Soviets; though her grasp of the language is fragmentary at best, she embarks constantly on the most complex philosophic arguments in it. It is one of her great gifts to make herself understood even when vocabulary fails her:

"I need a schnip-shnop" became a standard way to demand scissors in Furmanny, and several poems began with her much-quoted request for "some material small and like the sky"—a phrase she used to describe plastic bubble wrap with its small compartments filled with air.

But Lisa's performance touched on a more meaningful truth where its fatalism ("Soon I will be dead") and positivism ("Everything is in a way all right") intersected at the rhetoric of elapsed time. All that is certain in Soviet terms is retrospect; even in this era of glasnost, nothing is so sure as that the moment that is now will become the past, and that our memory of it will be touched with pleasure. The anticipation of nostalgia can be the keenest form of self-knowledge. Perhaps the best one can say of the first years of glasnost is that they are likely to seem, from the hazy distance of the twenty-first century, to have been a time when things were all right. In retrospect, even Stalinism will have been all right, because it will somehow have bred whatever follows on its heels. If, as Nietzsche says, only that which is painful is truly memorable, then a society that cherishes memory must also, perhaps, cherish pain. Soon we will all be dead. But that certain knowledge earns, in the meanwhile, the pleasures of a cheerful retrospect; and that in turn does make everything, in a way, all right.

Lisa was in Moscow when the Sotheby's sale took place. I met her briefly at Andrey Monastyrskiy's Action in the woods, though I have only the vaguest memory of having done so. Certainly none of the Soviets told me at that time that they were coming to Berlin. None of them thought that they were. On September 1, 1988, Lisa's six months ended, and she set off for home, and on that day Ira Nakhova and Josif Bakshteyn were told that their visa applications had been approved. On the fourteenth, Ira and Josif came to West Berlin. A few days later, Sven Gundlakh and Sergey Vorontsov came; then three days after, Sergey Volkov and Nikola Ovchinnikov; and after that Sergey Anufriev arrived with some musicians who had also been invited, Vladimir Tarasov and Vladimir Sorokin. Vadim Zakharov came last of all but for Dima Prigov, who—because his mental-hospital imprisonment was so recent, because his KGB violations ran beyond the end of the Brezhnev era—was denied his visa and his passport. After months of delays, he received a call from someone he knew in the Department of Foreign Affairs. "Don't worry, Dima," this man said. "We have finally managed to clear your file completely. You will very soon be given a passport." Dima was delighted, and indeed received a passport by mail shortly thereafter. The day after that, because of a clerical error, he received another passport. Knowing that his passport number would be registered at the border, and that it would be extremely suspicious if he showed up with two passports, he went to the police to turn the extra one in—and was promptly arrested as a forger. In the end, he came to Berlin only after the opening of *Isskunstvo,* though he was later to win a scholarship and live there from March to August of 1990.

How to describe the process of arriving in the West from the East? The West was disappointing because it was not different enough, and it was intimidating because it was too different, and it was exhausting because it made too many demands, and it was uncomfortable because everything was too easy. It was wonderful and it was horrible. There were too many choices to make, and no one knew how to make them. "How," many artists were to ask me, "do you select one kind of butter over another?" In Moscow, you are lucky to find butter at all; if you do it is probably sour; in any event, it is marked, simply, "butter." The notion of brands, indeed the notion of choice, is essentially alien. The difference in the modes of shopping for food is an emblem for this. In the West, you have a recipe, and you go out and buy the seven ingredients necessary to prepare it. In Moscow, you go and wander through the streets, buying whatever food is available on the day you are out, and at the end of the day you are at home with seven items you have purchased. You have no choice but to try to put them together, and how well you eat is a matter of how creatively you can interpret and integrate this unsought disparity of comestibles.

For artists, it was frequently much the same thing. "One day," Sergey Mironenko once explained to me, "you go to a store, and you see gold beads. You are not working with gold beads, of course, but you consider and you think that you may someday want to work with them. You know that if you don't buy them at once, they will be gone. And perhaps you will never again find gold beads. So you decide to buy some. Now you have to decide how many gold beads to buy, and since you still don't know what you're going to do with the gold beads, or whether you're ever going to use them at all, it's very difficult to decide how many you want. So in the end, you just buy some beads, as many as fit in your hand, or enough to fill a sack, or maybe just three of them, depending on your mood and how much money you have. Usually, sooner or later, you are working on something and you suddenly remember that you have these gold beads, and you realize they are just the thing, and you use them." That is how creative people work in the U.S.S.R. It is oppressive to know that every store has only things that it will also have two months later, that there is no reason to buy anything unless you know what you will do with it, and that anything you might suddenly think of will be instantly available. To create richness out of plenty is worse than useless—it is boring.

More fundamentally alienating than this plenty, perhaps, was the distance at which they found themselves from their self-contained world. The people who came from the West to Moscow and to the studios of the artists, mixed bag though they may have been, were people who were interested in the art and the artists. To be in the West was to undergo a much more profound alienation from their old motivations for producing art than anything they had known so far. Sotheby's was a big bang. Arrival in Berlin was a bigger bang. When the privacy of the Soviet art community entered the public domain by way of works of art, the communicative language of those works was undermined. As the artists entered the public domain into which their work had preceded them, the urgency of their acts of communication was undermined as well, leaving them either exponents of a dreary repetitiveness—who could locate integrity only in the refusal of suspect but obsessive new experiences—or facile champions of a novel multiplicity whose apparent promise of breadth ultimately led only to narrowness. An acceptance of a confining and foreign system of values seemed naive, but outright dismissal of that system was equally naive, since nothing is so clumsy as self-consciously artificial inspiration. An informed recognition of the disavowals implicit in the broadening of a staled horizon could only be a matter of elapsed time and painfully surprising failures; but though expecting those failures was no substitute for realizing them, it was possible to turn awareness of them into a new subject for art. With increasing candor, the Soviets turned their irony on the comedy that accompanied the truncation of their easy and profound communication. This was, in its way, a tragedy, but it was like all tragedies a fine subject for art; and in the rigors of its hermeneutic circle of self-destruction as self-aggrandizement lay its significance, the latent genius of the artists, and the visionary resonance of their best work. The new locus of meaning in the new Soviet work—created by artists in exile, artists in transit, and artists in disjunction with their still-inhabited homeland—was here.

The first change that perestroika wrought in the lives of these artists was the geometric expansion of the audience for their work to include an apparently limitless influx of critics, curators, dealers, and collectors eager to examine, criticize, and respond to work designed to enact secret communications wholly inaccessible to them. But whereas it was comparatively easy for the artists to exploit that situation by renegotiating the relationship between apparent and encoded meaning in their work, it was difficult for them to sustain that dialectic once they began to travel to countries in which secrecy itself was not a priority, in which any multiplicity of meaning emerged as visible layering or as a frank and uncomplicated invitation to penetration, and not as a cipher. It rapidly became impossible for them to regard their Western audience as interlopers, as they had done in Moscow. At the same time, they were unable to treat them as equals, since their habits of recognition and identification always reflected alien values. Some artists, of course, took one of these two courses, but for most, the tension between them became an invisible secret to replace its antecedent—and more stringently controlled—ciphers.

The transformation of the work itself was in some ways more difficult to identify than the transformation of the situation that work reflected. Sergey Volkov's exploitation of Western kitsch, dramatized by carefully selected clichés, or Sven Gundlakh's constructions with Western domestic wall finishes, pointed up the essentially trivial ways in which the West shares the failings of the East, instead of penetrating to the more important failings of Western society, acknowledging its successes, engaging with the new difficulties in the East, or reflecting on the positive side of changes there. The works were clever—very clever—but they were so defensive that their defensiveness became their subject. This worked fine, except that it neither eliminated that defensiveness nor penetrated to its causes—which were perhaps more important than the cleverness with which it was treated.

Whether the confidence underlying a work of art is visible or palpable is almost a moot point. Yet the easiest terms for categorization of this work were to do with confidence, since it continued to be the strongly held belief of these artists—in what they could say, and to whom what they could say would be comprehensible—that empowered their efforts. In the pre-glasnost days, these categories were clearly defined, but the Western habit of taking literally scenarios designed as evasions, which seemed risible and even appealing in the Soviet context, became a strong threat to work created in the West to be seen primarily by Westerners. The typical response was a flux between self-negating acknowledgment of the inevitable Western reading of work—a counter-intuitive and ill-considered generosity with an audience that did not understand—and self-indulgent confidence that the West would ultimately be content with the slowly dawning recognition of its own ignorance—which relieved the artists of responsibility to include any meaning in their work as a counterfoil for its bearing of secrecy. The self-doubt of the first assumption eroded meaning to the same degree as the affected arrogance of the second one. In neither instance was there even a modicum of belief that what was important to say had been or indeed could be said; fundamental habits of transitive dissembling were wholly devalued. The pointlessness of this work recalled Socialist Realism, whose phenomenal obviousness was meant to promote, and not to impede, its educatory or even inspiring function.

Unlike the Socialist Realists, however, the artists of the vanguard recognized that what is reduced is not improved, and that to forsake implicit strength unnecessarily is to champion banality. Neither self-abnegation nor arrogance was an effective response to the problems of exhibiting in the West, but as the situation of the West became increasingly familiar, it became itself a new problem to be explored at both the frank and the subliminal level. The best works produced by Soviets in the West at that time were the ones produced after some considerable migration between the two contexts, works that communicated the new discomfort of disjunction, works that nobly recognized their own limitations and turned that recognition into a more thrilling subject than the one that inspired it. The best of these works began with the ecstasy of their novelty and turned, for their confidence, to the certain knowledge that the West could understand, if not the acts of communication, at least the will to communicate.

But these finest works were also not too much enthralled by the new to believe wholeheartedly in progress, and so to give up on nostalgia. That they looked forward to a brave new world never meant they were beyond reflecting back; the leap between future and past needed in the end to be so often repeated as to blur into a single moment in which the intellect Soviets use to signify the present would be tainted with both the cautious ebullience of the future and the bitterness they locate in their past. Elizabeth Bishop, in "Questions of Travel," wrote: "Think of the long trip home. / Should we have stayed at home and thought of here? / Where would we be today?" These works of art, at their best, were responses to that very question. They were in part about the realization of an impossible dream of travel, a

fantasy too long deferred to be recognizable when it was finally realized, which, like all fantasies, lost not only its familiarity but also
much of its charm in the realization. What is the difference between
the place imagined and the place discovered? The poetics of meaning
for these Soviet artists still lies in their nostalgia, and it is perhaps a
greater mercy than they know that one of their cultural attributes is a
tendency toward homesickness. It is when they are able, in their work,
to think of the long trip home, to recognize that a dream realized is
in the end a dream forsaken, that they are able to resuscitate both
their purity of purpose—the much-vaunted urgency of communication—and the sense of humor which we find so very moving. There
were hints of it all at the Bahnhof Westend, where *Isskunstvo* took
place, but only time and necessary, astonishing failure could breed
back into these artists the capacious self-reference that had operated so
effectively in their work; in rediscovering their country from the
standpoint of distance, they rediscovered their original reasons for
telling, secretly or otherwise, what had seemed to them to be inalien-
able truth. And so, at that point, it began to seem to us.

This process, which is still unfolding, was buried under simpler
issues in Berlin. First came the issue of arrival. The German artists
went to meet each Soviet at his arrival in Berlin. None of the arriving
artists had believed in the ready availability of artistic materials in the
West, and they arrived with stretchers and canvases and supplies in
tow, perhaps ten items of baggage each. "We knew that we had only
a little bit of time," Sven Gundlakh has said. "We were afraid that if
we came without anything, it might take weeks to get the materials
we needed, that we might not be able even to start our work until
after the day for which the opening was scheduled." Clearing these
things through customs was a perennial trial.

"If everyone had arrived when Ira and Josif came," Lisa Schmitz has
explained, "it would have been so much easier. But every day we were
in suspense about who would arrive, and when, and we suspected that
it would be a long and slow process, that some people would not have
time for their work. This gave us a feeling of tension and anxiety right
up to the day of the opening." It took each artist about ten days to
adjust to the climate, to the number of colors and noises, and to the
speed of life and rushing cars. As the opening drew closer, the strain

built. The Soviets hardly had time to explore Berlin if they were to be ready for the opening, and the Germans also spent long hours in the Bahnhof, trying to complete their work. The Soviets had conceived some pieces before they came, but others depended on the space as they found it, and so there was a flurry of changes.and new decisions and fresh ideas.

The Bahnhof Westend is a peculiar structure, built in the late nineteenth century for the Kaiser to use on his visits to Berlin. He would get off the train, walk down the platform, and then go up a tremendously grand staircase to an impressive waiting room with a double door at its far end, through which he would exit to his carriage and the street. The building has a number of small, undecorated offices and signal rooms, a walkway above the train tracks, and this odd, amazing waiting room and staircase. Lisa had obtained permission from the Karl-Hofer-Gesellschaft to house the artists in these rooms. Ira and Josif were given their rooms when they arrived; Nikita Alexeev had come from Paris the day before, and for a few days the great station was inhabited only by the three of them. It was Nikita's first contact with the friends he had left behind when he had emigrated from Moscow eighteen months earlier. On the first night, Lisa and the Bomba Colori artists had dinner at the Bahnhof, and everyone got on famously. Afterward, Lisa has recalled, "Nikita, like an old general, came and walked us down the staircase to our car, and then stood watching us as we turned off, closing the station door as we drove into the street." Everyone was full of enthusiasm. When Sven Gundlakh and Sergey Vorontsov arrived, things continued peacefully. The Soviets lived quietly, worked hard, and saw the city bit by bit. The Germans slowly befriended them. It was like the first days of school; everyone was full of wonder and everyone was shy.

But in the end, living and working in the same place proved to be fraught with difficulties for the Soviets. There wasn't enough space. There was no oven, no samovar, no place to wash clothes. People who had always worked together found that they were acutely uncomfortable living together. And as time went on, and more and more of the rooms turned into installation spaces, life became more and more cramped. When more artists arrived, they had to share rooms. Some wanted to work by day, and others wanted to work by night. There were disputes about whose installation should get a more prominent room, and whose installation should get a more obscure one. Several of the artists were annoyed with Lisa; they had imagined a train sta-

SERGEY VORONTZOV: *The Mariner* (from the series
"Dreaming of the Motherland: The Mariner and the Cosmonaut")

tion more like those in Moscow, buildings of unimaginable scale and
ornament.

The Soviets became embroiled in petty arguments. This was the
legacy of Sotheby's. In Moscow, there had been so little to argue
about; in Berlin, there was everything to debate. Some artists felt
instantly at ease in the West, and others felt extremely uncomfortable.
Some artists were offered large sums of money for their work, and
others seemed to be attracting no interest at all. Other problems began
to emerge. There had been hopes for a performance by Middle Russian
Elevation, since almost all the members of the band were in Berlin;
but the idea was abandoned for lack of enthusiasm. The group has not
performed since, because Middle Russian Elevation was really about
group activity, about working together; and in the West, each artist
began working for himself. This is one of the key changes that travel
brought. Already in these first weeks, the artists discovered that they
needed space to reflect on their history. They saw that they had taken

each thing that was true of some of them and treated it as though it were true of all of them. It came to each as a surprise that he was at some level his own person, and that he had his own system for extracting meaning from his circumstances. How to choose among all the variety the West had to offer, they may have asked themselves frequently; more fundamentally, they asked how to choose among all the roles they had assigned to themselves and had had assigned to them by the artistic community of Moscow.

What did everyone make and do in Berlin? Ira Nakhova did several large dramatic paintings of ancient ruined amphitheaters, and also an installation, for which she covered a room of four cubic meters in white paper and fragments of maps arranged in such a way that if you stood in the right spot you lost the sense of the cube and believed yourself to be at the center of a globe. Ira remained calm and a little distant throughout the exhibition, slightly aloof, almost regal. She made fewer demands on the Germans than did the other artists; she could immediately negotiate the West on her own. By day she slept; by night she worked. Every evening her mother telephoned from Moscow.

Sven Gundlakh did several painting/installations, the most successful of which was the *Monument to the Sky*. Four large canvases were painted in imitation of the sky; at the center of each was a white square; projecting from each square was a wooden slat, at the end of which was a slide-viewing box; and in the slide-boxes were slides of the sky. Between the middle canvases, there were a sort of altar, some blue glass, a reclining figure, and some further sky imagery. The transparencies of the sky—which were actual photos but were not, of course, actual sky—could be seen only when one stood too close to the canvases to register the work as a whole. The painted sky, created to exist outside its frame of reference, had at least the reality of the created surface, of the control implicit in streaks of paint deliberately placed in appropriate succession on a blank surface. There was an ideal distance at which one eye could see a transparency, the other the canvas; but when both parts were visible, neither was fully meaningful, and the eyes, unable to focus, went into combat, forcing one image over the other. The sky is an old image for freedom in the U.S.S.R.; but in Sven's work there were too many kinds of sky: as if nothing but the artist's confrontation could be made real, as if the symbol were in the process of overtaking its exponents. Sven in Berlin was very much like Sven in Moscow, eager to argue and debate, punning, clever; but he was also fascinated by money and by the business of producing things. Perhaps the reason that he so ardently opposed performing with Middle Russian Elevation had partly to do with his sense of commodity: you could sell a painting, but you could only enact a performance.

Sergey Volkov did large paintings in which he literalized figurative turns of phrase: one that said, simply, "Man does not live by bread alone" showed an enormous and unappetizing Soviet loaf. Volkov caught on faster than anyone else about life in the West. He had come originally from Kazan, and had already, with careful reserve, learned to understand one new world when he arrived in Moscow; to understand another came naturally to him. He watched; he understood; and then he did. His clothes, his hair, his way of speaking certain thoughts were, when the exhibition opened, fully Western. But he was never simply a fool imitating what fascinated him. With Sergey Volkov, you are always aware of the decisions that have been made; even when he is most Western, he holds the West at a careful and ironic distance. In his smart clothes, carrying his expensive video camera, he remained in some ways more self-consciously from the East than was Sven Gundlakh in baggy grayish trousers with an unkempt beard.

Nikola Ovchinnikov was always obsessed with birch trees. He has done many paintings of birches and performances with birches; in 1989, he was to make light-up birches by painting black streaks across fluorescent lightbulbs. In Berlin, Nikola did a whole room—the stationmaster's office—of birches. Each wall was completely covered by large canvases that showed a congestion of birch trunks—but no leaves. The middle of the room was empty. Nikola covered even the door; and then there was a crisis, because he could not get out and no one else could get in. So in the end, he removed the panel over the door and left it open. Nikola in Berlin was sweet-natured as ever; he was always at the periphery of the game-playing that preoccupied Nikita, Kostya, and Anufriev.

Nikita Alexeev did a series of very cleverly referential sketches and cartoons, and covered the floor of the room in which he had hung them—next door to Nikola's birches—with leaves. Two chairs were poised for conversation in the midst of the leaves. Sometimes Nikita would spend the whole day sitting in his room, writing notes; but on other occasions he was a sort of ringleader, somber in his manner but right at the center of the fun unfolding.

One of Sergey Anufriev's installations showed a series of toy metal hospital beds balanced on sugar cubes, and was called *Zucherdiabett* (a pun on the German words for "diabetes" and "bed"); the piece had overtones of drug experiences, the sweet things of life that send you to hospitals. Another showed a series of toy dumptrucks with headscarves around their cabs, a reference to the enormous working women (always in headscarves) who clean the streets or tend apartment buildings in Moscow, and an ironic reference to the many representations of such women in Socialist Realist work. Anufriev, when questioned, admitted to a terrible fear of these women. He was always the player of games. "Don't trust me," he would say, and then give you false confidences and artificial clues to his character. Pasha Peppershteyn always stood slightly behind Anufriev, towering over him though rather hunched, or following behind like an outsize puppy.

Sergey Vorontsov and Kostya Zvezdochetov were not among the artists originally included in *Isskunstvo,* but they came at the last minute and were asked to contribute work. Vorontsov did some paintings on strips of paper. Kostya had come directly from Graz, where an exhibition of his mythical Perdo paintings had been a great success. In Berlin, he built a model of Venice out of cardboard boxes taped to stilts and positioned above some overturned refrigerators full of water. All night before the opening, Kostya carried water to the refrigerators in two big buckets, and when the opening began, and people came filing in in their best clothes, he was still going back and forth. The guests said, "Who is this gnome with the buckets? Isn't there a hose he can use somewhere?" But carrying the water was part of his work, the performance aspect of what he was doing. In one of the boxes, there was a hidden drawer, and for the duration of the exhibition, Kostya kept things to eat in the drawer, often a banana. The cardboard Venice was unbelievably ugly; it was outside the Bahnhof, and within a few days it began to fall apart. "In Graz," said Kostya, "I was paid very much money for my works by people who bought them because they liked the way they looked. It was very good; I have some money now, and I don't need to work again for money for maybe five years. So now I don't want to make aesthetic works, because if I do, no one will think about anything except their being aesthetic. And for me that is not at all interesting."

The secondary effects of glasnost were the inverse of the primary ones; they posed an alarming threat to the work of artists whose strength originally manifested itself as resistance to what had become a semidefunct oppression. The first transformation for the artists of the Soviet vanguard was the multiplication of their audience. The second transformation was the multiplication of the choices and experiences of the artists themselves. The irony of this was not lost on them. No sooner had they come to terms with the frustrations of trying to articulate their values to a world with which those values were incompatible, no sooner had they manufactured a complex net of philosophies to exonerate themselves from the tedium of self-explication, than they found themselves at the other side of the game, striving to come to terms with a society insufficiently interested in them to bother with such masking, or with such a philosophical net. The most gifted (or, at least, the most adaptable, and hence the most gifted in terms of the situation at that time), with impressive grace, contrived to make what had always been implicit in their work explicit, and what had always been explicit implicit; which is to say that, without destroying the balance of clarity and secrecy which constitutes the strength of most Soviet art, they learned that by telling what was once secret, they could manufacture new secrets and absorb the luxurious terms in which the West defines privacy.

This development demands examination in terms of the traditional significance of apparent, contextual, and suppressed meaning in the Soviet vanguard. The great difference between the fictions perpetrated by artists and the fictions perpetrated in days of yore by the government was that the artistic fictions were constructed specifically to be penetrated. Whereas the artists were willing to accept fiction as an extension of or marker for truth, the Ministry insisted that it be a substitute.

Of course internal reference remained a crucial element in such works. The paintings were seen by the members of the vanguard at home in the U.S.S.R. as photos, or seen by them when they too traveled to the Western capitals in which exhibitions were taking place. What such works communicated was the particular nature of the new priorities taken on by newly liberated artists. More interesting than the effect created was the decision to create that effect. The artists feared that if their work were to tell secrets no one could read, it would be pointless, and that fear became their new secret, visible, like the old one, to those who knew them best. They were afraid that their own notion that art can communicate what can be said in no other way might itself be untrue in the West. And the fear of their own failure—of not being understood—took the place of their previous fear of failure within the terms they laid out for themselves—being understood too easily, or by the wrong people. The best works at *Isskunstvo* were the ones that acknowledged their own loss, that professed the new safe truths but that could not surmount their own uneasiness about such honesty, and that made reference, with truth and directness, to fiction and evasion. In fact, it is as easy to communicate an attitude toward the truth by speaking it as by avoiding it.

So the artists were intelligent enough not to believe in their own new priorities. The question, of course, was whether they would come to believe in them or cease to sustain them, since it is impossible and uncomfortable to sustain a body of work that is about its own insufficiencies at both the specific and the abstract level. If these artists began to create what they did not really believe, if they accepted Western values far enough to forsake their old ones, they were in danger of being left with nothing at all. They had to learn all over again to trust themselves, and to make that trust of themselves their first priority. What the West values and what they had valued had been categorically distinct from one another; when the line was blurred, all values became moot, and the art became clumsy, boring, and, in the long run, utterly pointless. Only their continuing migration—back and forth to the U.S.S.R., back and forth to the belief in their own fictions—could sustain their power as they sought for redefinition.

Before the opening in Berlin, the artists mostly stayed in the Bahnhof, building their works. Josif Bakshteyn, who had no work to prepare, decided one day to visit East Berlin. He found that prices there were very low, and, eager to contribute something to the hospitality he was receiving and to battle his reputation for stinginess, he decided to buy food. After some consideration, he purchased three kilograms of cheese and—despite the fact that he is a vegetarian—one big salamilike sausage. At customs on the way back, he was stopped and questioned; very few Soviets were able to travel at that time, and the idea that one of them had entered East Berlin and was now returning to West Berlin raised everyone's suspicions. But the idea that he had been on a shopping expedition was the last straw. He was stripped and body-searched and questioned and delayed, and in the end the customs agents said he could bring his cheese to West Berlin, but not his sausage; and they gave him a document, with many stamps and seals and signatures, as a receipt for it. He returned to West Berlin traumatized, but his document was duly hung inside the door of the Bahnhof, as his material contribution to the exhibition.

A few days before the opening there was a press conference. The artists were assembled, waiting for news reporters and TV crews, when Nikita Alexeev came in with a large bunch of bananas. Soviets are obsessed with bananas, which are almost never available in the U.S.S.R. Once in Moscow, I passed a shop at which people were literally fighting with one another in the street for a place in the queue to buy them. The Germans, unaware of this, had not bought bananas for anyone; when Nikita came in with his bunch, the mob descended on them, and when the media came in, there was a line of seven Soviets, each eating a banana, like a row of monkeys. It was the first inadvertent performance.

I arrived in Berlin two days before the opening. Everyone was installed; everyone was manic; everyone was trying to finish work that seemed at a great remove from completion. The night before the opening, I had dinner with all the artists, German and Soviet, in the Bahnhof; and after dinner, as a sort of staged entertainment to defuse the tension, came the hairdresser, a friend of the German artists. One by one the Soviets had their hair washed and cut into moderately trendy German haircuts. Ira Nakhova was not going to touch her long straight blond locks; but everyone else, including Sergey Volkov, who of course already had a smart cut, had a trim. It was like a ritual of transformation, something they undertook together. One by one they sat in the hairdresser's folding chair at the top of the Bahnhof steps, and changed from Soviets to half-breeds tinged with the West. It was their scant preparation for the world they were entering, a quiet gesture of acceptance of what was about to accept them.

Even at that time, the strengths and the weaknesses of the exhibition were manifest. The work was uneven, some of it unfinished; eighteen months later, in Prato, near Florence, the artists were to gesture at exquisite installations in an elegant museum and say, "This is a good show of our work; that was not." But Isskunstvo had great precocities and strengths. It recognized the idea that in days of ignorance and confusion, Soviet art shown in the West might best be produced in the West, and might best be displayed contextually with the work of Western artists closely acquainted with Soviet life. This notion turned the problem of travel into a structuring insight. The German work sustained an internal coherence with the Soviet work without attempting to program the Western response to it. Though the German work was not "important," though it was more often whimsical than astonishing, it was not without its strengths, and it helped viewers to respond to the Soviet work. The Soviets deemed themselves better artists than the Germans, and perhaps they were; that debate, which occupied many many hours, is one that it is not useful to attempt to resolve. The inconsistencies of the work reflected both the richness and the inevitable discomfort of the nervous dissimulation to which most of the artists had been driven.

More than two thousand people, including the Senator for Culture, the director of the DAAD, and people from all the banks and businesses that had underwritten the project, came to the opening of *Isskunstvo,* which lasted from eleven in the morning until five in the afternoon. Art historians were there; people who had written about the artists were there, including Boris Groys, and Jamey Gambrell from New York; everyone who was anyone in Berlin was there. There were friends of the Germans' and friends of Lisa Schmitz's and professors from the University and from the Academy of Arts. The Senator for Culture had hired a Japanese catering firm, and there was an abundance of food, all of it delicious. There was champagne to drink. The artists with their new haircuts stood by their works, looking urbane and amused and perhaps, by late afternoon, a little bit tired.

But the festivities did not end so soon. At six o'clock, a party in honor of the artists was thrown by Natan Fedorowskij, a dealer in Russian avant-garde art of the 1920s. This was another elegant event, with more groaning buffet tables, champagne, and wealthy Germans in expensive clothes, all looking the Soviets over rather—several of them observed—as though they were monkeys (this time without bananas). Kostya, Sergey Anufriev, Nikola, and Pasha decided that they had been patronized enough, and to ease the stress of the situation they got down on their hands and knees and began to bark like dogs. The other partygoers looked rather aghast; this too was a sort of performance, which deflated the guests at least insofar as it confused them. It was a profound gesture of rejection, of discomfort with their exotic status. Ira Nakhova, of course, preserved her dignity, and Sergey Volkov preserved his distance; they watched and smiled and ate crudités from the buffet.

After the party everyone except Ira, who was tired, went to the

Jungle. The Jungle is the chicest nightclub in Berlin and has been for perhaps too many years; it is not at the cutting edge, not counterculture, but rather full of prosperous young people in expensive clothes. An evening at The Jungle is nonetheless worth experiencing once; the space is slick and dramatic and high-tech, and the people are usually much the same: amazing hair is in evidence, and, in the German way, there is an acreage of leather. When we arrived, there were relatively few people, and the music was blaring. At first the artists were shy about dancing, but as the evening wore on they threw caution to the wind. Sergey Volkov stood apart, watching the Germans dance; when he finally joined in, he looked like a German. But Kostya, Sergey Anufriev, Pasha, and Nikola danced in a ring, kicking their feet up into the air. Anufriev, wearing a bell-bottom synthetic yellow pantsuit that he assured everyone had been the height of couture wear in Moscow in the seventies, put into practice a mad twisting gesture entirely his own that involved much leaping into the air. Nikola, Nikita, and Sven also found steps of their own, and danced with some of the German artists. There was much flailing of limbs, much pantomime and enactment, much travesty. The Jungle had never seen anything like it. With a certain grudging respect, the airbrushed-looking people made way for the colloquium of mad Russians. Later that evening came other nightclubs, a bar in which some of the artists got lost, and at last a streaky dawn. It was the first true day of the West.

I left the following morning; in the week that followed, the problem of the parties endured. Every night someone threw another soirée with the same people, gawking and asking questions and whispering to one another. The artists hated it. Hermann Wiesler, a professor at the Berlin Academy of Arts, asked the Soviet artists to his home, a book-lined apartment that looks like part of a library. He set the party up to be comfortably Russian, with beer, cucumbers, and peasant bread, and invited most of the same people who had been at Natan Fedorowskij's. The German artists were getting peevish by this time, since no one seemed to have taken any note of their place in the exhibition, and the Soviets were really beyond the outermost limits of irritation: irritation mixed with boredom.

Nikita mentioned to Dési Baumeister that he had been watching her closely for some days, and had decided to ask her whether she would be interested in joining a secret sect to which all the Soviets belonged. Slightly confused, she asked what sort of sect this was; Nikita explained that it was a Satanic order that dated back to the

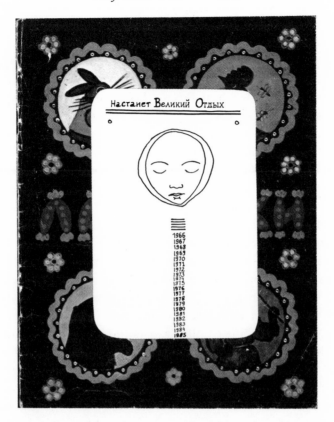

PEPPERSHTEYN (PASHA PIVOVAROV): *It Will Be a Great Rest*

Byzantine era. "But I can't tell you much more," he said. "You'd better ask Kostya, who is our vice president." She wasn't sure what was going on, so she went and asked Kostya. He looked a bit surprised; then he said that the cult was very ancient, pre-Byzantine, and explained some of its complex rituals. "I am only vice president. Neither Nikita nor I have the power to invite you to join. But we will consult with the president. Perhaps right now you would like to talk about this matter with Nikola."

One by one, each of the German artists was invited into the sect. Its rules were explained in dizzying detail. But the sect was actually just another game; moreover, it was an unplanned game. When Nikita had approached Dési, he had not discussed the matter with anyone else; Kostya had simply guessed what sort of entertainment was beginning, and had carried through the joke, as did all the others. Later on, the Soviets warned the Germans that they, the Germans, were being monitored by inspectors who followed them everywhere. "In the U.S.S.R.," they said, "this is normal. If you wish to associate with us, you will have to get used to having someone always watching you. Don't be self-conscious; your inspector is always there. Probably he will leave when we also leave." Like the barking, these games served to give the Soviets an upper hand. Art, for them, was communication; with these performances they communicated their disdain for the world in which they found themselves and also their puzzlement about its meaning. They wanted to explain clearly that what was held to be clear and significant and appropriate in the West made no more sense to them than these absurdities did to the Westerners.

This is not to suggest that they were not very fond of the Bomba Colori artists per se; the Satanic society and the vigilant inspector games were really a sort of mark of affection, an inclusion of everyone in the joke. Relations with Bomba Colori and with Lisa Schmitz went through ups and downs, but were essentially friendly throughout. Still, there was a certain amount of hostility toward German art as a category, and the Bomba Colori artists did not escape rebuke. The Soviets thought German art was formalistic. They thought that artists who had won scholarships and stipends, as the Bomba Colori artists had, were underwritten by the government and were producing a Western equivalent to Soviet official art. They said that the Germans liked coffee and the cinema more than they liked to work—an unlikely accusation from a world of people who had spent years meeting and drinking tea and discussing ideas that came to nothing. The Soviets accused the Germans of letting small talk take priority over serious discussion about art.

At the same time, the Soviets themselves talked more and more about galleries and money, and how to buy a computer, and how to get a computer back to the U.S.S.R. once you bought it, and how to buy a car, and which collectors paid the highest prices. They talked about what kind of work would sell and what kind of work would not sell; and even Kostya, who had made his cardboard Venice in protest of the commercial response to his work, volunteered endless information on Western tastes he had observed and their financial ramifications.

It had always been part of the plan for the Soviets to stay on for a few weeks after the opening, so that they could see some of Berlin. But several of them were so comfortable there that they did not want to leave. Sergey Volkov sold a lot of work, managed to find himself an apartment, and lived in prosperity and comfort. Other artists, in the weeks that followed the opening, became more and more self-assured in their game-playing, and played games on a larger and larger scale; Kostya and Sergey Anufriev (and his shadow Peppershteyn) stayed on with some of the German artists and staged pranks as a means of self-enactment.

They produced a wondrous array of projects: Kostya sketched a proposal for a pipeline to connect the Black Sea and the White Sea (in the north of Russia) to make them both gray. He and Anufriev went to flea markets with some of the Bomba Colori artists, and sometimes with Nikita and Nikola, and there they bought the most glittery and ostentatious clothes. Kostya obtained a sword and then a plastic crown —what he needed to be a king. He and Anufriev purchased the spoils of war, the things a general might bring to his people after battle in a foreign land. They bought Indian and Turkish clothes, which they wore to sit around and smoke in. With the Bomba Colori artists, they made clay sculpture of all sorts of things, of carrots and of gnomes, and they painted them. "It was more like theater than like reality," Dési Baumeister has recalled.

The Soviets, living on hospitality from the Bomba Colori artists, were constantly teasing their hosts for spending the day in offices or at jobs. The Germans were driven to the brink of distraction by the chaotic slovenliness of the Soviets; *gemütlich,* as a concept, was lost on them. The Soviets were often sexist, and they thought that cleanliness was a petty-bourgeois affectation. After one particularly strongly worded confrontation, Anufriev, as a symbolic gesture, set about cleaning the kitchen floor where he was staying. For three days he remained on his hands and knees, scrubbing every corner with a toothbrush. After that, he felt he had earned his rest, and didn't touch a cleaning utensil again.

Kostya became fascinated by demonstrations. He decided to join in every one he could find, making the most of this pleasure which had for so long been forbidden in the Soviet Union. He made collages, absurd and symbolic, heavy with media slogans and pictures of detectives, and photocopied them. Then he found demonstrations and walked in the opposite direction to the crowd, distributing these photocopies to the confused demonstrators, who were carried past him in the flow of people before they had time to ask what the papers meant. Sometimes he went out at night and posted his collages all over Berlin. It was like the Satanic society, like the inspector joke,

ХВОСТИК ОТ КЛУБНИКИ.

Sergey Anufriev: *The Little Tail of a Strawberry*

like all the games, a way to achieve brief power in an alien and abstracted world, a way to enforce his own system on what was foreign to him.

There is no question that the Soviets could be impossible in the West. Over and over again, I have heard them say, "We are like children. You must treat us like children. We know nothing at all, and we cannot take responsibility." In the long run, the attitude is an obnoxious one. It is tiresome in the extreme to treat like children people who are visibly not children. One accepts that certain quotidian matters—how to buy food or how to get from place to place—present technical difficulties. But sometimes the game-playing got out of hand, and the demands made on Westerners were unacceptable. "Do this and do that and also do this," Soviets would say on the telephone. To many of the people who met them they seemed ungrateful; one man I know negotiated a gallery contract for one of them, and after two weeks of solid work would accept no payment; he came in for sharp criticism because the photocopy he provided of the contract was on low-grade paper and because he hadn't insisted that the gallery write up the contract in Russian. Some of this behavior grew out of ignorance; the Soviets often didn't know how much effort or expense something involved, and they would thank you effusively for a sandwich in a restaurant and fail to express any gratitude for a three-month stay in your apartment. More of it was arrogance born of defensiveness; the Soviets were in a totally new world, and swaggered to prove they could take it.

Slowly I was also to see that the reaction to Soviet artists was deeply tied to the ambivalence with which the West greeted perestroika itself. That perestroika was essentially good no one would dispute. But we measure our freedom against the curtailment of other lives, our sense of continuity against other people's disturbances; for that reason, new liberalisms make us uneasy. There is nothing more frightening to us than the possibility that our own history is a fiction, that the meaning of the events by which we define ourselves has remained inaccessible to us. We structure our lives on the unstable foundation of what we ourselves remember and what others remember; it is the memory, and not the lost event, upon which we base our subsequent actions, and so it is the inadequacies of memory that compose the lacunae of history. Of all the many divides between Soviet and Western culture, the one that has been most significant for the West, the one from which our smug comfort has been derived, is neither military nor intellectual. Our composure depends on our insistence on remembering as much of the self-proclaimed truth as we possibly can, and the weakness of the Soviet Union has to us been most vividly manifest in the Soviet refusal to remember what has happened, in the apparently casual way in which fictive histories have been substituted for actual ones. Marx said that the point of intellectual work was not to understand the world, but to change it. For him, the study of history was not so much about documenting what had occurred, as about a kind of rhetorical performance that would create new history; the fictive histories of the Soviet bureaucracy grew from this idea, but fail most significantly for their slovenliness, their irregularity, and their inadequacy to the task Marx has set them. That is where we, with our less visionary documentary view, find ourselves far ahead.

The dawn of perestroika turned on the radical restructuring of the systems of information that we call history. Certain filters of obfuscation were eliminated to make way for the revised intentions of a government that professed, at least, to value memory over expedience. This development was frightening for the West, because it destroyed the yardstick against which we had always calculated our own nobility. The Soviets' forsaking their received history imbalanced our history, and their accord with us seemed to threaten our overdetermined future. We were obliged to find new fictions to replace the squandered and artificial confidence we possessed in the Cold War years, when our keenest pride was in our comparatively rigorous honesty; as old beliefs collapsed beneath the weight of new ones in the U.S.S.R., ours collapsed in concord. We even began to doubt our own history, and to mistrust our own collective memory; our response was a conservative celebration of the past both in our governmental policies and in the increasingly pedantic negativity of much post-modernism.

During the period in which the distortion of history was most relentless, the artists of the Soviet vanguard were guardians of their own knowledge, whose refusal to allow their own memories to be taken away from them was, in context, the most vigorous radicalism of all. The Soviet artists have been concerned, before all else, with the truth of what has happened, the truth of how we remember what has happened, and the truth of how we represent what we remember has happened. As outsiders, we are drawn into such work and denied a place within it, and the difficulty with which we accept it is neither greater nor smaller than the difficulty of its own circumstances.

In the days of perestroika, these artists began to recognize our dangerous gullibility, at the same time that they reveled in our rich openness. Work like that shown in Berlin recognized its audience and spoke directly to it; it was for the audience of Westerners to overcome fear of the new and discomfort with perestroika's partial triumphs. Because we measure our freedoms against other freedoms, ours too changed in the face of perestroika. Against the backdrop of these artists' luminary insistence on the multiplicity of reality, whining post-modernist complacence was suddenly revealed as totally unacceptable. That was the lesson of Berlin, communicated in dozens of codes, activities, works, prejudices, and biases.

After *Isskunstvo,* I did not see any Soviets until I went to New York for Christmas, and at that point I saw Dima Prigov. It was the first time I had seen one of these artists in my own world; Berlin is the West, but for me it is neutral territory in a way that the city where I grew up is not. Seeing Dima was surprising. There is a convention among travel memoirs, a tradition that started in the nineteenth century but that has carried into many modern texts, both sociological and anecdotal: the writer pauses in the midst of a protracted description of the life he has taken on, and observes that for some weeks or months he has been rising each day with the people he has come to observe, eating as they eat, washing as they wash, working as they work, and sleeping as they sleep—but he has known, nonetheless, that at the end of a specified period, he will return to his own life and leave them behind to rise and eat and wash and work and sleep as they do and have done time out of mind. It seems to be outside the convention for the people observed—usually a large tribe or community—to materialize on Seventy-second Street expecting to be received and fed, willing, with similar smiles of ironic detachment, to eat as the author eats, to work as he works, to sleep as he sleeps; to meet his family and friends and discuss their lives with them; to judge as cheerfully as they have been judged and to objectify as they have been objectified. Had Margaret Mead met the Samoans at her local newsstand, or on the train she was taking to a college reunion, or having lunch with her mother, she might, I think, have been given some moments' pause.

Not until I saw Dmitriy Prigov in the living room of my parents' house in New York did I understand to how great an extent I had looked at the Soviets as inhabiting a world apart; and it was only then that I realized that the criticism I had read about them—and some of the criticism I had written about them—treated them in this anthropological, distancing, and ultimately patronizing way. In Moscow, I would occasionally comment on an eccentricity of the Soviet system, or on a bizarre negotiation undertaken to purchase something, or on an extraordinary-looking man in the street. "Russian Exotic," the artists would say with a smile. They took an ironic position toward their status as foreign and unknowable. They pointed out the absurdities of Western life as casually as I had observed those of the Soviet system. Eventually the disparate worlds began to merge. In 1988 and 1989, there was an unending stream of Soviets coming through New York and through London. Some stayed with me; when my house was full, I often asked friends to house others. In Moscow, Kostya might say to me, "Maybe it's true, what you say. But I think your friend James doesn't think so." In Leningrad, Afrika observed that someone in the street looked like my brother. There is a sense in which people need not be dealt with as people so long as they remain outside the realities of one's life; one can see them instead as specimens of something foreign and ultimately unknowable. When they enter your life materially, that changes.

It is truly impossible to describe the artists and their lives, my engagement with them and my occasional disaffection, without indulging in some of the rhetoric of Russian Exotic. Communal apartments warrant a description, and they warrant a tone of incredulity and horror. If I were not to describe the physical conditions in Furmanny, no one from the West could envision life there. But it is important not to treat the artists purely as novelty: because their exoticism is as much a game as a reality. Every aspect of life could be as confusing as the Satanic society. "We have laughed very much," Larisa Zvezdochetova told me in Berlin in early 1990. "Some things you have published about our exotic lives, they were only jokes. It's not true," she said, and listed several details from an article—some of which were fictions, but some of which were really true. By blurring the line between what had been made up and what was so, she took a sort of forceful control of the artists' exoticism. One of the things Larisa mentioned was something that was stated ironically in my article. "So it is a joke also from you?" she asked. For them, there was such a thing as Western Exotic, and sometimes the exotic and the genuine faded together. It was a relief to discover the similarities of our positions. So long as we mistook and exaggerated one another in equal degrees, everything was fine. Larisa did a sculpture of me; Kostya and Anufriev recorded a dialogue about my skin (which they had decided was prototypical Western skin). I too could be literalized.

The day that Dima Prigov came to my parents' house I began to know the artists anew. If who they are were not incomplete without the Russian Exotic, it might be tactful to leave it out; but the game of Russian Exotic, which had begun in earnest with the monologues the artists gave to their Western visitors at the time of Sotheby's and had continued with the Satanic society, which had shown up in their dialogues with the Germans, and which was to play its role in their lives back in Moscow—the game of Russian Exotic became part of who they were. To leave it out now would be as patronizing as it might have been to include it in the days when they had had no contact with the West, before they recognized Russian Exotic as a category.

Dima and I had fun in New York. One clear, crisp day we went to the British consulate to try to obtain a visa for him to visit London. It brought home to me the harshness with which Soviets are often treated in the West, and it demonstrated at how basic a level they were unprepared for the details of our system. As if to punish them for the character of their motherland, we force them, when they come to the West, to endure protracted negotiation with badly run and unresponsive bureaucracies, bureaucracies that assume more knowledge than any Soviet is likely to have and that are less interested in the citizens they process than is any Soviet institution. I loathe waiting in endless lines to get visas of private invitation for long trips to the U.S.S.R., but I have learned that this inconvenience is as nothing compared to what Soviets must undergo to come to the West—not what they have to endure from their own government, but what they endure from those of the West.

Dima was to go to London as a guest of the ICA (Institute of Contemporary Arts), one of Britain's leading art institutions; he had all the relevant papers in order. At the British consulate, we were faced with pages and pages of forms to fill out, full of questions the correct answers to which would have been obvious to anyone from the West—anyone not required to fill them out—and wholly inaccessible to anyone unacquainted with the priorities of Western immigration authorities. After name and wife's name and mother's maiden name and date and place of birth and so on came a series of questions: Where will you live? What is your source of income? What is your annual income in UK pounds? How will you pay for your expenses in the United Kingdom? On what date will you leave? Dima said, naturally enough, that he would live with someone whose name he didn't know who worked at the ICA, that his income came from people's interest in his work, that its level was completely uncertain but that in UK pounds it was probably about four hundred a year (calculated to a realistic rather than an official exchange rate), that he hoped the ICA would pay him something but he didn't yet know, and that he would leave when he got tired of England. I reviewed these accurate responses, and said that I was not sure they would serve the purpose of the application. So we filled out a new application, saying that he would live with me and giving my address, that his income came from his work as an artist, that he earned about eight thousand pounds per year (at an official exchange rate), that the ICA would cover all his expenses while in England, and that he would leave within a month of his arrival.

We submitted the application and waited for several hours. We were told that Dima would have to be interviewed. Knowing that his interview would be full of additional trick questions, I asked whether anyone at the consulate spoke Russian. No one did. Realizing what was coming, I volunteered, after some discussion with Dima, to serve as a translator, though I had no qualifications to do so. In a small and rather dank room, a rather patronizing member of the consular staff asked what to a Soviet citizen could only be booby-trap questions. After each one, I would turn to Dima and say, *"Blini rachmaninoff stroganov shashlik kiev bucharin?"* and he would reply with a line from one of his poems in Russian, and I would then give the consular woman an appropriate answer in English. Afterward, we laughed a lot about the whole episode; a month later, Dima got his visa. If it is impossible to be honest and always within the limits of the law as an American in Moscow, it is equally impossible to negotiate in a straightforward manner as a Soviet in New York. It was moving to see how the artists tried; and it was disillusioning to see how soon they were obliged to give up. As it became almost a joke in Moscow that I was in some forbidden place, so it became a joke in the West for artists to call and say, "So, from today, I am an illegal alien; and Aeroflot says they have no tickets until March." And slowly the matter would be renegotiated, with many telephone calls, so that they could leave with untarnished records.

Lots of Soviets were in New York that Christmas. I saw Igor and Sveta Kopystyanskiy; at a party in their honor I met some émigrés, including Alexander Kosolapov. The Kopystyanskiys had been in the U.S. for three months and, like Erik Bulatov, they had acquired poise, an ease with their surroundings. Meanwhile, there were artists in Cologne and Basel, Paris and Brussels. Later, I would see many Soviet artists imported for an opening, a week of tourism, a moment with the press. These meetings always had the embarrassing, clinging air of fiasco about them. They were aesthetic shock treatments, occasions for the artists to identify their own distance from what rapidly became an attacking public. The artists could do nothing more than retreat behind the loveliness of their work, if it was lovely; communication was not undermined but eliminated, and defensive secrecy benefited no one. The consistent crude dismissal of work that was devalued by the pretense that artists, in their persons, could emblematize their nation and history was painful and unnecessary. Much of the very bad Soviet art that came to the West was overhyped, and much of the very good was not understood; in the art market, there emerged a kind of random conflation of the good and the bad, the interesting and the uninteresting. Too many of the people who imported Soviet art failed to recognize the extent to which their attitudes transformed it, and refused to take a responsible attitude in their presentation of it. The public, eager to exploit the vogue, was too often unaware of the complexities with which it is necessary to engage in order to come to terms with such art, and they judged it in ignorance.

So the value of the exhibitions that were well mounted can hardly be exaggerated. Ronald Feldman, Phyllis Kind, Thomas Krings-Ernst, Eva Poll, Danny Keller, Vanessa Devereux, Peter Pakesch, Sophie Ungers, Natan Fedorowskij—I didn't care for all of their shows, but the essentially responsible attitudes they adopted toward the presentation of Soviet art (though several of them did take advantage of the general confusion in their negotiations with the artists and the buyers) made an intelligent reception of it possible. Shows at the Pompidou, at the ICA, in several American museums, and in an exhibition center in Vienna were like shining lights in the murky forest.

T he whole world seemed to be coming under the sway of Soviet art, and the artists were increasingly in demand. Most prominently, they were collected by Paul Ludwig, a German confectionery magnate who had previously set world trends by being among the first serious collectors of American Pop art; he has bought work by every one of the new young Soviets, on grounds that after ten years some of the work will be tremendously valuable, and the rest of it can then be disposed of. The vast Ludwig collection is like the fuse on a time bomb of deflated prices and worldwide deaccessioning. Though the artists often say, somewhat relieved, that entire exhibitions have been bought out by Ludwig, they also see his enthusiasm as cause for fear. In his collection and in others, their work has been hung too quickly beside work by the most important Western artists.

Almost no figure in the world of contemporary Western art would refuse someone who called up and identified himself as an artist on his first trip from Moscow who had always wanted to meet the figure with whom he was now, to his stupefaction, talking on the phone. And so the Soviets met everyone. They were invited to the homes and palazzi of collectors, and they had dinners thrown in their honor in apartments at Trump Tower. Their work was regularly mentioned in the local press, but even when it was unpopular, they were popular: they were invited to appear on morning television shows and profiled in glossy magazines.

Sometimes they were aware of the monkeys-in-the-zoo aspect of this attention and were vocal in their resistance to it. They expressed the sage fear that seems to elude rock stars: they would ask what happens to the sensation of the moment when the moment has passed, and they would try not to accelerate the machinery of a fame that could only dwindle into disappointment. Of course there was much swelling of egos, much bombastic discussion of the galleries in which one did and did not wish to show. The artists were modest about genuine accomplishments, and overbearingly self-important about patronizing responses from the curious world, or about the bizarre occasions to which they had been party. In the East, they had lived in much privation; in the West, they were thrown in at the deep end of privilege. Some were in their element at once, and some were depressed; but many were like children drowning in whipped cream, spluttering inchoate delight even as they choked on the excess of their frothy glory.

Their fixation on consumer goods burgeoned. They could not buy homes because private property was still not an issue in Moscow. They didn't want to buy art, or fine furniture, or expensive clothes. The big items to buy were computers, cars, and video equipment. This proclivity, which had started in Berlin, grew into an obsession. Cars were purchased by people without licenses; Sven Gundlakh bought one and imported it in the name of Sergey Mironenko's wife, because she had a license; since she was also importing one for herself, the arrangement seemed straightforward. But when the crew returned to Moscow, they found that it was illegal to change the title on a car from the one who had registered it at import to another person, and also that it was illegal for one person to have two cars in his or her name. That saga went on for some time. I spent endless hours listening to conversation so boring and so greedy as to be painful: where to get which kind of computer, what it cost, where it was available for less, how to resell it in Moscow and make enough money to live on forever, how to import it, how to export it, what it could and couldn't do, what accessories were available for it. The material obsession became a driving, *the* driving force in these fragile Soviet lives.

Back in London I saw Sven Gundlakh and Ira Nakhova when they came over for an exhibition. Sergey Volkov came for a short visit but stayed for months because he had lost his passport and couldn't go anywhere without it. (One night, late, he told me that British collectors of art were like "post-Marx collectors," and I challenged him on the idea that Marxism could breed collectors of any description. It took twenty minutes for us to work out that he was referring to collectors of canceled postage stamps—"postmarks collectors." About British collectors he was at least half right; about communication and its complexities, we were both only just learning.) I also met dozens of émigrés, among them Ilona Medvedeva, a young woman not without talent whose inconsistent stories seemed to be largely figments of her imagination. I remember Ilona's coming to my house one day with a portfolio of drawings of melons. "When I first came to the West," she explained, "I was very poor, and I didn't have enough to eat. I was in Ireland, in Dublin. I was too embarrassed to beg, so I went each day to the market, and I said to the men with stalls there that I was a painter of still lifes, and that I wanted the spoiled fruit they were preparing to throw away so that I could paint it. There was one man who would always say, 'If you want something to paint, then I will give you my best and most beautiful melon.' I felt so guilty about deceiving him that I always painted his beautiful melons before I ate them."

Ilona is representative of a group of people I was to continue to meet, people who left the U.S.S.R. at the wrong moment. Artists such as Komar and Melamid were able to establish real reputations in the West; and even Viktor Skersis, Alexander Kosolapov, and Leonid Sokov achieved some notice in their adopted country. Furthermore, such artists were very much tied into the infrastructure of the avant-garde, and they did collaborative exhibitions with the artists they had known in Moscow. But an artist like Ilona, expert at negotiating her own prominence, could easily have achieved it in the West had she stayed in Moscow for three more years. Because she left too soon, because she became part of life in the West in the mid-eighties, she was of no interest to all the people who were buying Soviet art in the name of voguishness.

One day, I received a press release saying:

THE TRANSFORMATION OF KENSINGTON INTO ITALY

a constructivist ballet performed by THE ROYAL RUSSIAN AVANTE GARDE CONSTRUCTIVIST BALLET COMPANY based in London.

The ballet will begin at SOUTH KENSINGTON UNDER-
GROUND (in the shopping arcade) at 12 NOON TUESDAY AU-
GUST FIRST 1989. It will proceed along Exhibition Road,
through Hyde Park coming to a close at the park's north boundary at 1 pm also TUESDAY AUGUST FIRST.

DURING THIS TIME KENSINGTON WILL BE TRANS-
FORMED INTO ITALY by dancers dressed in constructivist
blouses carrying an orange cloth more than 10 meters in length.

Orange is the brightest colour and from satellites, an area of
more than 10 sq. meters can be discerned. At the time of the
orange harvest satellites are able to distinguish Southern Italy
because of its orange plantations.

On the 1st of August manned spacecraft and computerized
satellites in space will be thrown into confusion and will think,
on viewing Kensington that they, in fact, are looking at Southern
Italy during harvest time.

This was an event not to be missed, and Tuesday, August 1, found
me in the shopping arcade in question. I was immediately co-opted
into the performance. We all put on ludicrous orange smocks that
Ilona had cut and sewed, and so garbed we walked with great ceremony along the Gloucester Road and through Hyde Park, carrying a
long piece of orange fabric that Ilona had brought back from Moscow
(this reinforced the awareness that we were involved with Soviet art)
and that smelled strangely like curry. The press release was, in its
way, a stroke of amusing mad genius; the realization of the ballet,
however, was asinine, and the people involved a bit creepy; one of
them kept readjusting his smock and saying in a high-pitched voice,
"I think we are confusing local earthlings." Everyone in South Kensington stared at us. I felt like an idiot, and the event made me wonder
a bit about the Actions with K/D. Of course those Actions were the
product of a serious artistic intelligence, and they were part of a
continuing tradition. They were art of some substance; this was bad
art. But were the stares of the fishermen at my first action with
Monastyrskiy, or those of the passersby at an Action that I had recently
attended in Moscow any less embarrassing than the stares of the dapper
businessmen I encountered across the road from the Victoria and
Albert Museum? Less embarrassing for me, surely, because being
foreign is like wearing a protective coat of explanations for your behavior. It was odd for the Soviets to bark like dogs at Natan Fedo-

rowskij's party, but then again they were in camouflage, though a camouflage whose status may have eluded them.

The camouflage of the younger artists was to undergo a series of transformations; but stubborn refusal to engage continued to underlie it, a hostility that fluctuated between the overt—Kostya for example, got into several bar fights—and the covert. For the older artists, it was different; Kabakov and Bulatov were always gracious and responsive and eminently civilized, and Dima Prigov, less passive in his response than those two, was nonetheless able and willing to engage fully with the new cultures he encountered. In fact, Erik and Natasha Bulatov stayed with me in London for two weeks and were so kind and so warm, so attentive to keeping the house clean and the refrigerator stocked, that they gave me a new affection for London, for my home, for life itself.

Kabakov was always so frankly politic that my tremendous respect for him never passed into anything more. His wife, Vika Kabakova, is an inspiring woman, a pillar of strength, alive with the kind of brightness that makes everything around her seem more entirely alive. Kabakov himself is always amenable, agreeable; I have never heard him say a word against anyone or anything. But in the West he still behaves as though he were among pleasant aliens from a dream. He offends no one and commands everyone's attention and is polite and articulate but strangely noncommittal, as though the habit of allowing his work to subsume his actual opinions had left him without the ability to have opinions of his own. And with a sage manner of indifference, Andrey Monastyrskiy continued to refuse all invitations to travel. It was made clear to everyone: he did not need the West.

But the younger artists were everywhere. Of the dozens and dozens of exhibitions of their work that took place in the spring of 1989, three stand out: *10 + 10,* which opened in Fort Worth in early May and traveled to San Francisco, Buffalo, Milwaukee, and Washington, then on to Moscow, Tblisi, and Leningrad; *Mosca Terza Roma,* which opened in Rome in late May; and *Art Instead of Art,* which took place in Budapest in June.

10 + 10 showed the work of ten Soviet and ten American artists, and it was distinguished for the scale of its successes and its failures. The Soviet list included several of the Moscow conceptualists: Yuriy Albert, Vladimir Mironenko, Andrey Royter, Vadim Zakharov, and Kostya Zvezdochetov; younger Moscow artists: Anatoliy Zhuravlev, who was just emerging as an important figure in Moscow, and Sergey

Shutov, closely tied to the Leningrad New Artists; the mad and amusing but marginal Yuriy Petruk; the semiofficial quasi-primitive Leonid Purygin; and the radical Union figure Aleksey Sundukov. The American list included a number of big names: David Salle, Donald Sultan, Peter Halley, Ross Bleckner, and Annette Lemieux, among others.

The show was organized by Intercultura, an international cultural foundation run by Dee Smith, a sophisticated, intelligent Texan who has done ground-breaking work in opening communication between American museums and difficult or inaccessible cultures. Smith went to Moscow to organize a show of icons and another of avant-garde work from the twenties; when he got there, the Ministry of Culture suggested that he do a show of contemporary art, and he agreed, largely to win points with the Ministry. *10 + 10* was born as a bargaining chip in the negotiations for the twenties show, and only after it had been mooted for political reasons did it develop into something of artistic significance. Unlike *Isskunstvo,* or the Kabakov and Bulatov shows organized by Paul and Claudia Jolles, or indeed any of the other shows of 1988–89, *10 + 10* went through official channels. Smith and the curators, Marla Price from Fort Worth and Graham Beal from San Francisco, worked closely with Pavel Khoroshilov (the man who told Lisa Schmitz her project would never take place), and realized their show under the auspices of the Ministry of Culture. To their credit, they did not accept a list of Union hacks; Smith made it clear from the first meeting that he would work with the Ministry only if Intercultura and the curators were allowed to choose the artists. They did not press for the most radical figures of Moscow unofficial art, which is perhaps fortunate; but it is worthy of note that two of the blacklisted former Mukhomors were accepted under the official aegis of the Ministry. Given the constraints placed on them, the curators—intelligent and creative people in an impossible situation—did a terrific job. Sent to any Western European city and asked to choose ten important artists, they would have had context and a feasible rationale to make their choice; dumped in Moscow, they had to—in the words of Marla Price—"go for visual impact." They spent three trips of two weeks each going around Moscow in a big car, visiting studios for an hour each at the outside, attending dinners at the Ministry of Culture and at the American embassy. They heard everyone's patter-songs; I cannot doubt that they met more artists than I have met in several years of contact with the vanguard. They had some names from friends and sources in the U.S.S.R., and they listened to the artists they met, seeing everyone to whom they were referred.

There was some very good work in 10 + 10, but there was no reason for some of the artists to be included or for others to be excluded. The number ten, taken to fit with the exhibition's snappy title, had no further justification; it was a round, irrelevant number of artists to select. The criteria on which the art was judged had little to do with its strengths or demerits, and the exhibition did nothing to explain to those who visited it what it meant to encounter Soviet art, how Soviet art differed from Western art, what concessions it required and what triumphs it could achieve. The selection was like a crazy salad; it was apparently meant to show how various the work of Soviets might be, and how various the work of Americans. This agenda fails to make Soviet work accessible to ordinary American citizens; likewise, it fails to make American work accessible to ordinary Soviet citizens, who were to encounter the work of all the Americans and almost all the Soviets for the first time when the exhibition toured the U.S.S.R.

The artists who came to the United States for the various openings of 10 + 10 were treated like royalty, given tours around town, toasted at gala fêtes. They met the Americans included in the show, and discovered all the glamour of major art events in the West. Their work was beautifully displayed, perfectly lit, impeccably reproduced in a catalogue distributed by Abrams. At parties, they encountered members of the Ministry of Culture, people who had snubbed them for years, and who now chatted with them like colleagues and old friends. "[A major official] is like my pal, now, my buddy—it's uncomfortable for me. I don't trust this exhibition, I don't trust anything about it," said Volodya Mironenko; but he also said, "It's professional, how an exhibition should look. I met Peter Halley, and I liked him; he's funny and a good artist. I'm glad to be part of this." In some ways, 10 + 10 did more than anything else to suggest that the line between the official and the unofficial had been broken; but since that line *hadn't* really been broken, the exhibit made manifest a partial truth as though it had been validated, and paved the way, in a highly politicized context, to the enthusiastic complacence for which America was at that time richly primed.

The official/unofficial question came up again and again. Back in Moscow it was clear how unofficial the artists of the vanguard still were, but in the West, they found themselves being courted by people who had previously spat at them. They were sometimes amused but more often disoriented by this, and they responded none too warmly. Georgiy Puzenkov, heir apparent to the presidency of the Union of Artists, is a good-natured man, an undistinguished but not a terrible painter, someone who moved toward officialdom from his student days not because he believed in the politics of communism so much as because he wanted to lead the good life and knew on which side his bread was buttered. His timing was terrible; he was just rising in the Union hierarchy when glasnost came and official artists turned into *personae non gratae* outside of their own constricted circle. So Puzenkov tried to switch. When I first met him, he talked about years of oppression—despite his powerful status in Moscow—with more gusto than Dima Prigov. In April, I ended up at a party in London with Sergey Volkov, Sven Gundlakh, Ira Nakhova, Afrika, and Puzenkov. I was talking to Volkov and Afrika when Puzenkov came to join us. He spoke about his paintings in a slightly pompous way and produced snapshots of his gallery exhibition. Afrika looked at them and nodded sagely. "You have absorbed very well the influence of the great Moscow master Sergey Volkov," he said. There was a moment's silence, and then Puzenkov said, "We work together," and smiled at Volkov. Volkov did not smile back. He laughed, then frowned. And Puzenkov could only look embarrassed and stammer and change the subject to ask solicitous questions about the London art market.

Mosca Terza Roma (Moscow, the Third Rome) was in some ways the antithesis of *10 + 10*. Organized by Viktor Miziano, then of the Pushkin Museum, it took place in a desanctified church in Rome. The list of artists was entirely coherent, carefully chosen on the basis of a very deep knowledge of the Moscow scene. The artists included— Andrey Filippov, Boris Orlov, Zhora Litichevskiy, Kostya Zvezdochetov, Dmitriy Prigov, and Andrey Royter—were individuals whose conjunction gave definition to their work; with widely different poetics, they gave voice to closely related truths. Each artist did an installation specifically for the exhibition. Whereas *10 + 10* was a show of works snatched unwittingly from the safety of Moscow, *Mosca Terza Roma* was composed entirely of work manufactured to be seen in the West. It was rife with in-jokes; the favorite piece was Filippov's *Last Supper*, a table with a heavy red cloth and twelve places, each set with a black plate, a black hammer where the fork might have gone, and a black sickle for the knife. The play between what the artists knew and what they communicated was deliberate, tense, and eloquent; this was progress over *Isskunstvo*, where it was accidental, loose, and virtually meaningless. It was probably the most successful show of that winter.

At the time of *Isskunstvo* the fact that many artists who knew one another well were all living together outside Moscow had seemed natural—since they had been in proximity to one another for years. At the time of *Mosca Terza Roma* they were experienced in isolation, and their meeting was therefore both a relief and a source of tension. They had by that time done too many solo shows in strange cities, spent too much time sitting at tables full of serious people who spoke foreign languages slowly and loudly at them, seen too many exhibitions of alien or incomprehensible art. So while the carousing in which they indulged in Rome was a calculated gesture aimed at their hosts, it was also a way of reestablishing intimacy, a reforming of the codes. After drinking themselves into a stupor one night on the Capitoline Hill, Zvezdochetov and Filippov said that they were senators come from the Third Rome to the First Rome; and so, in a way, they were.

Hungary was the revelation of a possible future: a nation in advanced post-communism that had achieved sufficient prosperity to look almost like a Western country. *Art Instead of Art,* the exhibition in Budapest, was of work by the seven Furmanny artists and, as in Berlin and Rome, it was created in the weeks preceding the opening specifically for the exhibition space. The organizers of the exhibition had gone to Moscow in January, when most of these artists were traveling, the others recently returned and scheduled to depart, and had found to their dismay that they could not organize an exhibition along conventional lines, by choosing work and arranging to export it—not, this time, because export licenses were scarce, but because there was no work to choose from in Moscow. Only invitations to the artists themselves would result in work, and so, following on the pattern Lisa Schmitz had first established, the Hungarians invited the Soviet artists in the flesh.

There is, in any new field, a moment when the difficulties of certain basic accomplishments seem to drop away, a plateau before boredom sets in and new accomplishments are required. There is a moment in which the novice experiences only satisfaction at his own newly acquired abilities. It was like that in Budapest. Everyone was there; everyone was together; there were no real points to prove, and everyone had a good time. The exhibition was not troubled, like *Isskunstvo,* and it was not tense and energized like *Mosca Terza Roma.* In his introduction to the catalogue, Sven Gundlakh wrote: "Time seems to have stopped nowadays." In the absence of time, a richness of creative spirit bloomed. "Progress has silently changed from a spiral to a circular motion, and its speed has consequently accelerated." Sven

154 Kensington Park Road
London W11 2ER
4 September 1990

Yuri Albert, Andrei Filippov, Sergei Mironenko
Thomas Krings-Ernst
Goltsteinstrasse 106
5000 Köln 51
fax: 34-23-70

Dear Yuri, Andrei, and Sergei:

So how's things in Cologne? I have been trying to reach all
three of you for some months. I tried to call Moscow. I sent
letters to Moscow. I even sent Lisa Schmitz to Moscow, but it
was all useless. You can imagine that I am now very happy to
have found you in Köln, where I hope you are all having a great
time. I got Yuri's message on my answering machine, which was
great; unfortunately he failed to say where he was, and so I had
no way to get back in touch. I'm sorry I missed the opening of
the exhibition he mentioned; I was not in England at the time,
and got his message only after the opening had taken place, which
meant I could not have come even if he had said where he was
calling from.

I gather that Vadik may have mentioned to you the matter of
illustrations for my book, and perhaps some of the other artists
w███████████ work will ha██ told you s██ thing as ██████████
have ██████ from Kos███, ████ssa, S███, ███ Nach███ █████
Prigov, ████ ███ ███a, Serg████lk███ Medger███████ etc.). I
think you know █████████ now█████████ book ███████t art,
which █████████████████ in ███████ ███. I █████████████ of
the artists whose w████████████████████ ██████awings in
black-and-█████████████████████ ███████████████ the book,
and I wondered whether █████████████████████ doing a piece
for me. The i█████ ████ I █████████████████ ███████ which
people use like a mus████████████████████, in which I
illustrate certain ██████████████████████, that they are
the most important or███████████████████ Soviet art in the
world. The point ██make in ██████████████ i██ not useful to
judge Soviet art in █hose █████, ████ y ████ █████ are the best
and which are slight██ ████ g███████████h a██████inary. I want
each person to do a ████ which he████ is █████sentative of
himself in some way, ██████ough████████is, obviously, full of
my ideas about Soviet art,██ want ███ illustrations to be the
artists' ideas about themselves. ██████ illustrations don't need
to be fabulously intricate, or to █████everything you have always
wanted to say, but I want you to create the work for this book
which is partly about you.

ANDREY FILIPPOV: *Censorship*
(The text at the bottom of the page reads, "Verified/A. Filippov.")

wrote this as though he were the privileged one at the center of the circle, motionless despite the speed around him. "The present state of culture is similar to the state of mind known in psychology as *post coitus trista;* it is no coincidence that orgasm has been termed *la petite morte* by the French, who are both easygoing and rational." Sven, bound into existentialism by the realities of Soviet life, had always had a soft spot for the rationalism of Pascal and Descartes. Was the art in Budapest already sad, or was it the last spasm of orgiastic indulgence that winter, the first winter of freedom, an ecstatic contact with a new mistress now turning into a potential spouse? "It is life after death, shades in Paradise." More accurate, perhaps, to say that it was in between. Sven's essay ends with a sudden access of maturity, a new level of insight, and a flash of the optimism that, when love is true, must run even through *post coitus trista:* "In the end, I think these are virtues, since they are rooted in a striving for truth, clarity, and a new sincerity." Perhaps, in Budapest, the high price of calculated evasions had finally dawned on the artists. It was time for new ambitions.

Awash in a sea of new contexts, they began to drift back to Moscow. Their nostalgia led them home. But the place they had left behind, bleak and unchanging Moscow, had changed past all recognition. The more you have gone home in your work and in your mind's eye, the less you can go home again in the flesh, on a plane or a train headed toward the U.S.S.R. The artists came back like ghosts, to a city swept forward in time and swept beyond its need for them; and the fame they brought back piled high on their shoulders dissolved into the light summer air of Moscow. They had left like children, and came back like old men.

The fate of the Leningrad artists was different. They found a different kind of fame and fortune in the West. The Leningrad artists burned—it was often remarked—with the brilliance of shooting stars tracing spectral blazes across a crowded galaxy. They met pretty much all of the most famous people in the West, went to all the best parties, danced to the truest music and sang the songs of their hearts. They had been primed for the glamorous life, and they led the glamorous life, skimming across the top of society like birds of paradise. "Suddenly, I found myself dancing with Madonna," Afrika said to me when I saw him in the late autumn. "She asked *me* to dance." He paused, and then confided, "She's an amazing dancer." And though he had the good taste, at these words, to smile with an ironic glint in his eye, the depth of his satisfaction shone behind like the clear beam from a lighthouse.

Appropriately, the philosophic problems of travel were simplified, and reduced, in the hands of the more slick, but less probing, artists from Leningrad. Though they remained more on the surface than the Moscow artists, some of what had been their weaknesses in the U.S.S.R. became manifest strengths in the West. Their quickness and adaptability strengthened their acts of communication. Because self-indulgence had always been a candidly articulated part of their work, its permutations did not obscure the meaning of their activities in the West, as it so often did for the artists from Moscow. The difference in type came through even in petty matters: though I enjoyed most of my guests most of the time, everyone who entertained Soviets— except for the older generation of Moscow artists, who were wonderful to have in your home—encountered difficulties with Soviet symbolic adaptability/unadaptability. These, however, varied in kind. Unlike the messy, drunken, quarrelsome, impossible members of Moscow's younger generation, Afrika, for instance, would appear perfectly scrubbed, bearing flowers and chocolates and paintings as house gifts. He would tell beguiling stories and jokes to your friends, help the ladies with their coats, and make knowing comments to the men about the wine. He would also run up the phone bill by making four-hour calls to Japan, and bring home illegal drugs in disturbing quantities. The younger Moscow artists most often stayed in the West with other artists, or with students, and took advantage of them by eating all their groceries; the Leningrad artists stayed with naive millionaires and monopolized their chauffeurs.

The New Artists exhibited in the West, but their travel was primarily in the context of music-related activities; Afrika and Timur Novikov went to Stockholm, Berlin, and Liverpool with Sergey Kurekhin and Pop Mekhanika. The Scandinavian visit was hurried, and there was little time for tourism; the high point of the concert came when Afrika leapt from the stage and fractured both legs. He then spent some months in the U.S.S.R., where he made the acquaintance of the German dealer Ingrid Raab; on the next Pop Mekhanika tour, to Berlin, he brought a collection of work to the Raab Gallery. "*Isskunstvo* was taking place when I was in Berlin, and many of the artists were there. I met with Sven Gundlakh, but I never even found out that my close friend Anufriev was in town. If I had realized in advance, I would have tried to stay; but I didn't, and so my trip to Berlin was for three days only, and then back to Moscow."

Afrika and Timur's next visit, a full-fledged one for a concert and an exhibition, was to Liverpool, in late January. Why Liverpool? The question was asked dozens of times. Liverpool itself is like a lesser Leningrad; despite noble efforts at revitalization, it remains an agonizingly poor city in which a few spectacular, even bombastic, buildings recall a long-vanished period of prosperity. "For you, it's more depressing that the housewives here look very much like the prostitutes, or that the prostitutes look very much like the housewives?" asked Afrika one evening there—a question whose undertones do not render it groundless. Why Liverpool? Two Liverpudlians, Colin Fallowes and Pete Fulwell, of the independent record label ARK, had released a recording of Pop Mekhanika a year earlier, and they organized the visit. They tried to get financing in London, but the proposals of the London councils were insufficient, and the Liverpool council offered more. Then too, the Bluecoat, a noncommercial gallery, had agreed to show the New Artists, and the Tate Gallery Liverpool had agreed to mount an exhibition of work by Afrika and Timur. And so Liverpool it was.

The artists flew to London and then changed planes, and I met them at Heathrow for the second leg of the flight. It was in principle an ordinary shuttle flight to Liverpool, but the only people on it were the artists, the organizers of the concert, a large TV crew that was documenting the event for the *Late Show,* a dozen bewildered commuters, and a friend and I. The artists reveled in the attention being paid them, but the stewardesses did not; as they passed through the cabin with glasses of lukewarm orange juice they had to dodge cameramen trying to zoom in on Soviet drummers and guitarists reading their first Western in-flight magazines. So preoccupied were the filmmakers with their filming and the artists with being filmed that a fire in the plane's bathroom shortly before landing passed virtually unnoticed by all but ground control, who ushered the plane in in some haste.

We were greeted at the Liverpool airport by more cameras—regional TV—and every civic authority in town, and we were escorted through to the VIP lounge for a moving speech about how much it meant to the city to be welcoming these visiting artists. Sergey Kurekhin, Afrika, and Timur reciprocated with appropriate speeches about how pleased they were to be in Liverpool. The cast of characters was already extraordinary: there was someone from Radio Merseyside with a mohawk and fluorescent leather leggings trying to arrange interviews; there was Jane, organizer of everything, wearing a black fedora with some artificial flowers in it and promising that the event would be "the coolest"; there were Colin Fallowes and Pete Fulwell, who had arranged the whole visit, fluctuating between modest pride and extreme nervousness; there was the director of the Bluecoat, looking serious and kempt; there was the mayor of Liverpool, looking official. TV cameras were zooming in and out on everyone, a situation that was only to get worse; several enthusiastic teenagers got the autograph of the chef from the Bluecoat cafeteria, because he happened to be there and looked far and away the trendiest person of all, and several reels were devoted to him by the cameramen, who were never clear on what was happening or on who anyone was. Later on in the weekend, four TV stations devoted substantial amounts of film to my unwrapping of a Toblerone bar, apparently suffering under the misapprehension that I was a visitor from behind the Iron Curtain having my first significant encounter with milk chocolate.

After the airport ceremony, we were taken on a bus tour of downtown Liverpool. We arrived at the hotel where we were to spend the following nights, a building designed as an adjunct to a municipal parking lot. Afrika, in what he sincerely meant to be a gesture of tact, walked into the hotel lobby, breathed the air, gestured at the area by the reception desk, and said, "Plastic plants, like in the airport! It's a British thing?" The organizers of the event had received somewhat less money than they had originally requested, and had decided to economize on food. This is not the Russian way, and it is especially alien in the West, where the fruits of the earth are meant to overflow an abundance of figurative cornucopia. After depositing our things in our rooms, we went downstairs to a bar decorated with puffy quilted murals of clouds, where each performer was given half a hard cheese sandwich. "You remember, there is very bad food on the ferry in Leningrad?" Afrika asked me. "This is the same thing absolutely."

The organizers had also neglected to hire a translator, on grounds that Afrika spoke good English and that Sergey Kurekhin's wife, Nastya, was virtually fluent. Everyone sat down, and Jane—with the hat—launched into a baroque explanation of the agenda for the following days. She spoke quickly, and with a very strong Liverpudlian accent which I think most people from other parts of the British Isles would be hard-pressed to understand; I was awestruck when Nastya translated everything fluently. Later, Nastya told me, "At the beginning, I thought of asking this Jane to speak more slowly. But I realized that even if she did so I would never be able to understand her. And so I thought to myself: I have to do something or we will have a terrible situation on our hands. And I thought to myself, well, I am an intuitive woman. I looked at Jane. I thought, what would someone like that want to say to all these Soviets right here right now? And whatever I thought up, I said that in Russian. Everyone seems to have been happy."

So there was actually no communication at all. Pop Mekhanika concerts always entail roping together an unlikely assortment of performers, and so their Western concerts mirrored *Isskunstvo,* insofar as they were founded on principles of collaboration. It was neither feasible nor desirable to bring Georgian folk music ensembles and the orchestra from the Kirov out with Pop Mekhanika's principal musicians to play their small segments in the middle of the concert. For Western concerts, there was a madcap juxtaposition of Soviet and local performers. In Liverpool the participants included a forty-piece concertina marching band, some African drummers, whole sections of the city's orchestra, a bouzouki player, an Irish pipe band, an opera singer, a blues singer, and rock stars from Echo and the Bunnymen, The Christians, and It's Immaterial. The next two days were occupied with rehearsals in which no one knew quite what he was meant to be doing. Hours and hours passed in various inadequately heated rooms. Everyone was starved: at midnight the first night, I ordered room service in for a small crowd of Soviets who came to my room asking what to do about food. The "Chicken Surprise" turned out to be an unsurprisingly scrawny bit of chicken meat pressed between slices of Mother's Pride (British Wonder Bread); the "Chicken Surprises" consumed that night were numbered as the stars. The second night, we went to McDonald's—the only restaurant we could find—where a cheery man asked, "What do you want on your hamburger?" The artists and musicians said with one voice, "Hamburger with meat"; and just as the man had finished sorting that out, Timur Novikov, who is a vegetarian, piped up that he wanted, "Hamburger without meat."

There were more touches of the bizarre to come. The Liverpool concert hall, a magnificent nineteenth-century building, had for some reason been taken over by thousands and thousands of pigeons, which kept swooping down just when people were entering the hall, like something out of Hitchcock. The Soviet musicians included a few who played traditional instruments, a few who were in with Kurekhin on the dramatic ironies of the merging of all these groups, a drummer straight off *The Muppet Show,* and a guitarist like something from Twisted Sister, who played one solo with his teeth. The Western musicians were people who would never have met had the Soviets not come to town, and they kept eyeing one another with disdain. The guitarist from Echo and the Bunnymen clearly had trouble playing the guitar, and kept cribbing off the guitarist from The Christians. The guitarist from The Christians kept disappearing altogether to do mushrooms and other drugs with Afrika and Timur. No one seemed to be able to learn the music that was given to him, and in the end almost everyone played things they already knew, which Kurekhin arranged like a collage. Colin Fallowes wanted the concert to be completely authentic and, knowing that Kurekhin had sometimes had live animals on stage, arranged to rent a substantial supply of livestock from a nearby farm. The fire marshal said that it was illegal to have these animals inside, and so Colin tied them outside, where they shivered and watched the birds. Colin also said that he thought this was an evening when one could do anything, and he proposed to the Soviets that they throw raw sausages at the audience at the end of the concert. "I'm not sure it's such a nice idea," said Kurekhin, but in the event, Colin crept backstage with some of The Christians and threw the sausages himself at an audience that consisted of rowdy trendies delighted by confrontation and of a certain number of London art figures in fur coats who were none too pleased by the development.

The night before the concert, I sat up with Afrika and Timur flicking between an Andrei Tarkovsky film, on Channel Two, and *2001* on Channel Four. The advantage of the Tarkovsky was that it was in Russian with English subtitles and was therefore comprehensible to everyone. The advantage to *2001* was that it was a perfect emblem for the concert the next day: you kept getting really cool bits, but you didn't know why you were getting them, and it was cool that you were getting them, but they were still kind of boring. The concert itself was hilarious, and well outside the realm of the comprehensible. It opened with a Soviet army song played on a stereo system while Afrika and Timur, dressed as military officials, climbed up a flight of stairs and struck dramatic poses on the stage. Kurekhin, at a vast pipe organ, played a rather brilliant variation on this song. An Irish piper and a fiddler played a piece of British Renaissance music; Kurekhin harmonized with this on the organ. Then a string quartet joined in, playing a late baroque piece. The harmonies remained interesting if a bit strident. Afrika and Timur raised Soviet flags on either side of the organ, and a man with an amazing voice sang "Amazing Grace.' Then some drummers played in rhythm, and then came a piano solo, and then the brass section played, and then there was a sax solo, and then several more similar items. At that point—and I quote the program—there was "a big full billy rock 'n' roll piece" while Afrika scratched Soviet records on the stereo system playing overhead and chewed gum, and Kurekhin stumbled stiff-legged around the stage like Lurch in *The Addams Family*. The guitarist did his solo with his teeth, the drummer drummed, and a group of Liverpool born-and-bred traditional African drummers—in African drumming garb—came running down the center aisle toward the stage, led by a half-naked woman who was performing an exorcism which seemed largely to consist of blowing cornmeal at the audience. As she reached the ecstatic high point of her gyrations, the Bootles Concertina Marching Band (established 1904) came marching in playing a traditional concertina piece. Even the coolest of concertina bands has a certain innate nerdiness, and this one was no exception. They marched up like brave people fulfilling a contract, eyeing the rock guitarists and the African drummers and even the string quartet with calculated terror.

At this point, Afrika and Timur began beating Kurekhin with flowers while the Greek bouzouki player, recruited from a local restaurant we had unfortunately been unable to find the night before, played his dinner repertoire. Afrika and Timur took off most of Sergey's clothes and threw a bucket of water over him; then they ate the flowers used for the flagellation. (Later on, when Afrika and Timur were throwing up, they explained that they usually eat carnations, but had bought irises because they had been unable to find carnations. "Maybe this was foolish," they said.) There were a few moments of glory: part of the concert was to be a fashion show, and in the directions written out by the British there was a note that "At this point, the models should hit the stage." Unaccustomed to colloquial usage, the models did just that: they stood in a line and hit the stage with their fists for a good twenty minutes. The whole thing ended with the sausages.

On one level, the Liverpool evening was a great success: the effect of this hodgepodge, more easily negotiated in music than in the visual arts, was to disrupt the audience's sense of logic by underscoring the incoherence that remained inescapable for the Soviets: nothing meant what it had always meant. The concomitant exhibitions of paintings at the Bluecoat and Tate galleries in Liverpool were strengthened by the musical education of their audience to abandon all its habits of recognition, and the work by Afrika and Timur Novikov preserved its "in-joke" status by teasing its audience frankly, sometimes uncharitably, but almost always successfully.

The real tragedy of Liverpool, the thing that lay below the surface of absurdities and poor organization, was that the organizers kept dealing with Pop Mekhanika as though it were high art of the first order. They were the most earnest lot of people I have ever met, too intimidated by the Soviets to see that the performance they had negotiated was really high camp. The lack of communication at both the literal and the figurative levels was funny in a way, but it was also a bit sad: sad for the concertina band members, sad for the string quartet and the bouzouki player, and most of all sad for the ARK people, who were so anxious about political import that they failed entirely to understand that the Soviets were doing this to have a good time, because they enjoyed it, to *escape* the tedium of politics and political motives. "I don't know whether it's special to Liverpool, or to England, or whether it's like this for you too," one of The Christians said to Afrika and me at a party after the concert, "but you know, sometimes I just stare in the mirror and I think that life is pretty weird." Afrika said, politely, "I think maybe it's a universal thing."

ARK and the Bluecoat had planned a whole agenda for the artists in the week following the concert, but Afrika and Timur escaped to London as quickly as possible. One of the fur-clad ladies offered a ride in her car, and in no time at all Afrika had deserted ship; Timur followed a few days later. It was constantly difficult to help the Soviets to be well enough informed to make judgments without teaching them cultural snobberies. I will never forget a dinner in New York in the autumn of 1989, at which Kostya Zvezdochetov, Volodya Mironenko, and I were guests, along with several other people, of an undistinguished American artist. We had come for dinner; the food was disgusting, a stew made by the artist's wife, who kept trailing her greasy hair through what she was cooking and then standing up so that it slapped gravy all over her blouse. Halfway through the evening, in the course of an argument about American and Soviet TV, the host stood up, turned on his own television—which had a giant six-foot screen—and put on Channel J, then the New York porn channel. Most of the people at dinner tried to ignore this disruption, but the host's nine-year-old daughter came out of her room and sat transfixed about four inches from the screen. "Good for her!" the host said. "Teach her something!" I was trying to talk about an exhibition with Margarita Tupitsyn, who was dressed in a smart outfit from Yamamoto and looked sleek and sophisticated. "I think Kabakov is always the father," she said, her head in silhouette against a heaving vagina and the words: "Dial Now. 970-TWAT." Then the host and his wife got into an argument and yelled at one another while the rest of us sat awkwardly by. When we left, Volodya said to me, "Was that a nice party?" His own instinct—that it was not—needed to be affirmed because there was some question as to whether the apparent unpleasantness was simply in keeping with American values.

Afrika and Timur moved in a snobbier world than did the Moscow artists. I think they would probably have known for sure that such a party was not a nice party. But it was a constant issue with them: they were keen to understand snobberies even if they did not accept or adopt them. They loved the glamour of the people they knew and the places they went. In London, Timur wanted to go to the opera at Covent Garden more than anything. The Liverpool experience amused and delighted them, but it also frustrated them. And it was perhaps a sort of snobbery that allowed them to desert the ARK people without telling them that they were going, and to escape from under the eye of the lax Komsomol man who was supposed to be watching them on this trip. They knew that they wanted no part of the ARK crowd, that they had done Liverpool and were ready to move on; and they had no instinct that told them to stay because it was what they had contracted to do, no impulse that said it would be unkind to reject with so little ceremony the agenda prepared for them. And then— they might never get to London again, and they had so much to see, opportunity knocking at the door, a lady in a fur coat offering a ride down. Who could say no?

A month later, Afrika made a great hit in New York, which is still the place where Leningrad artists are most often to be found, the place, perhaps, where they feel most entirely in their element. The story of the early exports of Leningrad work is somewhat less complex than the story of the first Moscow exports. Whereas the interest in Moscow artists was originally evinced in Germany and Switzerland, the interest in Leningrad artists began in the United States. Joanna Stingray (née Fields), who is now married to a Soviet rock musician and has recently toured Siberia as a rock star in her own right, organized an exhibition in 1986 of work by Leningrad artists as a fundraiser at the Keith Green Gallery in New York. The show, called *Red Wave,* was a big success; lots of people came (at $125 per head) and lots of work sold, and the rock videos that were shown throughout the evening attracted bountiful positive attention. One of the guests that evening, a young man named Paul Alan Judelson, bought a painting by Andrey Khlobystin, and met and talked to Joanna Stingray.

Over the next few years, Judelson continued to buy work, mostly by Khlobystin, from Joanna, who was showing Leningrad paintings in Los Angeles. In the winter of 1989, shortly after the Liverpool event, she had an exhibition at the West Sawtelle Gallery, for which Afrika came to town. The Leningrad artists were already beginning to complain that they had problems with Joanna, that some of their work had disappeared; but for the moment they were more or less stuck with her. Paul Alan Judelson, curious to meet one of the Soviets, went to the exhibition, talked to Afrika, gave him his phone number, bought seven pictures, and went home to New York. A few weeks later, Afrika came through New York, called Paul, and proposed holding an exhibition in his apartment.

Paul Alan Judelson is just as earnest as Colin Fallowes and Pete Fulwell, but he is substantially more cosmopolitan, and whereas the seriousness of the Liverpudlians meant that they missed the point of the Mayakovsky Club, the seriousness of Paul Alan Judelson means that he is willing to go to extraordinary and often excessive lengths to inform the world of the point of the Mayakovsky Club. His career up to his first meeting with Afrika was a checkered one: he earned an M.A. in history at Brown University; then did archival research on Judah P. Benjamin, a man of some station in the Confederacy; and then climbed the West face of Mount Kilimanjaro, and wrote a long article about it which he failed to publish. He then started a fish company. A partner bought corbina bass in Central America and sent it to his family in New Orleans; they packaged it and sent it to New York; and Paul drove every day to La Guardia Airport to collect it in his Fiat convertible, stored it overnight on ice on the balcony of his Turtle Bay brownstone apartment, and then delivered it to the Four Seasons, Le Bernardin, and a number of other prestigious New York restaurants. "The flesh of that fish," he recalls with pleasure, "just melted in your mouth." This enterprise he called the Fin Boutique. When he got tired of fish—after about eight months—he turned his entire interest over to his partner and accepted a commission to write the annual calendar for the United Negro College Fund, which he did, and for which he received some accolades when the calendar was unveiled in a ceremony at the Equitable Building.

So Afrika had good reason to imagine that Paul Judelson might be

ANDREY KHLOBYSTIN:
Romantics Melchior and Sulpicius Observing an Atmospheric Event in 1804

game for a new venture, and he suggested one Friday afternoon that he arrange work all over Paul's house and invite some friends for a selling exhibition. They hung the work Afrika had brought from the Tate and Bluecoat exhibitions in Liverpool, a few pieces Paul had bought in previous years, and the seven pieces he had purchased from Joanna Stingray in Los Angeles. They priced the work together; the artists included were Afrika, Timur, Georgiy Guryanov, Khlobystin, Yevgeniy Kozlov, Yevgeniy Yufit, Inal Savchenkov, Vadim Ovchinnikov, Kuzim Maslov, Viktor Tsoy, and Boris Koshelokhov. Afrika had by this time befriended—and was staying with—Page Powell, an old friend of Andy Warhol's, a staff member of *Interview* magazine, and a force to be reckoned with in New York's cutting-edge cultural scene. Paul invited a few prosperous family friends, and Afrika and Page Powell invited the rest: Tama Janowitz, John Cage, Stephen Sprouse, and dozens of others of their ilk. The pictures were hung everywhere in Paul's apartment: some were on the floor, some were in the bathtub, some were behind the toilet. The trendy New York weekly *7 Days* ran a review of the show headlined "Art From Behind the Shower Curtain." By the end, seventy-eight of the eighty-five pieces in the show were sold, at stunningly high prices. Paul took no commission—"since I had no overhead and since it wasn't even my idea to do the show"—but instead used the proceeds of the exhibit to set up a fund for the Soviet artists so that they would have some money in America. Flushed with delight at his new project, he set off for Paris to make the acquaintance of Andrey Khlobystin, who met him at the airport with a banner showing the Kremlin reaching its hands out to shake hands with the Statue of Liberty, over whose head floated dollar signs.

So that was New York. Afrika published a long piece, the cover story in the summer issue of *Art & Antiques,* written as a letter to Timur, in which he took on the role of the naive young Soviet exploring the big, strange city. It was full of lines like: "If you picked up Rudolf Nureyev's apartment whole and added it to The Hermitage, it would fit right in"; and "John [Cage] introduced me to Nam June Paik, whom I thanked for his program *Wrap Around the World* on behalf of millions of Soviet people, who were able to see scenes of cultural life from all over the world, without our television's usual editorializing." Meanwhile, Afrika had plans for everything: he was to be in a film about Napoleon, playing opposite Robert de Niro; he was to be in every major rock video in creation; he was to perform at the Brooklyn Academy of Music. He had risen to the top like a cross between the proverbial cream and the proverbial froth. Later, because of a question about multiple entries on a visa, Afrika was delayed in Heathrow and held in custody. "I find that I feel very comfortable everywhere," he said. "No place is strange to me. I didn't feel very comfortable in the jail in the British airport, because I had been in places like that in Leningrad, but except for that I have been comfortable at every moment of my life in these last years."

The joy of Afrika is that this is true. His fantastic adaptability becomes a kind of profound art, thrown into sharper relief by the unadaptability of so many of his countrymen. He may never be a great painter, but what of that? He has more fun in the West than any Muscovite. He finds what he wants wherever he goes. When, later, I accused him of changing color as effortlessly as a chameleon, camouflaging himself through so many situations that he had almost forsaken his identity, he only smiled, and said, "I change color, of course, but not like a chameleon: like litmus paper." By the late springtime, it was time for him also to go back to an original color, and to Leningrad.

CHAPTER IV

Home Again

When will we ever get to Moscow? By the end of their travels, the Soviet artists asked this question as eagerly as the Three Sisters; they anticipated a journey, however, not into the unknowable world of glorious possibilities, but into peace, and calm, and all things habitual. Imagine their shock, then: had Sven Gundlakh said in Budapest, "Time seems to have stopped nowadays"? It was as though all the acceleration stalled in the West had taken place in Moscow, where time had moved a thousand times faster than it had ever been known to move before. The static society they had left had preserved none of its simple structures, and the artists were like a family of latter-day Rip Van Winkles, puzzled by hints of the familiar sketched across an alien landscape they knew had once been home.

I made my return to Moscow in a state of some trepidation, aware that the year since my previous visit had transformed my relationship to the place, but uncertain what that transformation would actually mean. The second part of *Isskunstvo,* a reciprocal exhibition in Moscow along much the same lines as the Berlin one, had long been scheduled for June 1989. The Berlin artists and the Soviets had agreed to be in Moscow by the end of May; this would allow sufficient time to make works for the exhibition opening in late June. I wanted to arrive before the opening, to see the artists working together in tense preparation for this culminating collaboration, this opportunity for the Soviets to re-create at home the success they had known abroad. I wanted to witness the return to the U.S.S.R., and I also of course wanted to see the project itself. But in late May, the only *Isskunstvo* artists in Moscow were German, and in mid-June, when I arrived, the few Soviets on hand were withdrawn, noncommittal, and uncommunicative. Some of the time they were downright hostile. Certainly they were in no frame of mind for jolly collaborations and the thrall of communication. When will we ever get to Moscow? They came in early summer, when the leaves were out on the birches and the snows were all gone and the days were so long that you could miss the night if you closed your eyes. They came bearing the pennants of their triumphs abroad; but few and far between were the fatted calves slaughtered in their honor. They came back not to a society awestruck by their accomplishments, but to a society in flux that seemed to have forgotten them. They came back to a world that had realigned itself, a world whose bleakness was made sharp by its startling unfamiliarity.

"It was not a shock for me to go to the West," Andrey Royter told me when I saw him a few weeks later. "I had imagined such a place so many times that each new detail seemed only a confirmation of my dreams. No, the shock came when I returned here after my months abroad, and I saw this country for what it is for the first time." He said it more succinctly than anyone else, but the experience was almost universal. You can't go home again. The Soviets had seen too much of strangeness in the course of the winter, and they were tired. They had returned at the brink of summer because they wanted things to be easy in the way that things are easy at even the least comfortable home for the person whose home it is. But they had not reckoned with the fact that when you leave a place you dissociate yourself from its changes; and they had left the U.S.S.R. in a state of transition that was such that almost nothing they remembered was in its familiar place. You can't go home again; but you particularly can't go home if your home has been reinhabited and your family reeducated and the name of your street changed. What was scary for them was the speed of it, how quickly their lives had disappeared. None of this seemed like a challenge, like an emblematic fruit of perestroika. Nothing that was new seemed like an improvement. Inflation and food shortages clearly did not constitute progress; but even the few changes for the better brought home only how what has vanished becomes more valuable for its disappearance, how its rarity surfaces and its banished

ANDREY ROYTER: *Untitled*

pleasures glitter in the slanting rays of retrospect with seductive purity and simplicity. Theirs was the misery of leaving one kind of alienation only to arrive at another; it was as if the buildings and the soil, the fabric of the country itself, had betrayed their unthinking trust.

This disillusion spread from their minds to their lives, and from their lives to their work; though many things were different for external reasons, others were different for internal reasons. What was the point of making works of art to show only to friends, to enact secret communications, when one could do work to be shown in the great museums of the world? To be clandestine and secret when that had finally become genuinely unnecessary, when there was no real need to hold off the West and no need at all to hold off the KGB, seemed stupid and self-indulgent. All they had to declare to one another was affection, and you can articulate that just so many times and then no more, or it becomes boring and sappy. And also—when all you have to offer people is affection, you grow bored with the affection itself, and it withers into nothing. A few of the artists were afraid of success, and others were afraid of failure, but in Moscow there was no one against whom they had to defend themselves, and there was simply no fear that warranted making a work of art about. To sit in one another's rooms and drink tea again—what was the point? It was in this way that old friendships were deformed beyond recognition. As for genuine artistic concerns: those were distilled in the West, where serious work was done. It was an affectation to work with bad paint in just four colors on tiny scraps of canvas that would be impossible to export when everyone knew perfectly well that high-quality goods would be available on the next sojourn to make work for museums and major galleries.

There can be little doubt that *Isskunstvo* took itself too seriously. The Germans, quite reasonably, felt that they had been good, even indulgent hosts to the Soviets, and they expected their hospitality to be reciprocated. They thought people would invite them for dinner, would take them out for amusing afternoons, would introduce them to their families, would absorb them into the life of this foreign country. More even than that, they thought the Soviets would commit themselves seriously to creating important works of art for the exhibition. The Germans did not reckon on the Soviets' disaffection, and they found it difficult to understand that it was focused on the realities of the Soviets' own lives. The Germans thought they were being dismissed, and were understandably dismayed; they had almost fallen in love with their idea of the U.S.S.R. If it is difficult to go home again, it is also difficult to go to a place that has captured all your affections in this way; to be excluded further by the actual people you have come to see is an inhuman blow.

I went to Moscow on June 14. I had for some weeks been out of touch with everyone: with the Soviets, who were scattered across the globe, and with Lisa Schmitz, who had gone to Moscow sometime earlier to organize the details of *Isskunstvo*. Since, at the time I was planning my trip, none of the Soviets seemed to know exactly when they would be returning to Moscow, and since their Moscow apartments were tiny and crowded, I arranged to stay with the German artists outside the city in a dacha that Lisa had rented. I had given Lisa my flight number in May, screaming across a terrible connection to Moscow, and she had volunteered to meet my plane. My subsequent efforts to reach her in Nikolina Gora had been to no avail. It is almost impossible to get a phone call through to Moscow; there is a desperate insufficiency of international phone lines, all of which are almost always engaged with official phone calls. The dacha, of course, was not even in Moscow, so calls there had to be routed through the capital and passed on from there to Nikolina Gora, where there is such a shortage of lines that one is shared by perhaps a dozen houses. When a call comes through, the phones in all these houses ring. Each house has a shift: phone calls for one are to be received between nine and ten, and so members of that household are permitted to answer the phone only between nine and ten; for another house, it will be between ten and eleven, for another, between eleven and twelve, and so on. On the other hand, anyone can make an outgoing call at any time, so that someone in another dacha could easily keep the line engaged through the hour allotted to you for incoming calls. It would have been easier to pass through the eye of a needle on a camel than to get a line from the West to Nikolina Gora within the prescribed hour.

So when I boarded my flight to Moscow, I was clinging to the slender hope that Lisa had remembered the date of my arrival, had remembered that she was meeting me at the airport, had remembered my flight number. I had no idea where the dacha was; and I could not call on the day of my arrival because I would have missed the reserved telephone hour by the time I landed. I knew, of course, that I could depend on any of dozens of Soviet friends, but many of the artists don't have telephones at all, and others had told me they would be moving and would therefore have new numbers. Others yet were still in the West. Furthermore, though calls from a private phone within Moscow are free, calls from a public phone cost two kopeks—about a tenth of a cent—and require two-kopek pieces. I had no qualms about spending the kopeks, but I knew it would be almost impossible to get the coins, and that I would have to keep seeking out change and then returning to the phones. If I were seen by the police to be wandering around the airport without any apparent purpose, I might well be asked who had invited me to the U.S.S.R.; but my private visa had been arranged for me by Galina Main, and I knew only that the paperwork had been done by a friend of her sister's. Its terms strictly prohibited a night in a hotel; my spending a night in the airport or in the streets of Moscow with a large dark blue suitcase was likely to attract attention. Aware of all this, I determined to befriend the person next to whom I was seated on the plane at absolutely any cost, on grounds that I could slip off to his hotel and phone around from there without attracting too much obvious attention; I thought I could perhaps hide under his bed for the night if I couldn't reach anyone.

I was, naturally, seated next to an evangelist from South Africa who was trying to establish a right-wing cult on an island off the coast of Scotland and who hoped to find some sympathetic Christians in the Soviet Union. Her carry-on luggage included a guitar, on which she planned to play "hip hymns" to raise up the spirit of the Union of Soviet Socialist Republics. This item would not fit in the overhead luggage compartment, and it would also not fit under the seat in front of her, and so it spent the better part of the journey balanced delicately across both our laps. There was excessive turbulence on the flight, and the stewardess had overfilled the cups; one drink the evangelist spilled on the guitar, from which it dripped everywhere, and the second she poured directly into my shoes. She too was traveling on a private invitation, and she had members of the faith coming to collect her at Sheremetyevo. "Of course we'll take you along if your friend isn't there to meet you," she said. "We always want new blood for the Church. You can help me with the Russian campaign."

Gruesome though the episode sounds in retrospect, it was a relief at the time that there was someone along who would help me if I needed help at the far end of the journey. But there are not words enough to describe my joy when I came through customs and found Lisa standing in the crowd of nervous Russians at the far side, like a splash of color in a black-and-white photograph. "The dacha is very beautiful," she said, "but the situation with the artists is a little bit strange. You'll see." We took a bus from the airport to a point at the western edge of Moscow; an old man threw up all over the bus shortly after we pulled out of the airport, and only the breeze coming in the driver's window kept us from passing out in the oppressive stench. A crowd of stubby old women set to berating the man, who was quite drunk and began to sing. The bus driver was also singing. The bus, painted orange and apparently made of tin, creaked its way along a road so pocked with holes that it was difficult to calculate the level of its original surface. I was back in Moscow.

After the bus, we took a taxi. The taxi ride was different. We argued with the driver about how much to pay, then set off through the outskirts of the city, and a few minutes later took a sudden turn onto a wide road, almost a highway, which was lined with Socialist Realist sculptures of bears and deer, all painted dark red, and with clumps of trees. In the U.S.S.R., you can be stopped by the police at any time when you are driving, whether you have committed a traffic offense or not, and be asked to present your identity papers. The road to Nikolina Gora was lined with policemen because, as I was later to learn, it was also the road to Gorbachev's dacha and to those of the politburo members; for this reason the police were very strict, and would sometimes subject drivers to long interrogations. One night, my taxi was pulled over for almost an hour; when the driver came back, to drive on to the dacha, he was crying and shaking with relief. I asked whether he had done anything wrong. He told me he had mispronounced the name of the street where we were going. Often when we were driving to or from the house, we would hear the sound of sirens, and we would be obliged to pull off the road to allow the enormous black cars of Gorbachev or his chief advisers, with escorts of smaller cars and motorcycles, to rush past at superhuman speed. That business of driving into the mud until the motorcade had gone by brought home as vividly as anything that we were living in a country that was far from democracy, in which the ordinary people still had to make way for the important people. Near Nikolina Gora itself were beaches reserved for the diplomatic community. I used to joke that I was staying just a bit beyond the East Hampton of the U.S.S.R.

After a forty-minute drive, Lisa and I arrived at Aleya Martynova, the dirt path we called a street; this was the address of the dacha. We got out of the taxi at the bottom of the road, despite my suitcase; Lisa explained to me that there had been too many attacks on foreigners and thefts of their property in the previous months in Moscow, and that we were therefore not to let anyone who was not a friend know where we were actually living. And so we walked the last leg of the journey. How to describe the dacha itself? A house in the woods in American or European parlance is a house with perhaps a garden, a bit of a lawn, a stone path, and maybe a driveway, with woods beyond it, or before it, or beside it. A house in the woods in the old Russian tradition is just that: a house in the woods, with trees pressing against every side. Our dacha was beyond the one that belonged to Tanya, our landlady; you walked past her house, along a twisting path through the trees, and then suddenly you saw the bulky wooden building, weathered by the years, misshapen with its peculiar balconies, like some eccentric growth of the forest itself. On the left and right sides of it were glassed-in porches; at the front there was a big porch, not enclosed; and upstairs were two balconies, a big one and a little one. Of course, like everything in the U.S.S.R., it was falling down. The interior was full of strange primitivisms. There were two toilets, one that worked and one that didn't. There was a refrigerator in the kitchen, in which we kept fresher food, and one on the porch in which we kept food that was about to go bad, or that had recently gone. To have hot water, you had to turn on the cold full force, then pull one lever across on the boiler in the kitchen—a structure apparently made of spare parts from the Tin Man in *The Wizard of Oz*—put in a lit match, wait for the funny sound of a small gas explosion, then pull across another lever, which resulted in a great rush of gas and an enormous glowing blue flame that seemed certain to blow the place sky-high. We were warned by Tanya that if we turned off the water before turning off the gas, we would immediately incinerate the dacha. The walls had been papered with pages from an American magazine of the early seventies that someone had somehow acquired at the time, and these were protected by sheets of crumpled plastic wrap, the sort you might use to pack sandwiches. The ads were for products whose names I hadn't heard since my childhood, full of exotically painted women pressing Eve cigarettes on you and fat men dressed for the ball game standing next to absurd-looking old Chevrolets. Toilet paper was usually about to run out; you could not buy it for love or money in Moscow that summer, and many was the time that I swanned into a hotel by showing my passport at the door, stood at the front of the dining room as though considering, and then left, pockets bulging with rolls of paper I had lifted from the public facilities.

The dacha was impossible, but it was also charming. The rooms were big; the color of the wood of which the place was built was warm; the organic layout—you felt the smaller rooms were the children of the larger ones—felt familiar almost at once. From the balconies at night, you could see the silhouettes of the white trees all around you, silvered by the moon; sometimes we would sit there with candles, drinking tea and telling stories almost until dawn. In the big middle room the sofa was so comfortable that someone fell asleep on it almost every night. Andrea Sunder-Plassmann took over one glassed-in porch as her bedroom, and Dési Baumeister took over the other; these chambers were delightful, full of leaf-filtered light by day and passing shadows by night—though they were also full of water when it rained. Outside there were flowers among the weeds, and the birches stood massed like a sea of columns supporting the dappled green and blue above. To know, on a quiet afternoon, that no one would come to disturb you and that the phone would not ring for you, that you could simply let the hours drift past while you thought, or talked, or absorbed the sunshine—it was magical. At the end of a day of Moscow, where it was hot and crowded and everything was difficult, the dacha was like an answered prayer, and though there was sometimes argument there, there were more often crows of complacent contentedness. Ten minutes' walk away was a beach on the riverbank. The water was cold and apparently badly polluted, but we paid little attention to that, wading in and then floating downstream under the overhanging branches of birches and pines. The Russian love of nature, and of the eternal birches of the countryside, is deep and obsessive, and in the dacha we came to understand how every one of those trees is a miniature Soviet landscape; life went on in Moscow—things happened there —but the dacha was like a fragment of a lost paradise, where everything reached new heights of peace and serenity.

The renting of the dacha had been arranged by Josif Bakshteyn and a critic called Lena Kurlyandtseva; they operated under pressure from Lisa. Though it was not then possible to own property in the cities of the U.S.S.R., it was possible to own country houses; these most often remained in families by descent, though it has recently become fashionable to sell them to people able to pay in Western currency. A number of the artists I know had dachas: Ira Nakhova, Sergey Volkov, and the Mironenko brothers all spent time in country places. Our rent for the month was negligible, and was covered by the funding Lisa had found for *Isskunstvo, Part II.* When Lisa and I arrived that first evening, Werner Zein was cooking dinner with some odds and ends that had been available in Moscow that afternoon. Food was enlivened all summer by an odd assortment of spices that the Germans had brought from Berlin, potent enough to cover the sometimes dubious condition of local goods.

Lisa was expert at hunting out things worth buying, and she was tireless about carrying: if at ten in the morning she saw someone selling bundles of fresh dill, she would buy all of them, and if at noon the same day she saw a truck of chocolate cakes, she would buy a dozen or two dozen and lug them with her for the rest of the day. She would carelessly toss five two-liter jugs of plum juice into her shoulder bag along with thirty onions and bring them back for general consumption. The rest of us tried to do the same thing, though we usually kept our purchases to a smaller scale. Some of Lisa's purchases—those chocolate cakes in particular—ended up by turning slightly disgusting in the porch fridge; we were hungry, but not, perhaps, that hungry. But mostly Lisa's enterprise kept us better fed than one would expect possible in Moscow.

There were ten of us in the dacha: Lisa; Sergey Vorontsov, musician turned artist, who had become her lover; Marie Mannschatz, an old friend of the artists and a Reichian therapist who was documenting the project; the six Bomba Colori artists, and I. The Bomba Colori artists are a curious lot. They have been friends for years, more or less since high school, and they lived together until about the time of *Isskunstvo,* enjoying the communal lives of eternal students. They are in their late twenties and early thirties, the best sort of idealists, arguing subjects of the intellect with an intensity of purpose which, in most eyes, unresolvable questions do not warrant, proposing solutions, sometimes half-baked and sometimes convincing, with an appealing ingenuous fierceness. They have never had to confront their own limitations because each bears the others up; this provides for the splendid optimism that underlies their continuing engagement with art. Their seriousness is very exciting and very appealing, but it sometimes seems groundless, almost self-indulgent. As artists, they have clever ideas that they realize well, but though their work is fun and sometimes gives occasion for pause, there are many fundamental ways in which it does not question itself, and that is why the Soviets ultimately found it alien and uninteresting. The Bomba Colori artists are funny, and their jokes strengthen their work; they would say that art is the center of their lives, but their notion of themselves as artists is perhaps closer to the center, art the entertaining activity that justifies their sense of themselves. What they undervalue in themselves is their profound openness. They can turn anything into a performance or an installation; they can absorb any influence, and they can accept from the world whatever it has to offer and be happy. Their artistic projects are like postcards of friendship. They were artists for the sheer pleasure of it: they liked the paint and the mirrors and the wonderful variety of plenty on the green earth. If they someday contrive to communicate that—and Andrea Sunder-Plassmann, Dési Baumeister, and Werner Zein have sometimes come close—then they could approach the seriousness they so avidly desire. My studies of Soviet art have given me access to many people, Soviet and otherwise, but there are few whose friendship I value as much as theirs.

"Well," Werner said when I came in the first night. "What a treat it is to find that there is someone in the Soviet Union who, even if he is not Soviet, is at least not German." And the story began to unfold: how the Germans had come to Moscow full of energy and projects, and how they had found the place deserted. Lisa was sure that it would be all right, but the others were less sure. Lisa said, "Give them time"; the other Germans said, "We have given them time, and attention, and hospitality, and money; and where are they?" Where indeed? They were in Budapest, or in France, or in depressed states in their Moscow flats. Even if the Soviet artists had not been suffering from the Rip Van Winkle syndrome, the situation would have been a strained one. Imagine that you had gone on a trip around the world that lasted an entire year, and that in the course of that year, someone had been particularly kind to you at one of your first ports of call, and you had invited that person to come to visit any time. When you finished your journey, that very week, the kind host appeared to claim his promised hospitality. While some people in the West might dutifully shepherd such a visitor around local sights, the delight would be unlikely to be unexceptioned, especially if the visitor was so confounded by the alien land that he was hardly able even to shop for himself.

This problem needed to be resolved. *Isskunstvo, Part II* was funded and ready, and feeling ran high that the show must go on. The day after I arrived I went into Moscow proper for the first time since the previous year. To get from the dacha to Moscow, one walked to the bus, took the bus to Perkhushkovo, and then took the train to Belorusskaya, a train station on the Moscow circle line, from which it was possible to travel to other destinations within Moscow. It took about an hour and a half, assuming you didn't miss a connection, that the train wasn't canceled, and that you didn't get off at the wrong stop. We all went together to the site of the exhibition, a building in Frunzenskaya that was supposed to be finished well before the project began, but that I feel certain is far from completion even as this book goes into production. It was a big hall, part of an elaborate exhibition complex near the water. There were long debates with the *dezhurnaya* —the woman who opened the building in the morning, sat there all day to ensure that no damage was done to state property, and then locked up in the evening—because she was very rigid about closing times and refused to let artists in the grip of inspiration work late on their own. The Germans decided to woo her, not so much so they could stay after hours as because her dour presence was so depressing. It is very revealing about the situation of Soviet workers that this woman could not understand that the bunches of flowers they brought were for her; she kept setting them up on a table in the hall, assuming they had been brought for use in the installations, or to attract visitors, despite the Germans' insistence that she keep them. When she did understand, at the literal level, she seemed puzzled; and when it dawned on her that the Germans were trying to make friends, she responded with the mistrustful pleasure of a straggly stray dog taken in by a kind family.

Those of the project artists who were in Moscow—Dima Prigov, Sergey Volkov, Ira Nakhova, and Nikita Alexeev, who was making his first visit to the Soviet Union since his emigration to Paris—had come along for a meeting at the exhibition hall when we arrived that day. It was June 16; the opening was scheduled for June 20, and the pressure was on. Lisa had compiled a list of grievances, and she sat everyone down and tried to talk through the complaints, enumerating faults with a rhadamanthine sense of justice. It was not a great scene. The Bomba Colori artists kept interrupting Lisa with additional grievances of their own, or with dismissals of particular grievances of hers. Everyone was struggling for the last word. Angrily, the Germans spoke of communication as the goal of the project, said that for them to work on their own in Moscow was the same as for them to work alone in Berlin. Nikita, wearing sunglasses, watched the whole thing with an ironic smile, like a parent watching other people's children bicker. Prigov kept dismissing the criticisms. "All right, so we'll go home and get some work together and put it up for the exhibition," he said. The Germans were not content with that. "We need to work together," they said. "This is a collaborative project. We don't want you just to come in and hang up some work." Prigov remarked a bit tartly that he had missed all the collaboration in Berlin and that he had other plans in Moscow. "Let's stop talking about the past," he said. Volkov was making a genuine effort to be helpful, and had in fact already done some work for the exhibition, and he looked embarrassed and uncomfortable as Lisa droned on. He, Sergey Vorontzov, Josif Bakshteyn, and Ira Nakhova were the only ones who had been friendly to the Germans; but Ira was depressed, and then she had a cold, and she went off to her dacha (which was nowhere near the *Isskunstvo* dacha) and stayed there, coming back to do her rather good installation in two days before disappearing again.

Nothing was settled, but the artists were shamed into contact. As more came back from the West, the atmosphere brightened a bit. The greatest awkwardness of all was that, at that moment, the Soviets liked the Germans less than the Germans liked the Soviets. And though the Soviets did not articulate that in so many words, they really made no bones about it; it was not part of their system of tact to equivocate over such issues. Furthermore, the Soviets believed themselves to be better artists, and behaved like famous people. They patronized the Germans, who were clearly not famous. The fact that no one in the U.S.S.R. was interested in the Soviets' successes abroad made it particularly important to them to keep up such strutting. If they were still not Union members, still could not get supplies, and were unable for all their wealth to arrange decent places to live, they had to find some way to prove to themselves and to their country that they had accomplished something. They would not have wanted to show in an official place had one been offered to them, because that would have been giving in to the Union, but they also didn't want to do an exhibition organized, as *Isskunstvo, Part II* was, in the Soviet way, with all the awkward amateurishness that once had been their hallmark and that now seemed so shoddy. The prospect of an exhibition with German artists whose work they didn't much like in an unfinished exhibition hall in the middle of nowhere didn't do much for them. Who would come to this exhibition? Westerners, who could see the work in the West with equal ease; friends, who had seen enough work already; and sycophantic young artists who wanted to see what had gone on in the West and who perhaps would try to horn in on the Western dealers expected for the opening. No: the whole thing was terrible.

But in another way, it was not so terrible. How difficult, really, to do a few light, maybe humorous works, to accommodate these Germans? Slowly at first, the Soviets began to thaw. Sergey Volkov was a gentleman throughout, aware of his debt to the Germans and eager to repay it in kind; he did an enormous painting, called *It Is Better to Listen Once than to Hear a Hundred Times,* which showed a hundred ears neatly arranged in rows. Nikola Ovchinnikov, on his return from Paris, drove out to the dacha with his wife, and ate dinner there. He did a funny, kitschy, rather slapdash installation. Sven Gundlakh came back from Budapest, waving his catalogue triumphantly, and expressed much incredulity at the situation between the Germans and the Soviets; he came every day to sit at Frunzenskaya and chat with the other artists at work. His own project for the exhibition, he explained, was being planned; the day of the opening he went to the Arbat (where street artists work) and bought little oil sketches of flowers on tables and verdant landscapes from the street peddlers there, and he arranged these in a row with a sign saying, "20 kopeks." It was an irony, often remarked on, that red velvet ropes had to go up around Sven's installation, because Soviet visitors to the exhibition kept trying to steal these paintings; the actual works of art by the other artists, of course, they never touched.

Vadim Zakharov did not return from Budapest until after *Isskunstvo, Part II* had opened, but he sent a work ahead of him with very elaborate instructions saying just how and where it should be installed. Sergey Vorontsov, whose work in the Berlin part of the project had been rather undistinguished, did far better this time, with several really clever installations, mostly realized with his friend Sergey Smakov. Nikita would often come in the afternoon, wearing a pair of Parisian green suede shoes, and sit and smile meaningfully. He said that Nikita Alexeev had died and an alter-ego, Alexei Nikitin, had been born. "You can imagine that after I left Moscow, I found myself in absolutely different surroundings, and had to explain to myself, why am I am here, and what am I doing here, and what was I doing there—so I just divided myself into these two people." During his time in Moscow, he remained Alexei Nikitin, but glimpses of Nikita Alexeev also shone through, and later, in Paris, he would speak of weeks when Nikita Alexeev, "resurrected in the mode of Sherlock Holmes," came to visit. His installation was called simply *Fish, Cat, Cat, Fish* and was made of items he had brought with him from Paris that were totally unavailable in Moscow that year: some washing powder, some loose change (French money), a checked tablecloth, some sugar, and a bottle of alcohol. "A really nasty piece of art," he said to me later.

Prigov's installation looked a lot like his installations from the previous year, bearing an almost uncanny resemblance to the one he had done for *Mosca Terza Roma;* he situated it and then left Moscow to give a poetry reading in Siberia. Anufriev had been dropped from the project for personal reasons, and was keeping a low profile. And Kostya returned from Budapest only on the day of the opening, with no work and no apologies and many stories of drunkenness.

By that time, there was an exhibition in place. It was not a good exhibition. Most of the Soviet work was stupid, badly made, or sloppy; but it was, at least, an exhibition. The opening itself was an interesting contrast with the Berlin opening. Some diplomats were there, and all the artists, and some friends of the artists. Kostya and his wife, Larisa, were there. It was the first time I had seen Larisa since the previous summer; in the first piece I ever published about

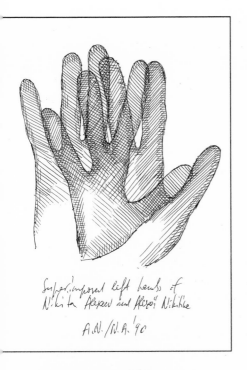

Superimposed left hands of
Nikita Alexeev and Alexeï Nikitine
A.N./N.A. '90

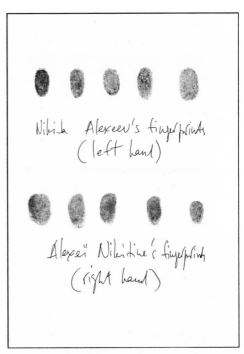

Nikita Alexeev's fingerprints
(left hand)

Alexeï Nikitine's fingerprints
(right hand)

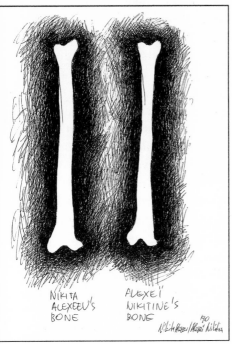

NIKITA
ALEXEEV'S
BONE

ALEXEÏ
NIKITINE'S
BONE

Nikita Alexeev/Alexeï Nikitin

Nikita Alexeev
in disguise

Alexeï Nikitine
in disguise

NIKITA ALEXEEV: *Four Works by Nikita Alexeev and Alexei Nikitin*

Soviet art I had described the couple as "teeny and wry"—a description that does not do them full credit but that is also not inaccurate. Seeing me for the first time that year, they came rushing, joined hands, and danced around me in a circle singing, "Teeny and wry! We are teeny and wry!" There was music, and there were a few bunches of flowers, and Lisa made a short speech. There were no Japanese hors d'oeuvres. People got very animated and very overexcited, and the room shook with the sound of reunions. Alexander Kosolapov, having returned to the U.S.S.R. for the first time in more than ten years, was with his daughter, whom he hadn't seen since his departure. Boris Groys was also making his first return since he had left in 1981. Jamey Gambrell was there, and Margarita Tupitsyn, and the German dealer Thomas Krings-Ernst, who bustled around with an important look on his face offering contracts to various artists. As at many events that summer, the Westerners on hand were introduced to Soviets who were in fact unlikely to enjoy conversation with someone from the West, because the introducing reflected well on the person performing the introduction. At the opening of *Isskunstvo*, I, like everyone else from the West, was besieged with people saying, "Hello! Please come with me and meet my old school friend, who is an expert on Russian Empire furniture. You can talk to her in French." This went on despite the fact that there were dozens of people there whom I hadn't seen in months and with whom I was eager to chat. Conversation became frenzied. And then, at the back of the room there was a slight hush, because Pavel Khoroshilov had come in, the man from the Ministry of Culture who had told Lisa almost two years earlier that her project would never take place. "Lisa," he said with a warm smile. "What a very fine exhibition. Many congratulations to you for managing to put it together so very well."

After the opening came the first of the *shashlik* parties, and it was the nicest one of all. Later on that summer, I reached a point at which the very mention of the word *shashlik* made me run screaming from the room, but at the beginning it was a great novelty. Lisa had recruited a technician from the Stroganov Institute, a man called Akop, who apparently had an extraordinary gift for cooking *shashlik*. Akop missed the opening in Moscow because he was busy building his bonfire in Nikolina Gora. He had obtained an enormous quantity of lamb, which had been cut into cubes and marinated. Remember that we had not seen meat in a week at that point; popular opinion held that there was no meat at all in Moscow. When the bonfire was really going, Akop put the meat on long skewers and grilled it over the open fire. Everyone came to the dacha that night, even Vika Kabakova (though Ilya was still in the West): it was such a gathering of the vanguard as had not taken place since before the travels began. We had enormous quantities of Soviet champagne to drink, and as it was a warm summer's evening near midsummer in a northern latitude, the light lingered for hours. Some people went swimming, while others sat around at the house. Georgiy Kizevalter took photographs, perhaps to remember the party, perhaps to document it. Later, we sang, and once we had begun we could hardly stop; we sang for hours, a hodgepodge of Russian army songs, German anthems, and American tunes from childhood. Sergey Vorontsov had a sort of miniature synthesizer from the West, and Werner Zein had a super-high-tech one; they played backup and rhythm.

The party was a little bit manic. There was more food than any of us had seen in a long time, and Akop went on cooking for hours and hours and hours. We all overstuffed ourselves; we had grown accustomed to being hungry all the time, and now suddenly there was enough meat to go on eating until you were ready to burst. There was a lot of story-telling, everyone relating adventures to everyone else. The Soviets who had never been to the West asked, from time to time, "Is this what parties are like in your country?" And we said that parties could be like this. There were familiar faces, and there were also faces I had never seen before, many of which would soon become familiar. They were the faces of the new vanguard, the young people who had befriended and been befriended by the older ones. Late at night, after most of the guests had driven home, a few collapsed on sofas or on the floor or on other people's beds and stayed the night. We fell asleep late. In the small hours around dawn we heard strange knocking sounds coming up through the floor, and went out to explore; Kostya had managed to crawl under the house and was "impersonating a poltergeist."

I loved the dacha, but I was aware that by staying there I had associated myself strongly with the Germans, living at a remove, and so when Larisa said to me, the following morning, "Maybe you come and live with us in Moscow, like a real Soviet," I decided to go. So it was that I came to Furmanny, to Kostya and Larisa's studio; and though I continued to spend occasional nights or weekends in the dacha, I was based in Furmanny for the rest of the summer. To have witnessed the heyday of Furmanny is an experience I will remember as long as memory serves. It was like being at the center of the world, and to be in Kostya and Larisa's studio was to be at the center of the center. In the winter of 1988–89, tourists from the West who wanted to buy art had come to Moscow knowing only the word "Furmanny," which led them to the building near the Krasnye Vorota metro station; but the men who had made Furmanny famous were of course abroad at that time, and the structure, slated for redevelopment by a cooperative that had agreed to sell it to the army, stood abandoned while the terms of its sale were debated. Even the School for the Blind had been relocated. Younger unknown artists quickly recognized the potential of this situation, and they established themselves as squatters in the many unoccupied rooms. Their agenda met with success; the befuddled tourists were in most instances delighted to have found any artists at all, and left, still not quite sure whom they had been meant to see, with paintings under their arms. This success bred interest among other young artists, and by late spring of 1989, there were more than a hundred of them established in Furmanny, which had turned into the center of Moscow artistic life. Savvy Westerners went there to see the variety of new Soviet art. When the original seven artists returned from their travels, they claimed large studios at the front of the building, and took their place at the upper end of the rapidly emerging Furmanny hierarchy.

Artists who were good friends of the original seven, artists who had exhibited with them in the West, came and worked at Furmanny to be companionable: so Nikola Ovchinnikov, Sergey Volkov, and Medgermenevtika all had studios there. Some artists who knew the original seven but were not their close friends, people who had reputations of their own but had never had adequate studio space, came also to Furmanny, including Zhora Litichevskiy, Nikolay Filatov, Sergey Shutov, and Pertsy. Some young artists came to study at the feet of the masters. More came to snare dealers and curators. The place developed its own self-regulating structure, almost like a co-op board: by the spring of 1989 you could not come and take a room unless you knew some of the people in residence and had been accepted by general consensus.

The Furmanny building was a squat: it was illegal to be there. Though the authorities kept an eye on it, life in Moscow was by then sufficiently relaxed so that no one did much about the artists. None-theless the place had all the disadvantages of any squat anywhere. There were no phones until Nikola Ovchinnikov managed to reroute a wire destined for another building and put a line in one studio; that lasted about two weeks before it spluttered out. The water and the electricity, though not disconnected, were irregular, and there were no lights in the hallways or on the stairs. There was no garbage collection, and the slow accumulation of refuse reached a height of unimaginable disgustingness in the heat of July: inexplicable rotting things of various description were piled in every hallway, and all the vermin one associates with decay had come to explore. When it rained hard, the ground floor flooded, and so whatever had been piled there was in a state of constant moist decomposition. Cooking was done in most studios on semifunctional burners in the corners; there was no refrigeration, and most of the time people drank from broken mugs or smeary glasses that had previously been used for rinsing brushes. Men in army uniforms were often to be seen standing in the concrete courtyard looking purposeless. There was gas in only one apartment, where the authorities had forgotten to turn it off; this was, therefore, the only place where there was hot water, and many was the morning that I woke up, trudged through the soldier-filled courtyard in Larisa's bathrobe, and climbed five flights of unlit stairs to wash. The building was under constant threat of destruction: it would be torn down any minute, according to some artists; by October, according to others; not later than November, according to others still. While some tried to organize official occupancy of the place, to save Furmanny, others reveled in the inevitable next disaster in what they glorified as their continuing oppression. It was fashionable to say that the place had had its day, that its destruction was necessary for the progress of Soviet art. Meanwhile, Larisa organized the payment of token rent so that the building would stay up at least for the summer, and she enforced payment. She was the only one of the artists from the old vanguard who saw every studio and had contact with all the new faces.

People from the West came in droves. "It's a real relief," Sven Gundlakh said one day, "that the ones who don't know what they've come to see get grabbed by the people downstairs, because it would be very exhausting to have to see everybody. You'd have to be crazy or desperate to have a studio on the ground floor." Some young artists would take it upon themselves to shepherd Western visitors around, telling the history of the place in tones of hushed melodrama as they went, entering certain apartments with a degree of ceremony that would have been more appropriate to the Kaaba in Mecca. The critics and dealers and curators drank endless tea from broken cups and took copious notes in large notebooks; they were often to be found looking nervous among the soldiers outside, comparing information, and whispering to one another. Though the established artists depended on established contacts, the younger ones were occasionally heard whooping for joy as these people departed, clutching invitations to leave the U.S.S.R. at last, and go on a trip to a festival outside Glasgow, or to a place near Warsaw, or to a town north of Helsinki. The older artists found all this a bit dreary, a bit depressing. "All these people know is that their art brings them money," Sven said. "They go to the stores early, get there first, and buy all the paint and all the canvas and all the stretchers, and when I say to them, 'Can I buy some paint from you, because there is none in the stores?' they say, 'I will sell it to you in exchange for an introduction to one of your dealers.' "

This sheer commercialism was the product of Gorbachev's reforms; everyone assumed perestroika meant that it would be easy to get rich quick. The Champions of the World, which Kostya Zvezdochetov had left some time before, had gone on without him under the leadership of Boris Matrosov, Giya Abramishvili, and Kostya Latyshev, and it had turned into a sort of club for young trendies with calculated self-glorifying objectives. Their work was churned out of tiredness, and the discourse that was developed to go with it was completely empty. Being accepted as a Champion—and there were more Champions every time you turned around—was like getting in with the popular kids in school; it was a matter of no aesthetic import at all. But at least the Champions thought it was a good idea to pretend to a high critical tone. The Fish Mafia—so called because its leading figures, including the prominent Valeriy Yershov, had names that resemble the names of fish in Russian—were artists who had sold out and made no bones about it, artists who had figured out what the West really wanted and did paintings in office-size and drawing-room size, in colors to coordinate with post-modern interiors. The drear of these people and their work was exceeded only by their wealth; you would be hard-pressed to find a Western corporation with a Moscow office not given a touch of authenticity by Fish Mafia paintings. Westerners were not the only ones to buy such work; Soviets who had obtained permission to emigrate would come to Furmanny following along

SVEN GUNDLAKH: *Kopecks*

behind the Western dealers, and would spend their life savings buying pictures to take to the West, because modern art was one of the few things they could take with them, and they thought they would be able to liquidate it easily when they got to Vienna or Tel Aviv. With their lack of artistic and business knowledge, however, it is unlikely that many of them were able to do anything with their pictures, if they got them out of the country, besides hang them on their walls.

For all that, Furmanny was the center of the world. Yuriy Leyderman was the one who said, "Furmanny is like a *pelmeni* [Russian ravioli], in which a smooth casing contains everything all chopped up and mixed together in quite a delicious way." Each day there was as full of tension and drama and exhilaration as a year in a soap opera. There were parties in Furmanny all the time that summer; I remember that on Kolya Filatov's birthday we danced all night and well into the following day. Some artists who had been to the West wore jeans and old shoes, and others had stylish Western clothes in peculiar juxtaposition with old Soviet things; the ones who had stayed at home wore borrowed T-shirts and homemade chic. The idea of wearing black only had caught on in a big way. Everyone drank all the time: alcohol was almost unavailable that summer to the general public, but though the artists resisted many of the ostentations their wealth might have provided, they spent their hard-earned currency unstintingly on a constant supply of harsh cognac. A high level of intellectual discourse was also sustained in Furmanny, and so, too, was the wistful nostalgia that the artists had developed in the West, a perennial homesickness that was little assuaged by the fact that they were once more at home. A Soviet woman called Olga Sviblova was making a documentary film about the place, and she was at every event, in every studio, always having some kind of elaborate problem with her camera or her assistants; her probing interrogations and cumbersome equipment gave one a constant sense that one was part of living history.

Kostya and Larisa's studio was the hub. So many people came to see them, to borrow a paintbrush, to have a chat, to have a drink, to ask for advice, to tell a story, to hijack a visitor, that they came up with a secret knock, like Morse code, to be used only by their closest friends. Many was the time that someone else banged on the door and Larisa froze, turned to me, and whispered: "Don't move. Quiet." And we would stay frozen like mimes until the caller had given up and gone back downstairs. I had a set of keys, but no matter how late I returned I found the studio full. Larisa would cook for whoever happened to turn up. Sometimes there were six people for dinner, but more often there were ten or twelve, sometimes forty. There was no fixed hour for eating; at some point she would start giving people bowls of food, and she would go on feeding whoever came at whatever time he came until it was late and everyone was well fed. The cooking was all done in a corner on a one-ring burner, and the food was served on plates or in the inverted lids of pots or sometimes on sheets of paper. It was often delicious. When you asked Larisa where it had come from, how she was able to find the ingredients, she would just shrug and say, "I found them"; for anyone else, this feat could have been a full-time career. There was always more than enough. She spent the day shopping for food and talking to friends, the evening cooking, then serving half the artists in Moscow, and then cleaning up. In the small hours of the morning, after everyone had left, she painted. Some hours after dawn, she would suddenly say, "I'm maybe tired, a little bit," and she would lie down. Kostya was always awake as well, talking, rambling, smoking, drinking, complaining about his health, looking out at the streets. In the course of those evenings we would talk about everything we could think of: "So," Kostya would say to me, "Why are you a writer?" or perhaps, "What does it mean, honesty?" or, "Why do all Western people love so much Gorbachev?"

Friends came to call, and we talked about glasnost and perestroika. We talked about the German artists and *Isskunstvo*. We talked about money, whether it's the source of all comfort or the root of all evil. We talked about the different republics of the U.S.S.R. and their respective characters. We talked about the backgrounds of various artists, about the experiences of their childhood. We told funny stories, and I heard all the tales from the old days. The favorite subject of all was which artists were good and which were not so good. "Of course, no one's work is interesting now," Kostya said in the halflight of the hour before sunrise one morning in late July. "Including mine."

The passionate connectedness of the members of the Mukhomor generation was less strong than it had been. Nikola Ovchinnikov came by Kostya and Larisa's a lot, and Yuriy Albert and Andrey Filippov were also regular callers, but Sergey Mironenko was away almost all summer, and Volodya Mironenko had found a Belgian/American girl named Raisa—who neither liked nor was liked by the artists—with whom he spent day and night. Sven Gundlakh had gone into a depression and stayed at home watching porno films on video. Vadim Zakharov, trying to make up to his children for the time he had spent away from them, went with his family to the country. Sergey Volkov worked long and disciplined hours, dropping around when he could for a short visit; Nikita Alexeev came to call from time to time and stayed talking all night. Kostya and Larisa were still closest to their old friends, but they spent more and more time with the younger artists in Furmanny, who were less sophisticated but more energetic and more readily available; these were the people with whom Larisa had passed the months while Kostya was in the West. In the studio downstairs from Kostya and Larisa's, Pavel Fomenko and Igor Kaminyuk worked together very closely under the joint name Fomskiy. Igor (called Kamin by his friends) came from Odessa, and so he and Larisa had a strong connection; Kostya would always accuse them of "scandalmongering like all the miserable Odessa people." Anton Olshvang, who had the studio with the hot water, was as good an artist as any of the young ones. These people created art with whatever came to hand, and what they did was not very distinguished: Olshvang did a lot of strange shapes in aluminum and papier mâché, and Fomskiy did a portrait of Brezhnev in drag. The work had nothing to do with gestures of communication or hidden meanings, and it did not come out of profound experience of an oppressive regime; by the time these people became artists, the career was a fine and respectable one, part of a good way of life. Pavel Fomenko said, "What do I want with my art? I want money, a little bit, fame, a little bit, and to make something good, that also a little bit."

There were a few young artists not based in Furmanny who were also part of the new generation. The most highly regarded of these were Tolik Zhuravlev and Masha Serebryakova. Tolik had been included in *10 + 10,* and so he had been to New York and Fort Worth. His experience of the West in the first year of general travel had given him a substantial edge over the other artists of his years. His work was literary (ostensibly in the Kabakov tradition); he used letters and numbers almost like figures of abstraction. Masha's work was full of the devalued signs of daily life, such as illustrations from Soviet cookbooks for recipes requiring ingredients and equipment obviously unavailable in the U.S.S.R. Larisa said, "There are now a lot of schools. A lot, and they are all the same. If before it was the renaissance, now it's mannerism. I think our movement is not so strong as the renaissance, and so our mannerism is not so good as theirs, but it is also not so bad."

The middle line, between the banality of the new mannerism and the exhaustion of the older generation, was the difficult one to find, and artists from Odessa managed it best. Pertsy—Oleg Petrenko and Lyudmila Skripkina—were based in Furmanny that summer, and they were always in the midst of the most theatrical arguments with everyone around them; it was their way to declare themselves great friends of certain artists and then to refuse to speak with anyone else. In the middle of the summer, Ronald Feldman decided to take the pair on board, and their egos grew out of all control. Pertsy's work was in the Monastyrskiy tradition, and depended on charts and scales, frequently painted onto ordinary everyday objects to smoothly surreal effect. A jar of the processed peas that one seems to be forever eating in Moscow was painted halfway up with mathematical and chemical tables, its significance inflated, obscured, and confounded by the addition. Medgermenevtika's work was less elegant than Pertsy's, but it was perhaps deeper and funnier. Sergey Anufriev, Pasha Peppershteyn, and Yuriy Leyderman continued to generate texts for one another's enlightenment, and did their taped interviews and refined their rhet-

АЛФАВИТ

ANATOLIY (TOLIK) ZHURAVLEV: *Alphabet* (Author's note: This drawing
was produced by superimposing all the letters of the Russian alphabet
on one another.)

oric of discourse. There was a subtle shifting of roles; whereas at the
beginning the others had seemed to depend on Anufriev to energize
them, now they seemed to energize him. Peppershteyn turned himself
almost into a new version of Andrey Monastyrskiy, serious, extravagant, at ease in the pompous rhetoric of genius. The work was so self-
referential that there is little point describing it; the artists of the
vanguard would tell Westerners that it was interesting and then
watch, grinning at how desperately they tried to puzzle it out.

The best artistic surprise was Larisa. A year earlier, she had been
"Kostya's wife," making occasional tiny figures out of clay; but while
the men had been off in the West, she had begun to work more
seriously, and had become—to borrow her own phrase—a "very beautiful artist," as good as any in Moscow. Her massive paintings were
done in imitation of the kitschy accessories of communist propaganda;
for a large series of works, she copied the idealized silhouettes of
athletes to be found on Soviet athletic medals onto synthetic velour
carpets printed with grazing deer, which her mother had bought for
her in Odessa. The wit of her work, its sheer inventiveness and brilliant humor, was balanced by a great seriousness. No one else in
Moscow worked so constantly or so productively in the summer of
1989 as Larisa Zvezdochetova, who was the only artist in that immediate circle who had yet to travel West.

Soviet kitsch is a tragic inversion of Western kitsch, because it does not simply reflect an unplanned sociological phenomenon, but is rather part of a deliberate process of indoctrination. It is an affront to the constraints of tastefulness, but it is also a clumsy version of propaganda, one in which the absurdity of what is said is matched fully by the absurdity of its means of expression. Kitsch in the West always appeals to the snobberies that recognize its aesthetic inferiority. It confirms our status as tasteful individuals who would not for a second find beauty in certain objects manufactured specifically to be celebrated as beautiful by people who clearly know nothing of beauty. The ignorance of those who genuinely like it makes us feel superior, and that is the origin of our laughter. But in the Soviet Union, where most kitsch is government produced, the appreciation of kitsch extends to a different kind of snobbery, because those who are amused by it are too sophisticated to believe the larger message of a successful communism that underlies it. It is a reminder that the system is ridiculous not only in abstract terms, but also in the pettiest of concrete terms. In the face of Soviet kitsch, we find that we cannot forget that communism itself is not tasteful, that for all its idealist exponents, it finally appeals to the lowest common denominator among the Soviet people, and that it is to this element that it has always been addressed. Tastelessness unto itself is the least of Stalin's evils, but it is an emblem for the most fundamental betrayals of communism.

Larisa exploits these truths throughout her work. With the works that represent Soviet political kitsch in conjunction with the simply visual kitsch that is so common in the West—like the state medals for athletic and artistic performance on their velour ground with its grazing deer—she locates the natural proximity of two kinds of snobbery. The result is a trenchant commentary on both art and politics, and on their inevitable entanglement. She reminds us that nothing is produced outside of the circumstances of its creator, and that an artist's tastes are always a patchwork of acceptance and rejection of the tastes of his society. In this context, aesthetic knowledge is both a gift and the basis for delusion, since one's response to an emblem and one's response to its object do not always correspond. In Soviet culture, it is often impossible to distinguish between the emblems of truth and the emblems of fiction, and so the only safe course is to treat all emblems as fictive, to live in the space between failed beauty and failed meaning. The grazing deer become as dangerous as the idealized athletes.

The interest of Larisa's work lies in this flattening of distinctions. Though Western viewers of her work frequently imagine that she has exaggerated the things she imitates, a few days in Moscow prove that she has taken only the most modest and moderate items and re-created them without violating their own terms. Unlike the Sots Artists, she will not take the more obvious modes of state Socialist Realism and demonstrate their absurdity simply by copying them. No—she sticks with enamels and embroideries and souvenirs, the most simple and smallest kinds of kitsch, the ones that no significant mind dictated, the ones that are lowest on Lenin's list. These are the works that couldn't make the Plan for Monumental Propaganda, that formed instead an insidious and omnipresent phenomenon one might call "miniature propaganda." Much of this material is so grotesque as to preclude caricature. Larisa's genius is that she engages with this work not by attempting to exaggerate it, but rather by forcing it into unlikely juxtapositions and alien contexts. She always insists that her work conform to the standards of beauty set by what it imitates; and since Soviet society at its most purely Stalinist insists on the perpetual celebration of its redoubtable technologies, she captures the meticulous precision of idealized industry, reminding us that such precision applied without intelligence is not a triumph for a communist or, indeed, for any other society. She insists on a very high technical standard; her colors are always strong and clear, and the field in which they are painted is always precisely defined. In her mock-embroidery work, she recreates the effect of stitchery so deftly that at any distance from the canvas one might mistake it for the genuine item.

But the fact remains that the objects she creates are strangely beautiful. One approaches them and is amused by the jokes they tell, but one lingers in front of them because they often have a quality almost of fairy tale. Like much kitsch, they recall the uninformed tastes of childhood. The false enamels and embroideries are fascinating for their very technical achievement; the colors seduce; the absolute wit of Larisa's *Self-Portrait as Nefertiti* made me laugh not once, but every time I saw it. Her work reminds us that it is not easy to operate always in terms of one's high beliefs, that one wants to continue to look at what one knows to be laughable. It reminds us over and over again, that the knowledge that something is absurd does not necessarily strip it of the pleasures it may provide. Those of us in the West who are charmed by her work are forced to recognize that we too could have been charmed by the dictates of communism, which, like her paintings, have a certain shimmering beauty to them, a seductive simplicity that is no less seductive because we know it to be absurd. Laughing at ourselves, we stare a long time into the depths of her brilliant colors, as if unable to move on; and the weakness we recognize in ourselves when we do finally tear ourselves away is the real message of her work. For beneath an exterior that is only playful is a profundity of insight, into the society in which she has lived her life, and into the many people who have come to study and reexamine that society. In telling us all about herself and her world, it tells us all about ourselves and ours.

Larisa had her first big show not in the West, but in Moscow, at First Gallery, which mounted a one-woman retrospective in July. First Gallery was another phenomenon of 1989. It was billed as a Western-style gallery selling the work of Soviet and Western artists for hard currency to whoever chose to buy it, and in principle it was just that. How it really functioned is anyone's guess. First Gallery was set up by Aydan Salakhova, the daughter of the head of the Union of Artists, with her friends Aleksandr Yakut and Yevgeniy Mitta. Aydan is dark and beautiful and mysterious, catlike, with enormous eyes, dramatically short black hair, and a quiet self-assurance that allows her to skate through the most difficult situations. She does not use her last name, partly because she has decided that to have only one name, in the mode of Halston, carries a certain chic; and partly because it is an oft-repeated "fact" that she has severed all ties with her father and hates him.

You never know whose side Aydan is on. She negotiates and arranges, and in the end things always seem to happen as she wants them to happen. Only in her early twenties, she is the best that perestroika has to offer, a businesswoman, an artist, a socialite, replete with ambition you have no doubt she will fulfill. Her gallery is a wonder in Moscow. It looks like Bloomingdale's, albeit in miniature. It has exactly that level of fun chic, of wealth put to reasonable use, of clichéd urbane sophistication. Remember that in Moscow all the old buildings are falling down, except in the Kremlin, and that all the new buildings are shoddily constructed out of cheap materials. Even the great showpieces of more recent date—from the Mezhdunarodnaya Hotel, where the Sotheby's sale took place, to the new work of architectural cooperatives—have a repellent thickness about them and are unpleasantly lit. But at First Gallery there are marble floors, gilded half-pediments over the doors, and a coffee bar that never runs out of coffee, where you sit on pale bentwood barstools with rose-colored upholstery and drink from Villeroy and Bosch cups. There is track lighting, and in large upholstered armchairs just inside the door

LARISA YURIYEVNA ZVEZDOCHETOVA: *Untitled*

you can consider your purchases while you leaf through the copies of recent Western magazines that are scattered casually on the coffee table. First Gallery is actually owned by a cooperative, which also operates a restaurant next door. The gallery is a status symbol for them, and draws people into the restaurant, but why they really operate it, and how they could have afforded to do it up so expensively with what must be imported materials, remain unclear. It is obvious that Aydan's contribution at the construction stage was taste rather than money; the restaurant was done just as expensively as the gallery and looks like the set for an amateur production of *Salomé*.

Perhaps some tourists bought work at First Gallery that summer, but the vogue among canny ones was for visiting artists in their studios, observing their lives, and taking work away as a souvenir, while the real pundits knew it was easier to buy work created by artists in the West from galleries in the West. Aydan's gallery offered a complete export service, but this was exorbitant and not always dependable. The prices seemed high; a picture Larisa might have sold well for a few hundred dollars in the spring was in Aydan's gallery for twenty thousand a few months later. This had its use for Larisa; though little was sold at the First Gallery exhibit, her work sold for similar prices in Berlin in December because the precedent had been established. What was most riveting was that though the gallery showed Bulatov, Kabakov, Chuykov, Vasilyev, Nakhova, and the Mironenkos, it also showed a picture by Robert Rauschenberg that he had given to Aydan, and mounted a big exhibition of Helmut Newton, for whose work the usual high prices were asked. Who would buy Newton photos for hard currency in Moscow? What were they doing there? The slightly pornographic flavor of some of his work meant that there were lines around the block to get into the gallery. Was the show a publicity stunt, a public service, or a subtle business arrangement? Did the fact that the gallery had shown Newton make Western buyers more confident about buying work there?

What First Gallery did was give the Soviet artists a place to show in Moscow. Though the cooperative would in principle have been willing to do business with Soviet citizens, there are no people in the U.S.S.R. who have enough Western currency to buy work by Soviet artists with it; and the few who have enough currency to buy Helmut Newton photographs can afford to go to California and buy them there. But First Gallery was open to anyone, and as people had once gone to Nikita Alexeev's apartment, or to the Kindergarten, so they now visited First Gallery to see what the masters of Soviet art were doing and to see who was coming up. Western dealers took Aydan very seriously, and frequently peeked in at her place, wrote down the names of artists shown there, and then hunted them out at Furmanny. Aydan had her finger on the pulse; between showing the most highly acclaimed members of the vanguard and Helmut Newton, she mounted exhibitions that included Tolik Zhuravlev, Fomskiy, Anton Olshvang, and the other new Furmanny artists who warranted some notice. The members of the vanguard met one another most often that summer in the courtyard at Furmanny or at Kostya and Larisa's, but when there was nothing else to do, they would go to First Gallery and find friends gathered at the coffee bar, drinking juice (which was cheaper than coffee) and discussing the strengths and weaknesses of the work on the walls. The gallery was air conditioned and comfortable, and for the young artists who had never traveled it was as close as they could get to a Western experience without a plane ticket. Artists not in residence at Furmanny met the living legends if they could get up the nerve to cross the gallery's marble-and-gilt threshold. Aydan, who became something of a celebrity, sat watching like a queen, or drifted over to tell about some new show or event of general interest. People who knew neither the artists nor Aydan came and struck up conversations. She showed her own paintings and those of her two partners; the other artists turned a tactful blind eye to their flatness, though the excess of vaginal and menstrual imagery in Aydan's "feminist" work fascinated less-sophisticated Soviet citizens who came to First Gallery. The gallery was all that *Isskunstvo, Part II* was not: it was a space such as most Soviets had never set foot in, which the artists could treat like the most ordinary second home, and its shows had high prices that reflected successes abroad. Though most artists scoffed at its chic, they also loved it: there was a studied casual way that some of them had of discussing loudly the negotiations they were undertaking with people from the West while they sat in the corner. No one quite trusted Aydan, but they all liked her cucumber-cool poise and her ability to rise to the surface like fresh cream; everyone made friends with her at least halfway.

While First Gallery was coming into its own, dreadful institutions that called themselves galleries sprang up across Moscow like corn shoots in springtime. Among the noisiest of these were the Gallery Mars, Art Moderne, and the National Hotel Salon, none of

AYDAN SALAKHOVA: *Untitled*

which was done up as First Gallery was, and none of which sold the caliber of work Aydan sought out. They were full of kitschy neo-Surrealist fantasy nightmares beyond all imagining. This art had enormous price tags attached to it, and was sold mostly to people too confused even to find the Fish Mafia, including many visitors from Eastern Europe. Other nonselling exhibitions ran parallel to *Isskunstvo, Part II.* Tanya Saltsirn, a young protégée of Viktor Miziano, put together an exhibition of the Champions of the World which confirmed their mediocrity in the eyes of many Moscow artists, but which had tremendous TV coverage from local and select international news. The Bulgarians did a feature on it; one of them said to me, "You have come here from the West. What makes this art good?" He also volunteered to show me work next time I was in Bulgaria, "Not as good as this—we are a small country—but also very interesting for you."

Then there were several exhibitions organized by Josif Bakshteyn, whose position had been both rationalized and undermined by the events of the previous year. They were less flashy than Aydan's shows, but they were also better; in fact, the best work shown in Moscow that summer was at Josif's exhibitions. The first of these was called *Dear Art,* a double entendre in Russian as well as in English, since "dear" means both beloved and expensive in both languages. The show took place in May, and included work by many of the artists who had been most successful in the West, made of the most mundane and shoddy materials, but calculated to grab the Western imagination. The expensiveness of these articles was a matter for ironic speculation among visitors. By the time *Isskunstvo* got under way, Josif's exhibition *Perspectives of Conceptualism* had opened at Avtozavodskaya. Like *Dear Art,* it combined pieces Josif had found during studio tours and new work he had commissioned. *Perspectives of Conceptualism* included Kostya and Larisa Zvezdochetov, Sergey Volkov, Georgiy Kizevalter, Igor Makarevich, Yelena Elagina, Pertsy, Masha Konstantinova, and Kolya Kozlov. Kozlov and Konstantinova, like Pertsy, had been members of the vanguard for years but had lingered in relative obscurity during the early days of glasnost. Josif's exhibitions revealed these people to Western eyes, and inscribed them on the list of artists included in every significant Western exhibition.

Important art-world visitors from the West were, as a matter of course, referred to Josif. He was not interested in giving tours of Furmanny to people who wanted souvenir pictures to take home, but he was always willing to help with the organization of major museum exhibitions, or to discuss the real infrastructure of the vanguard with influential dealers. He knew where everyone was at any given moment, and he could tell you at what time you would most likely reach any by phone. He knew which artists should be shown together and which works complemented one another. He told the artists which galleries were good and which were not, and he told the dealers which artists were good and which were not. And he negotiated to take his own exhibitions to the West, to organize the sale of the dear art he had commissioned. Artists knew that work Josif exhibited was likely to be seen by the people who counted, and that he had the power to push for some people and to let the word out that others were past their prime. He didn't press that prerogative too far; he said what was popularly believed more often than he made it up himself. But the power was there.

His position was awkward because people from the West wanted practical advice out of him more often than they wanted curatorial judgment, and he resented being used as an information service. Though Josif was able to organize things, he was also lazy, and in the summer of 1989, like everyone else, he wanted to sit and drink tea and chat and remember. He could be very short with people who made demands on him, even if he had initially discussed their plans with enthusiasm; having undertaken a project, he would casually fail to fulfill his obligations to it, then grumpily come through at the last minute. As he saw his friends growing rich, he began to ask more and more money for his services, and knowledge he would once have shared to be friendly he now shared for currency. The artists were consistently obnoxious about the money he received. "Why pay him? Has he made a work of art?" they would ask, though Josif earned far less than they did and worked about as hard.

It was into this fray that Lena Kurlyandtseva stepped gingerly. People were harsh on Josif because he seemed greedy and lazy. Lena was neither. She was intelligent, kind, warm, and very industrious, willing to do whatever was possible for whoever asked her, with payment or without. With her husband, she introduced and orchestrated everywhere she could, drove Westerners to their engagements, helped them to buy paintings. She was constantly helpful and attentive to the *Isskunstvo* Germans at a time when everyone else in Moscow was giving them short shrift. But, like Viktor Miziano, she had come to the vanguard too late and from the wrong quarter. Like him, she had had a semiofficial career for some years, and had moved fully into the circle of the vanguard when the move was fashionable, not when it was dangerous.

The relative impatience everyone evinced with Josif, Lena, and Viktor—"They are like educated dealers, not critics, not curators, not even historians," one of the older artists said—was a combination of arrogant condescension and a positive dislike of people who were willing to play the game. Aydan, of course, played the game to the hilt, but then she never pretended otherwise; Josif and Viktor tried to sustain untarnished friendships while they ingratiated themselves with the right people under the right circumstances. Josif's exhibitions, at least, were held in high regard; and after all, he had been married to Ira Nakhova, who had been married to Andrey Monastyrskiy; and besides, he had been involved with the vanguard for years. Viktor Miziano was not so easily redeemed, though everyone agreed that *Mosca Terza Roma* was one of the year's best exhibitions. He had published several catalogue essays for big exhibitions in which he failed to challenge inept curatorial choices, and the artists took him to task for this. In the catalogue for *10 + 10*, for example, he tried to link together Soviet artists who were, in their own eyes, unlinkable.

But that was hardly fair; almost everyone was playing such games by that time. The fact that the vanguard artists had suffered did not give them a monopoly on the exploitation of the profitable situation around them. Kostya would say that he wanted to stop negotiating with the West, with all the fuss and bother it entailed, and then he would go on meeting with Westerners and joking, and joking and meeting, and meeting, and meeting. Sven Gundlakh and the Mironenkos were busy negotiating with mafiosi and with the directors of cooperatives to get better housing and black market food and subsidized plane fares. Which of these people were really honest, free of the taint of self-interest? Sergey Volkov, who had originally provoked much suspicion because he made so much money so easily and seemed to understand so quickly how to live with money, was among the few who preserved both honesty and dignity. "What's nice about him is that even when he is making money, he is always willing to talk about art, while others, with less money, talk about money all the time," Nikita Alexeev said to me. "Volkov doesn't imitate Western artists, but he also doesn't try to hold them at a distance; he learns a lot in the West, but at the same time is able to preserve his identity. He doesn't want to preserve his ethnicity, his exoticism, like many others. He can change, and he changes. And he never interferes with other people's lives or decisions." Andrey Monastyrskiy was the only one who had refused point-blank to go to the West. But was this bravery or was it fear? Kostya once said to me, "I want to make tragic work, ultimately, and I think I must have a happy life to make tragic work. Monastyrskiy's work becomes more rarified and in a way more comical because he is turning his own life into a tragedy by hermeticizing himself. Your life and your work have to have an inverse relation to one another." But Ira Nakhova said, "I don't think that he's afraid. He's very self-confident, and a very clever man, one of the cleverest people I've ever met, and he knows quite well how to do things at the right moment. He has patience, and when it is right for him to travel, he will travel. He's the only one who has that much control." And indeed, in 1990, Monastyrskiy married a Western woman—Sabine Hänsgen, co-author of Kulterpalast—and thereafter kept homes in Moscow and abroad.

The situation with money was not good that summer, and it was having an effect all around. On the black market—and no one was fool enough to trade money anywhere else—a dollar bought fifteen to twenty rubles; officially, a ruble cost $1.50. Luxury goods that had been altogether unavailable at the time of the Sotheby's sale were suddenly there for the asking, but at absurd prices. You could get a kilo of apricots for sixty rubles, which for people with plenty of

Western currency was not so bad (about four dollars); but when you think that a doctor in the U.S.S.R. was at that time paid less than two hundred rubles a month, you realize how inflated a price that is. Art had turned into pure commodity in everyone's eyes; the American critic Jamey Gambrell wrote, "The Soviet government now officially treats art as an export barter commodity, up there with vodka and caviar on the short list of desirable Soviet products. An Asian conglomerate that recently signed a deal to provide the Soviets with winter clothing was offered a selection of goods in lieu of foreign-currency payment: 'art,' as a generic category, was reportedly on the list along with nails." Certainly it is the case that the same taxi drivers who a year earlier would have announced that they could change your money and introduce you to a beautiful sister/cousin/niece ripe for marriage were more likely by the summer of 1989 to volunteer to change your money and to introduce you to a sister/brother/cousin who was an artist and would sell you paintings at a good price.

The vanguard artists by and large chose not to get involved in the ever-increasing complexities of export, and this was a further reason not to do any work that summer. It was not so much that the taxes were prohibitive as that the process of paying them was so slow and so agonizing as to make exporting works hardly worth the ordeal. The U.S.S.R. was supposed to be desperate for hard currency, but if you wanted to buy a work of art there, even if you bought it through official channels and spent a lot of dollars which the law would route to government coffers, you had to spend weeks filling out papers, signing forms, waiting in lines, and getting permission, and when it was all over you might be able to get the piece out, or you might get turned back at the border because someone had forgotten to stamp something. So the Westerners found it easier to pay money for art in the West, which the Soviet government never heard about, and the artists found it easier to create work there. The lines for any bureaucratic activity were unbelievable that summer; when I went to get my Moscow visa stamped to permit me to travel to Leningrad, I waited for five hours one day and four the next, shoved and jostled by all the other people who had come. Only by pushing hardest could you get to the front, and when you did, you turned over your passport and crossed your fingers that you would see it again. Small wonder the Soviets chose to avoid this, that only Larisa and the new faces were willing to be bothered to make work under such unpromising circumstances.

By the middle of the summer, the frantic atmosphere had calmed

down a bit, and though no one did work to sell, artists began to do
little pieces for their own edification, much as they had in the old
days. Sven came out of the apartment to which he had withdrawn for
most of the summer, and organized the third boat ride, part of a
continuing tradition by now, on the Moskva/Volga Channel to the
same park we had visited the year before with its same paddleboats,
and he invited all the *Isskunstvo* artists along for the ride. This time
the boat felt empty; where there had in previous years been hundreds
of people, there were now no more than thirty. Nonetheless the sentiment and the sense of ritual prevailed. In mid-July, the artists
attached to *Isskunstvo*, German and Soviet, did one-day installations at
Furmanny. These did not have the same pretensions to seriousness
that the exhibition in Frunzenskaya had had, and they were far more
successful; the reestablished friendships between the Germans and the
Soviets were manifest in the jokey way the artists played on one
another's central themes. The work was done by the artists for one
another; members of the public were not informed of the show, and
did not come to it.

In late July, Andrey Monastyrskiy organized an Action in Moscow,
and invited a number of guests to take part, including such old friends
returned from exile as Nikita Alexeev and Margarita and Viktor Tupitsyn. Though we did not have the "frame" of a trip to the country,
we did have the mystery and the ritual of old. We met outside a metro
station at a specified hour shortly before dusk, and stood in knots and
clusters waiting for the Action to begin. After some minutes, Josif
approached the first person, and pointed to Monastyrskiy, who was
standing some distance away. "Follow him, maintaining the distance
that is now between you," he said. Then he went up to the next
person and pointed at the last person and gave the same directions, so
that in the end we formed a long single-file line, each of us at a fixed
distance of about forty feet from the one in front. In this way we
walked down a long and busy street, attracting some curiosity and
some looks of confusion, then climbed through a disused train station
and went across its platforms (this part was almost like Follow the
Leader; sustaining the forty-foot gap became more and more difficult
as one drew closer or moved farther away depending on the physical
challenge of the next bit of terrain), and then walked along a path
through an inexplicable wood at the far side of the tracks. After some
moments we were told to stop, and we all stood about in little groups
again, staring into the dusky trees. Josif Baksteyn looked through a
pair of binoculars into the distance and asked us all to move forward

when we saw a red flickering in the distance. We strained our eyes, and eventually we saw this light. We walked down the path until we came across a string blocking our way. Hanging from this string was a red lantern. Below the lantern was a small ring in which two toy motorized vehicles moved chaotically, banging into one another. Over the whole thing was draped a sheet of plastic. We stood for a while and looked at this, and then we all moved on, leaving it as an installation in the woods, that would last until people came and stripped it of its useful components. The Action was called *Homage to Nikita Alexeev;* but Nikita had gone to the wrong metro station, and had missed the entire event.

In August, a number of artists, including Nikola Ovchinnikov, Andrey Filippov, Larisa Zvezdochetova, Yuriy Albert, Kolya Kozlov, and Sergey Mironenko, went to the district of the New Jerusalem monastery and did an outdoor one-day exhibition, in the mode of the *Bulldozer Show* and *Aptart En Plein Air.* This time, there were no authorities to be offended, and very few members of the general public were on hand; the artists did the exhibition, like the small collaboration at Furmanny, very much for themselves. The pieces were clever, nostalgic, and strikingly unsellable. Sergey Mironenko spent the day carving into the earth a slogan he failed to complete; it was to say, "No Amount of Reform Will Save the Bolsheviks from the Judgment of History." This was as much a performance as an earthwork. Andrey Filippov put a cross at the end of a fishing line and dangled it in the river, while at the handle of the rod he placed various ritual objects of the Orthodox church; he called the piece *Fishing for Souls.* Kolya Kozlov built a short road between two hillocks and dug what looked like tunnel entrances into them; a stream of toy tanks ran from one labeled "Moscow" to the other, labeled "Berlin." Kozlov is the "degenerate alcoholic" son of a four-star general in the Soviet army, and his work almost always uses toy tanks, guns, and other military objects.

When the artists bickered with Josif Bakshteyn, Viktor Miziano, and Lena Kurlyandtseva, they rejected almost everyone within the Soviet Union who could reasonably be called a critic of their work. Theoretical writings by Andrey Monastyrskiy and Ilya Kabakov were praised to the skies, but they were not really criticism; work by the

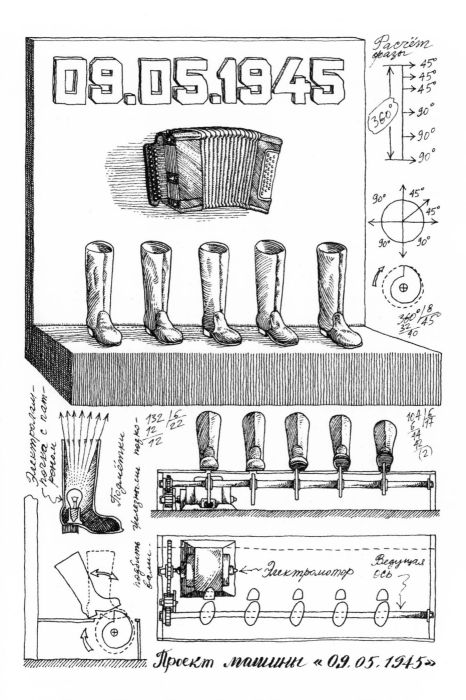

NIKOLAY (KOLYA) KOZLOV: *Project Machine "09.15.1945"* (Author's note: The Soviet victory over the Germans at the end of World War II was declared on May 9, 1945 (Victory Day). The incidental text in this drawing is all technical instruction for the building of the machine.)

philosopher/critic Mikhail Ryklin was tolerated; and the writing of Vitaliy Patsukov, Yevgeniy Barabanov, Leonid Bazhanov, and Dmitriy Sarabyanov, though only marginally connected to the situation of the vanguard, was respected. But there was no critical focus. Margarita and Viktor Tupitsyn spent much of the summer organizing a Russian-language edition of *Flash Art,* which contained translations of articles by regular *Flash Art* writers about Western work, and articles by Soviets about Soviet art. There was argument about who would write what, but the publication of the Russian *Flash Art* in the autumn was a real triumph, its glossiness and its complex critical vocabulary a matter of fascination to people in the U.S.S.R. The existing Soviet art magazine *Dekorativnoe Iskusstvo* ("Decorative Art") also took advantage of the new liberal atmosphere to tell the history of the vanguard and discuss its status. Much of what they published was written in an eccentric new Soviet style of criticism in which artists were fictionalized and their works deconstructed by way of hypothetical stories told about them. The effect of this writing was seldom illuminating; the artists continued to depend, for serious criticism, on writing from the West.

Glasnost is in part about allowing what was hidden within the Soviet Union to come out, and in part about allowing what was kept out of the Soviet Union to come in. As members of the vanguard traveled West, artists from the West were for the first time shown in the U.S.S.R., and so experience of radical work from Europe and America ceased to be the luxury of only those hailed outside their own country. The Union of Artists was host to major shows of Günther Uecker, Robert Rauschenberg, Andrew Wyeth, and Francis Bacon, and was, in the summer of 1989, preparing to invite Jeff Koons and Gilbert and George. The selection was eclectic at best, incoherent, even, but it gave people in the U.S.S.R. an opportunity to see work that would otherwise have remained inaccessible to them. *10 + 10* also promised to bring American art to the U.S.S.R. when it began the second half of its tour. Donald Kuspit announced plans for a major exhibition of American artists in Moscow, to be negotiated through official channels.

But what was the world that Western artists and writers and cultural figures saw when they came to the Soviet Union? Though some went to the studios in Furmanny, and had a clear or muddled experience of life there, far more came to the U.S.S.R. under official circumstances and witnessed the official version of the country's cultural life.

Once, the distinction would have involved seeing different artists; by the summer of 1990 it had become more subtle but no less strong. Sven told me a joke one afternoon. A man comes to Moscow from the provinces, a naive fellow with shoddy clothes and an eager grin. To the first Muscovite he meets he says, "Excuse me, but can you tell me where I can find Principle?" And the Muscovite, being rude, as Muscovites are, glowers at him and walks away. All day he wanders through the city saying, "Excuse me, please, but where is Principle?" And all the people he asks mumble irritably or cross the street or ignore him. Finally, toward dusk, he approaches someone and says, "Perhaps you can tell me where I can find Principle?" The man looks at him, puzzled, and says, "What are you talking about? All day you have been wandering around Moscow, asking this question. What is it you want to find?" And the first man replies, "I have been told that in Principle there is fresh meat readily available for all the citizens of the Soviet Union, that in Principle you can buy fresh vegetables for very little money; that in Principle a ruble is as valuable as a dollar. And more: I have heard that in Principle there is justice for all men now in the Soviet Union, that in Principle life is much better than in the old U.S.S.R. So I am looking for Principle—it must be an amazing place."

The official visitors came to Moscow and saw Principle, and they never noticed how little it had to do with reality. State visitors to any country are shown that country in the most favorable possible light, but in the West, the favorable light does not throw long enough shadows to hide the customs of the country in question. There are too many ways of life in Moscow, and they stand at too great a distance from one another. Western visitors never noticed that they were living in Principle because it was easy for them not to notice, because the Western media had abandoned so very quickly the image of the U.S.S.R. as the dread nation of enemies and spies in favor of a picture of the U.S.S.R. as the land of ecstatic new freedoms. People came from the West for the excitement of those freedoms, and their self-satisfaction prevented them from seeing how different the country they were visiting was from the country they had imagined. The organizers of official or semiofficial shows usually imported groups of interested people from the West for the openings. Such events, staged with almost as much drama as the Sotheby's sale, took place in a similarly enclosed, artificial world. The British shows of Francis Bacon and Gilbert and George were negotiated by a rather pompous young man so preoccupied with his image as the London-Moscow connection as to be beyond noticing any of the ramifications of what he was doing. "Situation? What situation?" he asked when someone tried to discuss with him the difficulties faced by artists in Moscow. At a party I attended for a visiting Western artist, someone approached a high-ranking Soviet official to say how much he admired the change in the U.S.S.R. The man smiled and said, as though someone had admired his necktie, "Isn't it lovely about glasnost? Everybody seems to like it." And the gypsy music played on in the corner.

It was not that the government was trying to keep people from seeing the squalor in which artists lived, trying to suppress information about the unavailability of materials to non-Union members, trying to obscure the fact that the artists had lost their belief in a Soviet way of life without gaining faith in a Western way, trying to conceal the news that communicative language had been undermined by a year of travel that had proved to be as destructive as it was constructive. No one went to lengths to deny that the integrity of the artists had been compromised, that they were suffering in consequence, that the manic fever in Furmanny had a down as well as an up side. The problem was an inaccurate category-equation made by Western visitors and unchallenged by official Soviets. The international art world of the West is essentially an upper-middle-class phenomenon. Struggling artists in the West are not part of the New York–Cologne–Paris–London–Milan set until they capture its imagination and earn its often condescending patronage. Even artists whose work is about resisting these circumstances end up participating in them in positive or negative terms. Once they have done that, they exist in relation to a world of wealthy collectors, earnest dealers with enviably exciting life-styles, and economically restricted but intellectually engaged curators—a world of cocktail parties, receptions, openings, and high-paced dialogue. Some of the people throwing the parties and having the dialogues are nice people; some of them are self-involved and horrid. You have to be in with the right crowd to get an invitation; you have to be, at least in relative terms, self-assured and self-directed to be in with that crowd.

Though the members of the Soviet vanguard managed to enter that world with the ease of people to whom it made sense, it remains very different from anything in the U.S.S.R. The Soviet artists knew that; they could never forget it. But the people who were part of that world and who came to Moscow did not know that. People who should have been smart enough to know better mistook the relation between the official and unofficial worlds for a replica of the relation between the wealthy and the poor in the West. They thought that being driven in big Z.I.L. cars or eating in hard-currency restaurants in Moscow was like being driven in Mercedes limousines and eating haute cuisine in New York. The Western system is full of corruption and injustice, and each week's news seems to carry information about another disgrace; but the Western system was not born and structured out of the madness of Lenin, the evil of Stalin, and the selfish pomposity of Khrushchev and Brezhnev. Gorbachev is a great man whose interest in universal good has yet to filter down through the ranks of his subordinates, most of whom—because who else has the training to do the work?—entered politics, as he did, in the Brezhnev days. The people who have administrative posts in the Union of Artists and the Ministry of Culture are not, by and large, demonically evil, but they are people who willingly took part in a system that was unabashedly and cruelly unjust. The people who are living depressed lives in the U.S.S.R. are not people of limited education, limited ambition, or dangerously extreme social circumstances; they are people whose inability or unwillingness to take part in an oppressive system has excluded them from its privileges.

It is unfair that rich Americans have summer houses with air conditioning while poor ones broil in the heat. It is horrifying that some Americans have maids and chauffeurs while some are homeless. But though, in the West, the rich may oppress the poor by dint of irresponsibility, they do not oppress them as part of so carefully schematized a system of self-glorification at any cost as the one that held dominion in the U.S.S.R. for years and years. And though racial prejudice may more frequently have echoed the enormities of the Soviet system, there too, the conspiracy, though horrifying, was less public, less powerful, and less brutal. Being a guest at an official party in Moscow is a way of taking part in this Soviet system, and only the blindness of such guests kept them from understanding that.

In July 1989 I spent a lovely and yet disturbing time with an American performer about whom I had written an article for a British magazine some months earlier, and whose entourage I had met during my research. There is a romantic story of our day: I found myself on a wet morning in Moscow walking along the Prospekt Marksa, unshaven and a bit depressed. "What a pleasant surprise," came a pleasant voice, and I turned to see one of the publicity people I had

encountered in America looking pert and elegant and smiling a friend-
lier smile than I had seen in some weeks. "Come in, come in," she
said; and inside I discovered, installed in the grand suites of the
National Hotel, the entire crew of people I had met while I was
writing my piece: the performer, his family, his friends, his assistants,
his publicists, and an assortment of subsidiary figures—nurses, the
pilots who had flown the private jet, a crew of translators, and some
inscrutable domestic staff. They had brought with them a microwave
oven, enough basic food supplies to open a supermarket, American
toilet paper and Kleenex, French mineral water, and a host of other
civilizing supplies. Everyone was wearing clothing that made the
outfits at the previous year's Sotheby's sale look dowdy. There was a
grand piano in the suite, and more than a thousand roses were arranged on every available surface.

The star's first performance was a benefit for Mrs. Gorbachev's
Cultural Foundation; afterward, there was a reception with the Gorbachevs, at which KGB men stood around the periphery of the room
whispering into their shirt cuffs. The second concert was "for the
people," and was played to an audience of foreigners and well-
connected semidiplomatic figures interspersed with aggressive elderly
ladies, invited to give the whole thing the resonance of legitimacy.
In the Green Room, afterward, the performer made a brief speech,
charming, articulate, appropriate, and deeply warm; and then presented the proceeds of his performance to the hall where it had taken
place. We were once more taken out, this time with the highest
security of all, and hurried into the enormous black limousine that
waited for us below, a twin car to Gorbachev's. Back in the suite in
the National Hotel, we ate chocolates and caviar and drank local
champagne. People observed what a nice country it seemed to be. In
the street outside the hotel, a crowd cheered and cheered; periodically
someone would go onto the balcony and throw roses down to the
assembled admirers. Everyone drank and smelled the flowers, and
agreed that the Gorbachevs were just lovely. There was much talk of
forthcoming performances in Leningrad, in Kiev, wherever they
might brighten the lives of a wonderful people.

But there is also another version of our day. I knew that the car I
was getting into after that concert was a car that most of my Soviet
friends could never enter, even though they had had success and
money and fame abroad. I knew that I was going into a hotel they
would not be allowed to visit. Each of us was given a military escort

to leave the hall where the performance took place; I had four people arranged around me to form a quincunx, and we were marched through a crowd of people who had been unable to get tickets (because they were not on the appropriate lists) and who were near tears with the agony of their exclusion. Perhaps rock stars are accustomed to marching in such a way under such a guard under such circumstances, but rock stars can affect the stance of being self-created. Comfort and glory in Moscow are always tied to power, and power there too frequently leads to abuse of power. We were a phenomenon in Moscow that evening that no Soviet could have created of himself, except perhaps by giving way to something that, much too much of the time, was evil. And the Western people with whom I was marched through that throng were unable to see that. Such blindness is as terrible as it is common.

Perhaps that is what became most clear that summer: the West is badly equipped to appreciate what is genuinely best about the people who are genuinely best in the U.S.S.R. because in our rage to be positive we have become so eager to forgive what is worst there that we forgive it by pretending that it no longer exists, that it has not existed for some time, that it is a phenomenon of the remote past, something as dead as Stalin himself. If the Soviets are at their most powerful when they are nostalgic, visitors from the West—official and unofficial, cultural and political—seem to think they are doing the best thing when they obliterate memory itself. It is wrong to hold Gorbachev at arm's length; we should do more than we do to strengthen his cause, egged on by the knowledge of how dreadfully wrong things can be in the U.S.S.R., and by the awareness that in despair even this most astute champion of freedom might sacrifice honor for the sake of control. The mindlessness of people who go East only to confirm opinions garnered from the daily press is not only depressing, it is dangerous. If you look deep into the work of the Moscow vanguard, you will find that it is a warning, a sustained message in transparent code that says, simply, "Beware, and remember." In the summer of 1989, the members of the original vanguard found themselves surrounded by credulous Westerners and ambitious young painters. In the thin language of exhaustion and nostalgia, they continued to pipe their steady SOS to a world tuned to different channels. Beware, and remember. Beware, and remember. Did they play jokes as well? It was comical to see how soon people had ceased to beware, or to remember. And if they wouldn't do either, they might as well laugh; the artists, strong men and women, could laugh themselves since their caution and memory were so unlikely to make a difference. But—since they were Soviet—they continued, always, to hope.

Leningrad in the summer of 1989 was bleak, much bleaker than Moscow. The Moscow artists returned home to reestablish their individual and collective identities. The Leningrad artists returned home because their visas were running out in the West. The primary way that they enforced their own glamour on the people who had never left Leningrad was by complaining constantly about every conceivable detail of Leningrad life. Whereas the Moscow artists came back from the West full of stories and eager for their friends to experience the world they had seen, the Leningrad artists came back as though their sojourns had transformed them into members of a superior race for whom the habits of a lifetime were now an agony of tedium. They were moody, and they sulked, and they didn't socialize much. People drifted in and out of one another's studios and smoked hash and talked about things that had happened to them in the West, repeating every episode as though it were part of a sacral text that sustained their superiority.

Afrika set up a large studio and hired a crew of assistants, all of whom were amazed and fascinated by him; he treated them like hired help. He would have an idea and then set his assistants to work on it, and he paid them what was by his standards of tremendous wealth a very small sum indeed. Like a nineteenth-century landowner, he did nothing but think; at irregular times he would show up with a new roster of demands to be met. With Timur he would recall happy times in the West, but he was short with many of the artists, once friends, who had not left Leningrad during the winter; it was as though they were no longer interesting at any level, as though dialogue with them was a gross imposition on his time. Timur, meanwhile, withdrew more and more into his own hermetic world, surrounded by beautiful young boys and usually high as a kite. Occasionally, on a morning when the spirit grabbed him, he would create two dozen works to be shown in the West; and beaming with satisfaction he would sink back into the softness of the world he had found for himself, and eat the exotic fruits and vegetables his admirers had hunted down in the markets to bring to him.

GEORGIY GURYANOV: *Self-Portrait*

Georgiy Guryanov longed for Paris, where he had spent two magi-cal weeks. He was becoming more and more famous as the drummer for Kino; the band, no longer oppressed and no longer secret, had become the top group in the U.S.S.R. Georgiy was a popular hero, recognized from Tbilisi to Mongolia, but his band remained unknown in the West, and he was the first to admit that in a Western context it would have been altogether uninteresting. But what then? To pur-sue a career as an artist, doing powerfully beautiful work and cultivat-ing his own personal powerful beauty, to go sometimes back to Paris, or to New York, to try to launch a career there that might or might not be a success? Or to remain a figure hailed and recognized in the streets of his own country as a teen idol? There was no question of the music going abroad, and there was no question of the art making him famous at home unless it made him famous abroad first. It was grow-ing increasingly difficult to sustain both. Only when Viktor Tsoy, the lead musician in Kino, was killed tragically in a car accident a year later was the decision finally made.

I went to Leningrad only for a few days, toward the end of my time in the Soviet Union that summer. I came back on the overnight train with Georgiy; Afrika and some friends came back on another train, and we were all together in Moscow at Larisa's opening at First Gal-lery, and again when the *Isskunstvo* artists, German and Soviet, did their miniature installations at Furmanny. The opening at First Gal-lery was full of Westerners visiting for official purposes, considering the meaning of everything they saw, working out their lists for future exhibitions, and preparing the anecdotes they would tell about the real lives of artists in the U.S.S.R. The installations at Furmanny were like a meeting of the Club of Avant-Gardists, and the only Westerners were the *Isskunstvo* artists and me. At Furmanny, the Leningrad artists seemed like interlopers; their clothes, their hair, their manner, their conversation all seemed to be of another world. But at First Gallery these differences were moot, and you could have substituted any artist for any other artist, from Leningrad, from Moscow, from the older generation, from the younger; at such an event, they might as well have been various manifestations of a single person. And that, cer-tainly, was something to remember and beware.

CHAPTER V

Hither and Yon

I do not think that I will forget the seventh of November 1989. It was the national holiday of the Soviet Union, and I was in Moscow researching an article about architecture. I was rather pleased that my visit had coincided with the celebration of the Revolution, and I assumed that I would join with friends in an ironic visit to the parades and other festivities planned for the day; I imagined that we would chortle about officialdom, about the ten-story banners of Lenin that had appeared everywhere, about the flashing lights—like Christmas decorations in New York—that were on every lamppost in Moscow, in the shape of the hammer and sickle. I thought that such events were the lifeblood of the people I knew in the U.S.S.R.

Two days before, Kostya Zvezdochetov had told me that there would be a demonstration for democracy on the national holiday. He had said that it was an important event, and that I, as a Westerner, was more or less obliged to take part in it. "It will be good for you," he said, "to fight for democracy." We talked about going to it to-gether; Kostya maintained that he was still keen on demonstrations, that his time in the West had made him a champion demonstrator. I no longer pursued a policy of caution in Moscow, no longer worried, as I had on my first visits, about losing my visa; it seemed to me that the bureaucracy in the U.S.S.R. could not keep track of its hopes or its promises, and I was hard-pressed to imagine that it might concentrate its short supply of efficiency on me. I knew that at a pro-democracy demonstration two weeks earlier, there had been police violence. Kostya had been there, and he told me all about it. But I imagined I could avoid the violence, and I thought of the whole thing as an art experience, a solid grounding for the irony with which we might treat the parade.

In the end, nothing happened like that. When Kostya found out that the demonstration was at eight o'clock in the morning, his enthusiasm waned. "You know, we'd need to be at Pushkin Square at daybreak," he said. I must say that I was also not keen on the idea of rising at dawn; if I had pushed Kostya, he might well have agreed to go, but the general ennui had begun to get to me also. I too had had enough ironic engagements with real problems, enough art experiences of suffering. And perhaps, after all, it was not wise to risk losing my visa.

The morning of November seventh, Sergey Volkov called me. "I have not been to my dacha since the end of summer," he said. "Today I think I will go to Peredelkino. Maybe you will come also?" And so I found myself, on the national holiday, far from the demonstrations and parades, at the train station near Kievskaya. Of course the idea of escaping the city on holidays is a familiar one from the West; it has always been a luxury of the jaded to leave New York and avoid parades. When I met Sergey, I asked about the official festivities, but he said only that in Brezhnev's time it would have been worth a visit for their ironic value, that in Brezhnev's time he never missed them. "But now," he said, "the color has gone out of it." What use is it to be only halfway pompous? "Today's celebration is the little party in the time of funerals, maybe a wake for the death of communism."

The ride to Peredelkino is a typical train journey out of Moscow, through industrial wastelands, and then through forests of birches and forests of pines. We arrived at the station after mid-day. Sergey's dacha was in the village, and the village was like something from a childhood story: little tumbledown houses painted in bright colors and positioned more or less next to one another, with little wooden fences between them and birch trees growing here and there. It was less smart than Nikolina Gora—though "smart" is hardly the word to describe where our dacha that summer had been—but more charming. We walked along a narrow path, by the side of the tracks, and then we reached the dacha itself. From the next yard, an angry dog barked at us and tugged at her chain. We went in: there was a little porch, then a kitchen, and then a room with a bed, an old oil sketch of a hilly landscape, and a few shelves. Over the bed was an icon in a silver case. The paint was peeling from the walls, and the room was chilly, but it had a welcoming, homely aspect. At one end of the room was a CD player, and piled in old boxes in the corner were Sergey's CDs. "In Moscow, there is a big risk that these things get stolen," he said. He left me inside for a few minutes, and then came back with jam tarts baked by a woman in a nearby dacha, "who always bakes something for me when I come to visit." We had tried to buy bread, but had met with a not-unusual story for Moscow at that time —the bread in the station shop had been made perhaps a month earlier, had gone very stale, had been soaked overnight in water, and had then been allowed to dry in the sun, so that to the unknowing buyer it seemed fresh; in fact, it would have been rotten at the core, hard and lumpish and pasty. So the homemade jam tarts were a relief.

Sergey put on a CD of Maria Callas, and her voice soared through the room while we drank tea and ate the jam tarts and some walnuts left over from a previous visit. "I like the landscape painting. It makes more sense here than my art," Sergey said between arias. But on the closed porch his old paintings were piled beside a few new works, done in the dacha, where it was quiet. Afterward, we went for a long walk, down winding paths and among the birches that grew beside the railway line. Sergey pointed out a city on the horizon that had been built post-perestroika, an inexplicable agglomeration of tower blocks interrupting an otherwise unbroken stretch of green. "That was the most beautiful village of this area," he said. "They tore it down to build these new buildings, forty buildings, all identical, like those buildings in Moscow all so similar that you can't tell which one is yours unless you count." We talked about the national holiday, and about patriotism. "Of course I love this country very much," he said, "but it doesn't make sense for me to be here, or to be living here." Like a man past the first flush of post-adolescence, who had rejected his home and family, then rediscovered them, and then found that the happiness he felt back among them was retrospective and outside life's useful realities, Volkov turned wistful.

We talked instead about the West, about successful and unsuccessful exhibitions, about people who had turned out to be true friends and people whom one didn't quite trust. As we walked, the sun was going down and the wind was coming up; on the way out we were

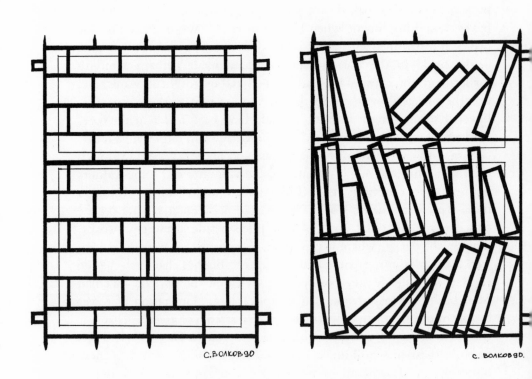

SERGEY VOLKOV: *Order and Chaos*

chilled from one side, and on the way back, chilled from the other. We scrabbled through a hidden tunnel under the railway line. It was an old joke that Lisa Schmitz turned everything around her into art. "We should make an installation with this," she would say about any street sign or plastic toy or funny-shaped rock that struck her fancy; or, "We should make a performance," about getting lost in the suburbs, or about dinner in a restaurant, or about a ride on a bus. And so with Sergey, discussing art while the wind turned around us and we sank into the mud, we joked about Lisa and wondered whether we were making a performance or not. Sergey had rented the dacha in Peredelkino every year since he first came to Moscow; this autumn the owner, who lived next door, had decided that he wanted to take it over himself. "Maybe the next time I come, it will be only to bring all my things back to Moscow. Maybe it is the last time in Peredelkino."

And so we went back to the dacha, had a last cup of tea and a few more walnuts, then locked the door, went past the dog barking on her long chain, and walked along the narrow lane back to the railway station. "Maybe it will be easier to take a cab to Moscow," said Sergey; but no cabs offered themselves, and so we climbed the platform to wait for the train. After a few minutes I heard a sound coming toward us, the familiar Soviet sound of a train that will not stop at the station where you are waiting, will not make the concession of slowing slightly as it passes, but will rather run by you at dizzying speed, creating a wind so strong that you will perhaps be knocked back against the wall behind you, at the far edge of the platform. This train came closer, and then with a dreadful sound it was in front of us, a train perhaps eighty cars long, each car a flat car, and on each one a military tank. They were the tanks that had been part of the traditional display for the seventh of November in Moscow; having had their moment of exhibition and glory in Red Square, they were now being taken back to wherever they were stored in the country.

It is more than disconcerting to stand on a train platform and see an unending stream of tanks whizzing past you. When they are all identical, when they go past at great speed, when it is that moment before nightfall on a gray day, when light is diffused and what you see is clear but black and white, then it is as though you are watching a film, in which the same image continually replaces itself. It is like watching one tank that will not move from its station in front of you. And when the image lingers, enormous and blurred, for more than a minute—since it takes some time for eighty cars to whiz past the platform at Peredelkino on a chill November evening—the tank becomes overwhelming, a universal tank. That day the tank was a reminder that this country in which love and friendship seemed to thrive was also the country that Western propaganda had time out of mind labeled the enemy, the country that had sent in tanks over and over and over again where liberty was coming into its own. This emblematic tank was an icon of Soviet prowess. Such as this had ended the Prague Spring, and had brought misery to the people of Afghanistan. This was the tank that shows up in American popular culture, in *Rambo* and in late night TV, the tank that sums up everything we fear in the strange world beyond our own experience. This tank was an emblem from earliest childhood for the evil force beyond our knowing.

As the train whizzed past, the single emblematic tank ceased to exist, and I saw instead a multitude of tanks. I have guessed that there were eighty of them, but it seemed like hundreds, like enough tanks for an entire army. I watched on and on, thinking that the train might never end; and then, four cars from the last, was a tank in all other regards like the rest, to whose projecting gun had been tied a green balloon on a long string. As I looked after the train, breathing the vacuum its passage had left behind, I saw that balloon, small, and beleaguered by the strong wind all around it, fluttering into the beginning of the night. It was the seventh of November, but it was also 1989, and power had become so confused with comedy that it was impossible to say where one ended and the other began. All we knew was that we were a little early for the train to Moscow, and that our day was like no other we had had or would have. Within minutes another train, our train, slow and mundane, came to the platform, and stopped, and Sergey and I sat in its harsh dim light and saw through a gap in the clouds how the moon was almost full, and talked about our time in Berlin when he came West for the first time, for the first part of *Isskunstvo*—not knowing that as we spoke other men were declaring elsewhere that the Wall would come down—and we talked about all the cities in which we might meet in the year to come, knowing how unlikely it was that we would ever find ourselves in Peredelkino again.

In the evening, Kostya and Larisa came to Sergey's Moscow flat, and we ate together. Larisa had just returned from Odessa, where she had been visiting her grandmother, who was ill and near death. Kostya was editing a magazine and was full of plans for it. I remember only that we spoke of friends, and that we had beef, rice, salad, and some good Rioja that Sergey and I had purchased from the National Hotel, and that everyone teased Larisa about her nationalistic enthusiasm for Odessa. Later, as we ate fresh fruit imported from China, we suddenly saw from the window the first burst of fireworks. Sergey pushed back the curtain, and as we continued to speak our faces were lit in pink, or in green, or in red. In this Technicolor, we remembered an older Moscow—so nostalgic already for the early days of our friendship, though I had known these people only a year and a half—in which fear had come more readily to hand, the Moscow in which the West had been an unknown and unknowable territory; and then the others remembered a much older Moscow, one I had never seen, the one in which they had met one another. Sergey took out a tape of Middle Russian Elevation, and played the first of their songs I had ever heard: "Gala goes away, Gala goes away, Gala forgets me. Fruit juice, water, beer, tobacco, *pelmeni.* Let me hide my face in your knees."

In the months that followed, everyone came West for exhibitions in Paris, Cologne, Berlin, Amsterdam, Australia, London, and New York. There were major group shows: in December, Margarita Tupitsyn's *Green Show* at Exit Art in New York; in February at the Centro Luigi Pecci in Prato, near Florence; and in April the third part of *Isskunstvo* in Stockholm. In May there was the Venice Biennale, and in June an enormous show, again curated by Margarita Tupitsyn among others, for the Goodwill Games in Tacoma. What was the feeling of all these meetings? It is hard, now, to remember how they began, but certainly by the time of the Prato show we had settled into the semidomestic routines of friends in perpetual transit. At each new place, I saw the Soviets, the critics from the West who were writing about Soviet art, and the dealers who were buying and selling that art. Like members of a bimonthly sewing circle, we greeted one another with affection and enthusiasm and discussed coming ventures. "Will you go to Washington for the Kabakov opening at the Hirshhorn?" someone would ask. "I feel as though I've been drenched in Kabakov these last few months," would come the reply. "But Stockholm I definitely want to catch. You'll be there?" "But of course."

The Soviets themselves were no longer foreign and alien; no longer did they require innumerable acts of cultural translation. When I arrived in Prato, it was Sergey Volkov who told me how to catch the bus back to Florence, where to get tickets for that bus, where to eat, and what the agenda was for the next few days. It was Kostya who said to me, "That woman, who you said was a curator, is actually a secretary." The Kopystyanskiys told me that they had found a new apartment in New York, and invited me to dinner when I next came through the city. Vadim Zakharov had befriended an Italian technician from the museum who spoke neither Russian nor English, and the artist was explaining his much-vaunted system with many hand-gestures and some laughter.

The opening of the Prato exhibition was on a Saturday. Curated by Claudia Jolles, it was in its way the best of that winter's group exhibitions in the West; if it was not entirely coherent, it was nonetheless a display of very good work by very good artists. Each was given a room: Bulatov, Volkov, Zakharov, Kabakov, Igor and Sveta Kopystyanskiy, Medgermenevtika, Pertsy, and Kostya Zvezdochetov. Volkov's installation—a set of metal open shelves with dozens of pickling jars of various sizes all filled with preserving solution and with the relics of a vanishing Soviet society: one full of busts of Lenin, another of *matreshka* dolls, another of half-burned candles from an Orthodox church—was a poignant tribute to the world they had all left behind, the world that was disappearing. It was probably the best new work there: some of the Prato pieces were old ones, Bulatov's paintings from Moscow days, New York paintings by the Kopystyanskiys. Kabakov's installation, in much the mode of previous ones, was dismissed by many of the younger artists as "museum art," a repetition of the "successes of Kabakov the Official Artist," but it was not without affect. Three days before the opening, Gorbachev announced that he would permit a multiparty system, and Kabakov repainted his room in a paler and more attractive gray, to make it less oppressive. This was a moving reminder to everyone that perestroika had not reached impasse, but it was also a strangely theatrical gesture from someone whose work had previously centered on a language above commentary.

In the course of the process of redefinition that was going on that spring, the artists of the older generation were often given short shrift by the younger. Bulatov was universally declared incapable of coming to terms with perestroika. Kabakov was accused of pandering to the West, and of repeating himself; he presented his usual impervious front in the face of these accusations, his regular mien of the man overwhelmed by all the attention, and unequal to all the demands. There is an old favorite story among the artists, told to me by Nikola Ovchinnikov, about Chagall. In 1918, Kazimir Malevich, who was running the artistic propaganda campaign for the new communist government, asked every local artistic committee to decorate prominent public spaces in celebration of the Revolution, which was then a year old. Marc Chagall was a great artist, and he was the chairman of the district committee for Vitebsk. He was sent an acreage of fabric and gallons of paint and told to cover the city with paintings. And so he created enormous paintings, and hung them, as he had been instructed, on the town hall of Vitebsk, and in the market squares. What did he paint? Did he paint the glories of communism, or reach toward constructivism? He did not. He painted flying cows and old Jewish men with violins and children flying before the moon. Malevich, saying that he was making fools of them all, sent Chagall to prison, but Anatoliy Lunacharskiy, head of Nakompros (the People's Commissariat for Public Enlightenment), wisely freed him, asking, "What else could he do?" The most radical young artists that winter said that Kabakov and Bulatov and Chuykov had betrayed their cause, but the more mature artists forgave them. And Kabakov, almost in spite of them, produced works that grew slowly but steadily more complex and more intelligently playful about his own situation, about the situation of the Soviet artist working for the West.

In fact, all the new work was clearly calculated in Western terms. It was not Western work per se, but it was finally tuned to internationalism. Sometimes with no explanation, sometimes with a little explanation, the intelligent audience from the West could say, "Right. I get it." And get it they did. It still had its secrets, but they were now the lightest of in-jokes. Robert Louis Stevenson once said of all literary works that "to the friends of the author, they seem like letters of affection, each page and each episode promising undying love or revealing unnurtured repose." If the works in Prato had secrets in them, they were such commonplace secrets as these.

At the opening in Prato, the first people I saw were the wives of the great originals standing and chatting: Vika Kabakova, Natasha Bulatova, and Nadya Burova (Dima Prigov's wife). Vika was wearing a leather skirt and a wonderful purple silk blouse; Natasha a black velvet dress with a lace collar, latter-day Laura Ashley; and Nadya a tweedy woolen suit and black pumps with grosgrain bows. They looked sophisticated, comfortable, and delighted to be all together at the same party, serene as they had perhaps looked when they met in the kitchens of their apartments in days gone by. Vika had come straight from Moscow; she said to me: "Two weeks ago, there was a big demonstration, five hundred thousand people marching against Pamyat (the Soviet fascist party) and against the communists and against oppression. They will not allow it to continue; it is the turning point; it is the end of our freedoms." Natasha said, "Two weeks ago, there was a big demonstration, five hundred thousand people marching against all the evil there has been in our country for these many years. It is the great turning point; it is the beginning of democracy for our people." And Nadya said, "You know that two weeks ago, there was a big demonstration, five hundred thousand people marching about all sorts of things all confused with one another, arguing in public the way they used to argue in private. Nothing changes, really, in our country. Democracy is still an idea, just as it always was, and we are no closer to it and no farther from it than we have ever been."

Three weeks earlier, I had been in Berlin, sitting with Larisa Zvezdochetova, when the news had come through that troops were entering Azerbaydzhan. "Oh, oh, oh!" Larisa had said with a theatrical flourish. "It's very bad news." I had mustered some arguments for and against the invasion, but she had shaken her head. "They will have to draft soldiers, and my husband!" she had exclaimed. "What will happen to my husband?" And once again I had remembered that this new life, on which these people had embarked with all the dignity of confidence, was as fragile as spun sugar. The greatest game anyone played was the one in which the old argument—there will be democracy, democracy will fail—was treated as though it were rhetorical. The secrets had gone; but to continue blithely producing art under these circumstances was an act as political as the production of unofficial art in the oppressive Brezhnev days. Sergey Volkov said, "Until now, even if we didn't like the future, we always knew what it was. We could do work which looked ahead toward the future because we understood that nothing ever changes, that life remains always essentially the same. But now we know that the future is an open terrain in which absolutely anything can happen. It makes things more difficult for us."

Kostya Zvezdochetov's installation in Prato included an army tent. Recalling how, when he was called to do his military service, he was put to work making propaganda posters and agitprop art, he placed the following words at the tent's entry flap:

Four years ago, I was taken very far east (I have never been farther east). I was surrounded by foreigners, and most of them were speaking in an incomprehensible language. I found it very uncomfortable and cold. I was homesick for Moscow, and longed for a cozy circle of friends, but it was precisely those friends who had gotten me to this remote place.

I was called into a room and was told: "A big day is ahead of us. This room has to be embellished. Write letters, glue photos, draw."

I started to do this day and night. I hardly ever went out. I was offered good food. Around me, everybody was doing hard physical labor; I was afraid that I would be sentenced to do the same if I couldn't manage.

But when the big day came, it became obvious that what I had done wasn't needed by anybody, that its only reason had been to perform a ritual.

Now I have been taken to the West (I have never been farther west), and again it is because of my friends. Around me is spoken a language I don't understand and it is cold.

Again I am told that it is a great day. There is a room, and I have to make something. I start to write letters, glue photos, draw. I do this day and night. I never go out. I am fed well. Again I am afraid of failing. Though I don't know why I am doing so, I repeat this ritual.

The most important thing is that nobody ask me to do difficult physical labor.

Once more there was a round of parties. The night of the opening, there was a gala dinner in a fifteenth-century villa whose walls were frescoed with flowers and vines and laughing putti. The food was "like for pigs," as Lyudmila Skripkina, of Pertsy, pointed out to our hosts (it was her first time in the West); but the setting was terrific. The following day, we were invited to the villa of a collector of Soviet and other art, Giuliano Gori, to see his famous collection. It was pouring rain, solid sheets of water that made driving a misery. After thirty minutes in damp Gori cars that smelled of dogs, we reached the great gates of the villa, which were opened by an old retainer; then we drove up a winding drive to the house itself, a palatial building perched at the top of a hill. Inside, we admired paintings by Picasso, Braque, Léger, and Chagall, all of which were hung in high-ceilinged rooms of astonishing grandeur. We were all cold and a bit wet, and the house, though grand, was as gray and stony and unwelcoming as any I have ever entered. We went upstairs, and walked through a warren of what must once have been servants' rooms, now all filled with quite fabulous installations by important contemporary artists. And then Signor Gori invited us into his famous sculpture garden. We looked at the rain, looked at one another, and went out into the wet for what we assumed would be a brief trot past a few major works. Nothing had prepared us for the pride that the Gori family take in their collection. For more than two hours we were led across fields and down hills to see astonishing and wonderful works which would no doubt have been the source of great delight on a sunny day. Nadya Burova was wearing elegant patent-leather shoes. Boris Groys was coming down with flu. We were sinking in mud. The path we were following was so labyrinthine that no one could go back to the house on his own. Repeated requests to return were met with a patient smile. "There's just one more work to see," Signor Gori would assure us.

Toward the end of the walk, we came to an ornamental lake. Signor Gori switched on the fountains, but the rain was so heavy that one could hardly tell whether they were working. Never in my life had I been so wet and so miserable. Signor Gori then uncovered a large rowboat. A "terrific piece" was apparently situated on an ornamental island in the middle of the ornamental lake. Erik Bulatov rowed; we all kept our umbrellas over our heads, though the wind was blowing the rain so hard that they were more useful as sails than as protection. It was, after all, February. We eventually reached the island and found that the installation was a Plexiglas wall that prevented us from disembarking. On it was inscribed a quotation from Nietzsche. We managed to retain our dignity, damp and muddy though we were, for the rowing back. And in the end no one minded the escapade very much—though almost everyone had a cold the following day—because we had by that time become so much aware of the process of manufacturing memories as we went along. If this liberal period was to end soon with the artists called to battle in Uzbekistan, such moments would at least remain vivid for them. If everything was to lead to fame and success, this would be a comical point of origin. Either way, it was worth having almost any experience in the name of mutuality. And whereas a year earlier, everyone would have had too much to drink and called attention to themselves, this year they felt no need to do that.

Thick and fast came the exhibitions after that. An Australian show of the original Furmanny artists provided "our best travel yet" according to Sergey Volkov, Sven Gundlakh, and the brothers Mironenko. Solo exhibitions of Vadim Zakharov and Viktor Skersis in Cologne, of Larisa Zvezdochetova in Berlin, of Nikola Ovchinnikov in Paris, of other artists in Italy, Germany, and New York were variously successful. Kabakov shows seemed to open every week, the installations following hot on one another's heels. Dima Prigov came to perform in the Brighton Jazz Festival. And in April, in Stockholm, there was the third part of *Isskunstvo,* called *Isskonstvo* (because the Swedish word for art is *konst*), including the original Germans and Soviets and a group of Swedish artists as well.

The Stockholm exhibition was excruciatingly badly organized. There were more visa difficulties for the Soviets, and so while Sergey Volkov, Sergey Vorontsov, and Ira Nakhova came within days of the Germans, Vadim Zakharov, Kostya, and Larisa arrived only a few days before the opening. The Kulturhuset, where the exhibition took place, is a capacious building near the center of Stockholm to which the city gives a substantial budget. It is run by the most polite group of women I have ever met, whose training had unfortunately failed to prepare them for the egotism and truculence of the Soviets and Germans. These women were significantly hampered by their inability to figure out what anyone wanted—"I thought this was a collaboration, and that you all loved one another," one of them complained at the end of a particularly trying afternoon—and by an incompetence that was almost a mode of performance. With the utmost grace and the purest intentions, they chose what can at best be called an uneven group of Swedish artists; they scheduled everything in the least convenient and most wasteful way; they gave the artists too little money to buy supplies but paid uncomplainingly the enormous telephone bills everyone ran up. They were defeated by the most simple questions. They didn't know where to buy paint, and they didn't know who might know. They didn't know how to get across town on the bus, or where you could get a cheap meal, or whether it would be a problem to plan large installations for the area ordinarily used by the Panorama Café on the top floor.

Everyone was lodged in a boardinghouse that belonged to a plump blond woman in her mid-fifties whose name itself became a watchword for terror among the artists. She was overbearingly maternal, unpleasantly strict, dishonest, greedy, and vindictive. She tried to pile as many people into each room as it would hold; we would leave in the morning, and return to find extra beds squeezed in where there had previously been chests of drawers or televisions, our luggage unpacked or repacked or moved, our foodstuffs confiscated. The establishment was decorated with kitschy posters of grinning models and luminous plastic decals of swans, and in one room someone had written all over the walls the word "confusion." It was sheer chaos.

The artists argued and argued and argued and argued. Much of their vitriol was turned against the Swedes, who seemed to have no clear idea of what a collaboration was or of why anybody would want to be involved in one; but in fact, the relationships among the German and Soviet artists were already so well-established that for a third group to join them at an equal level would have been virtually impossible. "Within our group," Lisa Schmitz explained to the puzzled Swedes, "we can insult one another with love." But the love was sometimes patchy. The Soviets boasted a lot. "Don't they realize that the reason they're showing in the Biennale and in all these expensive galleries is not that they're the world's greatest artists, but because they're Soviets, and it's the thing right now to show Soviets?" asked one of the Germans. Of course they knew that. It was the thing that terrified them most. On the other hand, there were a lot of artists in the U.S.S.R., and not all of them were reaching these pinnacles. How good were they? They didn't even want to think about it, and their boasting was the outpouring of their egotism and terror.

The Germans, because they arrived in Stockholm before the Soviets, were able to reserve for themselves many of the most dramatic spaces in the exhibition hall, and the Soviets were understandably annoyed; they accused the Germans of battling for territory "exactly as you did in the last war." The German work was consistent with previous German work, and hence, in the eyes of the Soviets, amusing but not very meaningful; the Soviet work was very uneven. Nikita Alexeev did the best installation, which included hundreds of drawings of a broad range of subjects: a blade of grass, a lightbulb, a crescent moon, a prostitute carrying the Romanian flag. Under each one he wrote: "God can be like this, #306," or "God can be like this, #12," or "God can be like this, #122." There is a government monopoly on alcoholic beverages in Sweden, which makes them incredibly expensive. Each artist had been given a budget for supplies for his installation, and Nikita, whose work consisted mostly of pencil drawings, had come in well under budget. He told the directors of the Kulturhuset that to complete his concept he needed three bottles of Scotch, preferably Johnny Walker Red. There was much discussion about getting empty bottles and filling them with tea; Nikita explained in solemn tones that this would not be adequate because it would undermine the integrity of the installation. When he at last got his way, we drank the Scotch; he refilled the bottles with tea; he bound the lids on them with bright green tape; and then he spent hours discussing with everyone ways to meet the greatest artistic challenge he had known so far: how to incorporate these bottles into the installation.

When we talked about the work, Nikita told me that he is a pessimist redeemed by faith. His work fights against both good and evil, but it is not aimed toward neutrality; with all the dignity of one of the horsemen of the Apocalypse, he rides toward the equalization of all things, which is also, in the end, their glorification. No Nietzschean, he; he is not able to imagine a point beyond good and evil, except in the end of the simple truths that are given voice in words and images. With considered distaste for the Stalinistic fallacy of labeling everything in black and white (he who is not with the Revolution is against the Revolution; he who is not with the Party is against the Party; he who is not with me is against me), Nikita hopes that by trying to determine the truth in more abstract terms and to give voice to it, he will in part redeem himself. So it will be that when he stands before the majesty of deity, he will be able to say, "Yes, I have murdered my brother and had incestuous relations with my sister; but not without reasons. No, I have not been a good artist; but I have made manifest those reasons. For this, and for my honesty, I beg your mercy."

Kostya and Larisa Zvezdochetov did sharp and somewhat comical installations; his was called *Sweet Azerbaydzhantsies* and was crudely constructed with lumps of wood, pieces of old clothing, and oversized nails; hers was called *Borscht and Space* and was a peasant-type altar (in the mode of Kostya) on which there was a typical Soviet electric burner boiling a pot of red paint and garlic which gave the entire exhibition an odor I will remember to my dying day. Ira Nakhova did a subtle and witty installation of camp beds in a black room, each painted with a classical figure, fragments of classical sculpture in a chamber pot beneath one of them. Sergey Volkov did a very well-conceived

installation in which images of a *matreshka* doll running along two
walls were hung at skewed angles to one another; but he had begun
by using Swedish paint with an inadequate siccative, and when it
became clear that the paint would not dry, he was obliged to repaint
the images without his usual thick impasto. The results were unim-
pressive; *Isskonstvo* is the only exhibition at which I have ever seen
work by Volkov that was not technically perfect, and he minded its
imperfection. Sergey Vorontsov did mannerist icons. Sven Gundlakh
and Nikola Ovchinnikov treated the exhibition as a bit of a joke, and
did sloppy, indifferent work there.

Vadim Zakharov did one of what he called the "marginal reflec-
tions" on his system. Zakharov and Volkov are always held up as the
two artists who have managed to do their work in wholly acceptable
Western terms. Volkov's work is simply addressed to a broad audience; Zakharov's work is as hermetic as it has always been, but it is
hermetic in terms which he sincerely invites the West to penetrate.
His work deals with his obsessive position as an artist perpetually
changing and refining a visual system in which characters/ideas in
rigorously defined relation to one another generate patterns by virtue
of their alternating areas of overlap and disjunction. For many years it
was his goal to establish the system itself, and he did this by taking
fragments from each work to use as the basis for new works, so that
what was structurally necessary but marginal in one piece became the
center of another, that center generating further systems of support.
So a painting of an elephant and a one-eyed man might give way to a
painting built around the elephant's trunk or the man's lost eye; and
those in turn might generate paintings in which these shapes become
abstracts rather than natural objects. By the time of the Sotheby's sale,
Zakharov had established the system itself; his work since then has
consisted in putting together the marginalia of the system, structured
in logical concentric circles around it, like Talmudic commentaries
around a single line of text. These margins bring back to life the
projects of the past, and by remaining outside the system itself, give
it new coherence.

The artists spent a certain amount of time enjoying one another's
company, planning how *Isskunstvo* might continue on into the indefi-
nite future, how it might be each year in a new country, until by the
time of *Isskunstvo*, Part Fifty, they would be leaders of an international
movement of communication. Ira Nakhova said that for the sake of
the continuation of *Isskunstvo* it would be necessary for everyone to

marry within the project, to be fruitful and multiply and produce the children of *Isskunstvo,* who would grow up knowing the circle of artists and realize their dream. Nikola Ovchinnikov came up with the slogan for the project: "Make love, not art."

But despite the rollicking and fun, the artists were exhausted. There is nothing so tiring as the realization that you do not live anywhere. Nothing is so taxing as the perpetual internationalism that makes all places interesting and none comfortable or satisfactory, the constant travel that means your time in each place is occupied primarily with arranging for your residence in the next. Nikola had just finished six months in Paris, and was talking about spending six more months there the following year. When I asked, "Is it in Paris that you live, or in Moscow?" he said mournfully, "If I only knew!" And the ambivalence showed in his work: Nikola Ovchinnikov, whose subject had always been the ironical treatment of Russian (not Soviet) sentimentality, the exploitation of the inflated symbolism of the birch tree and the winter landscape, had lost hold of his irony, subscribed to the very symbols he had previously desecrated, and was turning to a kind of delicate lyricism. Though his work in Stockholm was undistinguished, his catalogue from Paris showed a painting of a nineteenth-century peasant farm woman gazing at the infinite regress of her own image repeated and repeated and repeated, a Soviet equivalent of *Christina's World* in which Christina sees herself disappearing into the horizon.

Nikita Alexeev said, "I don't think the possibility of bringing Western money to the U.S.S.R. and eating well every day justifies or tranquilizes this tension of placelessness. I think that Moscow artists will have to make a choice, because I don't think it is possible to live as they are living for a long time. You see how much it is taking out of them already." But when I asked Sven Gundlakh whether he could imagine living in the West permanently, he said, "It's impossible for me. Here I would never have enough money to live well. But with my travels, I know I can live very well in the Soviet Union. It's dangerous, and life is strange there, but when I bring 10,000 deutschemarks to Moscow, this money allows me to live like the tsar." That was also untrue. The money he earns allows Sven to live much better than his neighbors, to live at the very top by Moscow standards. But it is only in contrast that he lives well. In the West, he could, with the income he could earn, eat well and have decent clothes and enough space to live, but by the standards of the West, he would be at the lower end of middle income, and so though the life would be better, he would not have the pride he achieves in Moscow. Where had this competitiveness come from, competitiveness about having things? How could it have come to exist so strongly in someone who threw away the life of received Soviet society for his urgent beliefs?

Sven's work was becoming less and less interesting. Sven is not an artist, insofar as an artist is a creator of solid and palpable tl.ings. He is an extraordinary journalist, an organizer, a commentator, a sort of inspired impressario who was pushed by perestroika into the production of artworks. Of course he was honest enough, and clever enough, to understand that he was incapable of producing self-sufficient works. For all those years of pre-Gorbachev history, with the Mukhomors and beyond, Sven generated ideas of his own and worked with people to make those ideas and their ideas more clear. His ideas were brilliant, the work of a real genius; but he knew that he was not competent to realize them, and he didn't try to do so. In the West, you do not get paid for inspiring the people around you, for changing the world by virtue of your ability to give urgency to other people's activity. You get paid for the things you make. What was Sven to do in the face of perestroika but keep his ideas to himself, and realize them in comical, sloppy, inadequate ways? And so though Sven and Sergey Volkov were both men of intelligence and integrity, Volkov was able to triumph in the West as he had never triumphed before, and Sven in some senses could only flounder there. He said one day in Stockholm, after Sergey had scraped the undried paint from his canvas and started to redo his work using flatter brushwork, "You should sell your thick-paint technique. You should offer it up for auction; there would, surely, be dozens of young Soviet artists willing to buy it. It's one of the great landmarks of the New Soviet Art." What had Sven to auction off? One day he said, "I am tired of this life. I need a change. I think I would like to be a girl of sixteen living in the country." I said, "And what would you do as a girl of sixteen?" And Sven replied, "I would stay that way for two years, and then I would write a book about it."

The artists became tired, failed to show up for exhibitions, slept for more and more of the day. They were no longer being rude or difficult as a defensive performance; they were simply worn out and tired of never being able to depend on anything. Mrs. Gorbachev's Cultural Foundation had announced a month earlier a joint project with the

Ministry of Culture to build a Museum of Modern Art in Moscow. They chose as a site a palace on the outskirts of town that was begun in the eighteenth century but never completed. "I think," Nikola said to me, "that this palace, which has not been completed in two hundred years, is not likely to be completed this year, or next year, or the year after that; its unfinished state is a tradition in Moscow. As for the people who are organizing it—they are this funny species, the new official people who have been given official positions since glasnost and perestroika, and who are about as official as I am. They are full of ideas, but nothing ever gets done just because they say it should be done." Nikita interrupted, "The problem is that there are now so many mafias in Moscow, so many people trumpeting themselves as artists, people who were in the Union of Artists, people who were not in the Union, people from small towns and cities, people from the center. If you put in one painting by each one, you will have nothing but confusion; but no one knows how to make the selection, and no one has any idea what the process of selecting would mean. It's a hopeless idea."

And yet, if everything was truly so desperate, then what were the artists doing in Stockholm at all? And why had they made works for *Isskonstvo,* and for Prato, and for all the other exhibitions? It was in part a matter of promises made that needed to be kept, but there was something more fundamental than that. This tentative mood, in which everyone articulated his pessimism and acted on optimism, was another kind of testimony to the need among these people to hope. They had never done anything but hope and laugh at the absurdity of their own hopes. What they had always hoped, and continued to hope, was that if they acted in good faith, despite their beliefs, then perhaps that faith would, in the end, be warranted.

What of Leningrad in this time of back and forth? "Moscow is a city in the mountains, and so the Moscow artists are organized like a pyramid," Andrey Khlobystin said. "Kabakov and Bulatov are on the top, and the young artists can enter this structure only at the lowest level; if you try to be an artist off the pyramid, you are nothing. But Leningrad is a very low city, with a lot of water, and everyone lives at the same level." So it was that every month brought a few new Leningrad artists, some of them very talented, others merely enthusiastic. While the vision of the Moscow artists was being compromised by the broadening of their vista, the same process was expanding the vision of Leningrad artists. The two types of art moved closer and closer together until, pyramid or no pyramid, they were often difficult to distinguish. Because the Leningrad artists had always made things, their work underwent very little transformation. "People see my work, and they think I am a Moscow artist," Afrika told me with a grin. "I think we are working toward the same tradition, the Moscow artists and I." Afrika began in late 1989 a series of collaborations with Sergey Anufriev. The two became obsessed with one another: Afrika represented effortless glittering success to Anufriev, and to Afrika, Anufriev was part of the exclusive Moscow intellectual tradition, the only one who seemed genuinely not to care about anything but his own contentment. His charm and his selfishness fascinated Afrika, and Afrika's ability to get what he wanted for himself fascinated Anufriev. They dedicated their pictures to one another, painted portraits of one another, collaborated on work. Afrika's studio approached the scale of van Dyck's, and was full of assistants who executed the ideas he and Anufriev devised.

Timur Novikov worked more quietly and explored the Western attitude toward his homosexuality; his interest in exhibitions waned. He spread the good word of gay liberation among Leningrad friends, and helped them to get to the West. A gay rights organization with which he and several other artists were loosely affiliated was formed to challenge the law against homosexuality, and, though the law remained on the books, their group was permitted to register officially. In the autumn of 1990, its members stood outside the Communist Party Conference and distributed condoms (of which there is a perennial shortage in Moscow) to the Party members as they emerged from the Kremlin. The first delegates took, modestly, one or two; but soon decorum gave way, and many paused to stuff their pockets with the precious things. When the gay activists were asked why they were giving condoms to these men, they said that they hoped to discourage Party members from reproducing.

Like the Moscow artists, though, Timur was very tired. There was no shortage of others to fill in for his exhaustion. Irina Kuksinite, Afrika's beautiful wife, took up artwork and graphics, became involved in feminist and lesbian exhibitions, and, in between, was photographed for American *Vogue*. Other women followed suit, and exhibitions took place in rapid succession of bold, brash work by

IRINA KUKSINITE: *Untitled*

proud, beautiful women, feminists and lesbians liberating themselves from the clichéd Soviet idea of the woman as a shapeless workhorse in a headscarf. Other priorities of the Leningrad artists were also shifting; Andrey Khlobystin, who had been deemed a bit humorless and much too intellectual a few years earlier, had become the critical spokesman for Leningrad. Both his writing and his painting were extremely well received, and the other artists found, to their suprise, that they had come to depend on him.

The high point of early 1990 was, surprisingly enough, an exhibition in Leningrad at the Russian Museum. It was curated by Yevgeniya N. Petrovna and Pontus Hulten. The show included work by Western and Soviet artists, but Hulten apparently missed Moscow on his tours of the U.S.S.R., so the sole Soviet representatives were the New Artists. Alongside work by Joseph Beuys, Daniel Buren, Hans Haacke, and Marcel Broodthaers hung a large collage by Timur Novikov in which he had constructed the New York skyline out of all the invitations to gay clubs he had received during a visit to America. This piece was bought by the Russian Museum. So officialdom had gone from the disapprobation of decades to the neutrality of a year to real support: at a time when no major Soviet museum had bought a work by any member of the underground, this piece—as decadent as Stalin's nightmares—was taken into the most jewel-like collection of them all.

The artists from Leningrad spent most of the year in Paul Judelson's house in New York, which was like an endless salon; artists and critics who happened to find themselves in the city would drop by for a cup of tea or a glass of wine and a chat. It was the good life at Paul's house, with a pretty roof terrace on which the visitors and the hosts could sunbathe while they considered which openings to visit and which to skip. Afrika bought one of Tchaikovsky's last letters with the proceeds from an exhibition; after you had seen his new work, and the new work of other Leningrad painters, you could look at the aged splendor of the letter itself, a piece of Russian history in Soviet hands. Paul Judelson's relative lack of sophistication as a dealer troubled no one. "The final verdict on the shows in the West, what everyone talks about on the way back home, is who sells the pictures, for how much, and where, and who bought them, and why they bought them," said Afrika. "So Paul is doing pretty well by me. It's enough that he's selling all the pictures that I bring here to good collectors. It doesn't matter whether we're in a third-floor apartment or in a gallery on the first floor."

The Leningrad artists became more and more obsessed with the idea of their freedom, and Paul's apartment was a symbol of that freedom. "I can understand Sergey Volkov very well, and it is very important that there are people like him," Afrika said to me one afternoon. "Maybe there are ten thousand people in the world with great collections, and maybe he can be in all of them. But we just want to have a great time in New York with our friends or in Leningrad with Anufriev. It's a short life, and you have to enjoy it. The important thing is not to be a slave your whole life." Though Afrika was never a slave, he was also never more than half present in his experiences of freedom. He had a take and an angle on everything. "When I came to New York this time," he told me on one occasion, "I was stopped at the border and grilled by your American customs agents for carrying hundreds of kilograms of art. I am a Soviet agent in America; in the

Soviet Union I am an American agent; in Finland I am a British agent; in Britain I am a Finnish agent. It's very easy for me to live here, and I understand this system completely; but when I am here, I don't have any feelings. In the Soviet Union you feel so much but you understand and can control so little, and so your feelings are no use at all. In the West you can understand everything around you, and you can get control whenever you need to control, but for the first time I don't have feelings about what I understand. For me, it's a little sad, but I am becoming used to it."

It had become clear by then that many artists were unable to "get used to it." It had become necessary by then to define a relationship between the artist and the work of art in the context of cultural neutrality in which everyone was living. No one cared by then what was secret and what was spoken. Urgent beliefs became moot. At what level can a work of art serve a high moral purpose in a complacently capitalist world? We all know that art can be angry, or intensely political; but how to invest it with truth? What was terrible about the Soviet artists' lives was no longer terrible enough to pass for a kind of profundity. Nikita Alexeev said, "The problem with our art history is that we have been preparing ourselves to be not great artists, but angels. We have been outside the ordinary idiom of art. And unfortunately, things have changed so that everyone has become an artist. Some have become, as Kabakov has, well-known international artists. Some have become, as I have, unknown artists in Paris. And some, like Sven, are traveling artists. But we all have to face problems which are strange for us. It was religious history, and now it's art history. And that's why there is all this confusion." The first time I met Vadim Zakharov, the week of the Sotheby's sale, he had quoted Dostoevsky to me: "Beauty, though, will save the world." I had looked at his gray paintings of fragments of elephants and one-eyed men and thought: what beauty? It was only later, much later, that I realized he had been speaking about the parareligious function of his art, in which beauty is the thing that comes closest to truth, truth a thing we know through beauty. In these terms, beauty has no point of contact with attractiveness.

The Venice Biennale, just a few weeks after Stockholm, was as much of an apotheosis as the artists were going to get. The Biennale is glamorous, a perfect event in its way, the best the international art world has to offer. The parties are beautiful; the art is beautiful; even the orchestra at Florian is beautiful. Venice in springtime is like a song of the heart, and there is so much art that you cannot hope to see it all, and in consequence do not try to see it all. At the 1990 Biennale, in addition to the Aperto and the pavilions themselves, there was an exhibition of Mondrian and Der Stijl near San Giorgio Maggiore, and one of Fluxus on the Giudecca, a Warhol retrospective at the Palazzo Grassi, a series of installations by Mimmo Rotella at Florian, a show of modern Flemish art, one of some young American sculptors, one called Homage to Chilida, and dozens of smaller exhibits and performances in galleries and in public places. Weddings, deaths, and the Biennale bring together entire webs of people ordinarily separated by geography and the other exigencies of their lives, people who defer to the solemnity of the occasion of their meeting but who nonetheless experience the anxious joy of the reunion itself with a kind of fullness that the complex ritual in which they are caught only magnifies.

The Soviets in Venice were in a strange situation; if they were at some level declaring their arrival at the international level, they were also having an unsought journey into the nostalgic region of their past. If they had spent years denying the accusation that they were the new official artists, they were now obliged to admit that they were, for better or for worse, exactly that. They were treated like the old official artists in more ways than one: the Soviet government transported their work and threw parties in their honor, but also watched their every move and regulated their activities. It was a splendid and strange time for the artists in the Soviet pavilion; and it was also a strange time for the other Soviets who came, those not in the pavilion. The structure of the Biennale is that each participating country has a pavilion, a building in the Giardini, which includes work chosen by the appropriate authorities in that country. In a vast nearby building is the Aperto, a display of work by artists from many countries that is selected by an independent international board of curators who have nothing to do with the authorities in the artists' own countries. The Aperto work is often by younger, less well known, and more radical artists; the pavilions usually have artists whose accomplishments reflect well on the countries from which they have come.

The Zvezdochetovs and Nikola Ovchinnikov were included in the Aperto. Nikolay Kozlov, Tolik Zhuravlev, Masha Serebryakova, Olga

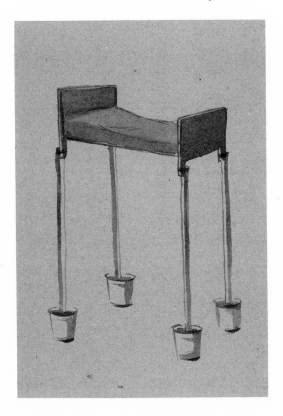

MARIYA (MASHA) SEREBRYAKOVA: *Untitled*

Royter (Andrey's wife), Tanya Saltsirn (who had organized the Champions exhibition in Moscow the previous summer), Aleksey Shulgin, and several other young artists were all in Venice more or less for the hell of it, most of them brought by dealers who were coming to the Biennale anyway and thought they should see it. Boris and Natasha Groys were there, and so were dozens of other people who had been involved in Soviet art directly or peripherally: such dealers as Ronald Feldman and Thomas Krings-Ernst; curators from the Centro Luigi Pecci in Prato and from the Kulturhuset; Western artists who had been in 10 + 10. The Soviet pavilion included work by Aydan and Yevgeniy Mitta and Aleksandr Yakut, her two partners from First Gallery, by Sergey Volkov, and by two of the Champions of the World, Andrey Yakhnin and Giya Abramishvili.

The story of the Soviet pavilion was deeply tangled. The first problem had been the selection of a suitable figure to choose the artists to be included. The commissioner for the pavilion (who administers it and takes, in principle, the curatorial role) was a man who had been in the position for years, a typical complacent bureaucrat fond of his life in Venice and anxious not to unsettle it. The invitation to choose the artists went, as always, to the Ministry of Culture and to the Union of Artists. What happened at that stage remains unclear; someone realized that the U.S.S.R. would make itself ridiculous if it chose any of the Union bigwigs who had traditionally been sent to the Biennale for a nice week in Venice, and accepted that unofficial artists would have to be chosen.

This in itself was a big thing. Since the time when Sotheby's and the curators of 10 + 10 had battled to show unofficial artists within the constraints of the official system, much progress had been made in the display of unofficial art in the West; the export of work and of artists had in some ways been facilitated; and it had been possible for the unofficial artists to show their work in Moscow in their own spaces. But the Union had toed its party line unfailingly, and it had never chosen any but its own hardliners for an official function. It was almost impossible to imagine that it could take the Biennale, the ultimate of all its sugarplums, and give it to someone from without. At the same time, it was inconceivable to do otherwise. Tair Salakhov, the Union's leader, was facing waves of racism from official artists, some of whom said that they, as Russians, refused to be led by an Azerbaydzhantsy, even one who had lived almost his entire life in Moscow and spoke flawless Russian. Salakhov's situation was delicate, and he knew that he could not choose the artists for the pavilion himself without incurring the wrath of the Union members he excluded and the condescension of the unofficial artists, who had made no secret of their disdain for him. But whom then to ask? The British artist was chosen by the British Council, the American by the National Endowment for the Arts. This was a decision made everywhere by official bodies like the one of which Salakhov was at the helm.

In the event, Salakhov's daughter, Aydan, emerged as curator of the exhibition. She continued to maintain that she had no connection to her father, that she had severed all ties. Maybe the settlement was only a business arrangement; all that anyone was told was that Aydan was choosing the artists for the Biennale. The news came through during the summer, and all summer Aydan chose and changed her mind and chose again and changed her mind again, so that every week someone else was given to believe that he would be in the Biennale.

Dozens of artists had a week of thinking they were the chosen before Aydan changed her mind again. At the time, this seemed like whimsy, but it is difficult to tell in retrospect how much control she really had of the situation, whether she was playing games or whether games were being played with her. It is likely that both things were going on, but it is impossible to know in what proportion.

Be that as it may, Aydan announced at some point in the late autumn that she had decided, after much consideration, to put her own work in the Soviet pavilion at the Biennale. No one knew what to say or think of this; Aydan had done a fine job with her gallery all along, but she was not at that time a good artist (though her work improved dramatically in the months that followed), and could only make herself ridiculous with such an agenda. She subsequently said that she would share the pavilion with her two business partners at the gallery, Yevgeniy Mitta (whose work is very graphic, very slick) and Aleksandr Yakut, and, as if it were the sugar to help the medicine go down, with Sergey Volkov. There was a lot of laughter at the time. "You know with whom Sergey now exhibits?" more than one artist asked me. "I think only in our country can the curator display her own works."

That Aydan was not entirely in control became apparent very soon after this. The decision was taken (by whom remains unclear) to re-create for the Biennale the theme of one of Aydan's first exhibitions at First Gallery, "Rauschenberg to Us, We to Rauschenberg." Robert Rauschenberg, as part of his continuing project to take his work to every corner of the globe, had gone to Moscow, and done a painting for the Soviets that Aydan had shown at First Gallery with responses to it by Soviet artists. It was a very strong show for Moscow, and the public thronged to see the Rauschenberg, which was partially explicated by the Soviet work around it. It functioned a little bit like a small-scale version of *Isskunstvo*.

It was a good idea for Moscow, but a ridiculous one for Venice. Rauschenberg did indeed do a painting, which was hung in the Soviet pavilion. It was the first time that a work had been in any pavilion by an artist from another nation. Around it were works many of which had absolutely nothing to do with it. Aydan had not been permitted to re-create her original show; furthermore, she had not been able to choose the new works. The worst difficulty was that the Ministry of Culture, panicked by the sense that it was losing control, announced a few months before the exhibition that the pavilion could include

1991

YEVGENIY MITTA: *1991*

only work then in the U.S.S.R. For Sergey Volkov, who had planned a site-specific installation, this meant that only some paintings left from the Moscow leg of *Isskunstvo* could be included. Of course no one's best work was sitting in Moscow; the proviso ensured that the exhibition was undistinguished. The Ministry further stated that they would transport the work in both directions, and that work included could be re-exported only if it were granted export licenses. "It's the new Ministry power principle, the principle by which the less power they have, the more they make you feel it," Volkov said.

So the pavilion in the end included second-string works by one good artist, a few acceptable artists, and a few quite bad artists, hung in conjunction with a Rauschenberg that had very little connection to them. Certainly better than the tired official art of previous years, it was still a mess. What was most peculiar was that the artists were treated in Venice as they had not been treated since the dawn of perestroika. They were shadowed by KGB officials—dressed up in the most imbecile way, like spies in films—and they were plagued with little difficulties and inconveniences thrown up by these men, who were nearly but not entirely stripped of power. "The same KGB guy who once withheld permission to travel and took away my apartment is now withholding my invitation to the reception at the Guggenheim collection and refusing to pay my hotel bill," Volkov said. I found it very odd to see these men at every event we visited. At the Guggenheim reception itself, Volkov and I stood looking out at the Grand Canal and drinking sugary bellinis, while, about ten feet away, a portly man in dark glasses and a lumpy yellow linen jacket talked to a svelte blond and kept an eye on us. Even in Moscow I had encountered very little of this kind of surveillance, and in Venice I found it not only disturbing, but also inexplicable. The KGB seems to me to have two missions: to get information, and to curtail the activities of those whom it surveils. There was no information they could have obtained from Sergey Volkov that he was not willing to share publicly: his politics and ambitions were all stated often and frankly. And there was nothing he might wish to do that they could prevent him from doing or had reason to prevent him from doing. The KGB had already announced to the artists that they would not pay their hotel bills, and they had omitted to book rooms for the overcrowded event, so that Aydan paid for a room in a pensione, one of the only ones available at short notice, with her ample Western currency, and everyone piled into it, sleeping several to a bed.

Still, everyone had fun in Venice. The parties were amazing and various, and there was lots of food and drink. The scene late at night at Florian was a festive one. Everyone went exploring, and everyone knew in advance which events to go to, which to avoid. At the British Council opening in the Palazzo Pisani Moretta—surely the most spectacular of the parties—we talked about being competitive, and agreed that there was not much point. Two days later was the official opening of the Biennale, and the Soviet pavilion won a prize. Was the award a considered political gesture on the part of the jury, an accolade to the East for managing to break out of the strictures of officialdom? Or was it a tribute to the apparent internationalism of the misplaced and unremarkable Rauschenberg? Or did they simply like Aydan's brushwork? We were never to know.

Afterward, we had lunch in a café near the Arsenale. "I want to win—not a prize, not against anyone, but in the purest possible terms," Kostya said to me. His work at the Aperto had been displayed in partial condition because the live dogs he had wanted to use were prohibited by the Italian equivalent of the ASPCA, while the sabers he had intended to incorporate were prohibited by an arms-control group. "At first, I thought I could bring the West around to an understanding of the Soviet way. Now I see that I must put the Soviet mentality in terms of the Western aesthetic. The Christians won because they combined the Word of Judaism with the ritual of Paganism. I will win when I can combine the truth of the Soviet mentality with the comfort of the Western aesthetic. Coming here has made me see that."

That, then, was the truth of the Biennale, and though more exhibitions were being planned and realized immediately afterward, Kostya's insight was perhaps the only thing left for the artists to understand. It is the truth he spoke that makes the Biennale as fitting an exhibition as any to conclude this book. The reconciliation of meaning and rhetoric is the usual aim of art; in Venice, the dynamic of that reconciliation was finally defined not as the readjustment of the truth, nor as the readjustment of the perception of that truth, but as the readjustment of its communication. Of course what the Soviet artists knew and understood could not be changed: the truth is not singular, but its core is singular for each person who believes that he knows it. The failed and naive gestures of secret communication, encoded meaning, and intentional evasion were finally irrelevant, games that had been played when they were needed and that could at best be dropped. You protect the truth by shouting it from the rooftops; and if circumstances make it unwise or impossible to visit the rooftops, then you wait, protecting the truth, until the rooftops are opened to you again.

These men and women have continued to resist the closing of the rooftops. In August 1990, members of the Soviet mafia came to the apartment in Moscow where many artists had gone after the destruction of Furmanny. They came with automatics, held Kostya, Sergey Mironenko, Giya Abramishvili, and Boris Matrosov at gunpoint, and demanded that they give them paintings, on grounds that "this is the only way left to us to get hard currency." The mafia men were prepared to pay for the work in Soviet currency, however, and gave Abramishvili, whose work had not been selling very well, twelve thousand rubles for seven paintings; but they also forced him to unlock the studios of other artists, and gave him similar (low) payments for their work. The mafia gangsters had come with a hit list, and the artists under threat were able to protect Volkov, who was at its top, only because his name had been misspelled; they assured the mafia members that the Volkov whose work was lying around was in fact another artist altogether from this "Boltov" on their list.

The artists reacted variously to this event, but no one called the police who "are like another mafia, worse than the real mafia, and too eager to interfere with too many things in our lives." Volkov was happily ensconced in Berlin, and he immediately arranged for non-artist friends in Moscow to hide his work in their apartments until he could return to the Soviet Union. The Mironenkos were furious, and set about organizing the publication in West Germany of an exposé, hoping that the mafia could be intimidated by press coverage as the KGB had once been daunted by *A-Ya*. Kostya and some others, the artists who were spending a relatively small part of their time in the West, contacted another section of the mafia and organized a protection racket. In the end, it was this protection racket that did the trick, but it was hardly any better than the original mafia. Each month, the "racketeers," as they were generally known, would come to the studios of artists under their protection and buy art for Soviet currency. They paid about two thousand rubles for a single work. This, at the black market rate, was about a hundred dollars; many of these artists were selling individual works in the West for over twenty thousand dollars. On the other hand, life in Moscow was not so expensive, and constant black market exchanges could be a nuisance. If you knew that you had two thousand rubles a month from the racketeers, you could leave your Western money in the West, to spend abroad, instead of going through the tricky business of smuggling it past customs and trying to exchange it in the U.S.S.R. So the setup was not without benefits for the artists.

Of course the racketeers didn't have much taste. When I was in Moscow in November 1990, I would go to the studios of friends and find them busily at work on undistinguished pieces. "That doesn't look great," I would say. "Don't worry," they would respond. "I'm just thinking through some new ideas, and the work itself is only for the racketeers." What did the racketeers do with all this work? The status of the artists of the vanguard had by that time become so confused and so exaggerated that no one in the Soviet Union could disentangle it or read it in real proportions. It is true that good Soviet work had realized high prices, but even good work by the best of these artists was not like currency, nor even like a Picasso drawing, which could be sold on any of a thousand black markets to any of tens of thousands of buyers. The racketeers did not have the connections to galleries and collectors which would have been necessary to place this work, and they soon found that they were not raking in the hard currency they had expected, that by offering work at lower prices than Phyllis Kind or Ronald Feldman or Aydan they could not immediately capture the Western market. "If they couldn't sell them," Nikita Alexeev remarked, "they could hang them on their own walls and enjoy them." But the racketeers were really not keen on this prospect, and so they paid off the director of a respectable cooperative, and, using his name, entered into negotiations with Mrs. Gorbachev's Cultural Foundation to mount a selling exhibition for hard currency in the Palace of Youth. "Raisa and the racketeers," said Larisa. "I think maybe it should be a pop group." This kind of chaos was endemic in Moscow in late 1990 and early 1991; in spite of it, the artists there continued to see their role as an almost sacred one.

Kostya cut a photo of a man and a woman gazing into one another's eyes from a Soviet magazine of the sixties, and showed it at an exhibition at Kashirskaya in November 1990, with a text that read: "She must always remember the name on the sword." The district commissioner, who had tolerated a naked photo of Georgiy Kizevalter at an exhibition a year earlier, said that the work was obscene, and threatened to close the entire exhibition if it was not removed. "Naked photos are not so obscene, because you can see at once what they are. But this work makes you think and imagine, and you can imagine anything." Kostya remarked only, "We will never stop fighting; there is no end to this fighting." He removed the work on grounds that the exhibition was very important to the younger artists included, and not so important for him. "But you have not heard the last of this," he warned. In that exhibition, and in the many others staged in Moscow at that time, thousands of young artists exhibited work with hopes not so far from those of the racketeers and the Cultural Foundation, but the slightly older artists sustained the vocabulary of visionary idealism.

But what qualifies the artists of the vanguard as guardians of the truth, and what, finally, is the nature of that truth?

Nikita Alexeev said to me, "You can write an arbitrary art history with everyone in it. You can choose the influences and do what you like." And Afrika said, "Ask us what you like, we will tell you what you like, and if you want to, in your book, you can change it." The truth is not a matter of facts, and the artists have no urgent sense that the historic details of their experiences need to be preserved. Once or twice I wrote catalogue essays for artists who said, "But it's so boring; it's just what happened. Why not change it?" In Sweden, Kostya asked me to write a paragraph about him and his work, and then he went through it and inserted "not" everywhere: "Kostya Zvezdochetov is *not* deeply engaged with the Russian folk tradition. His work does *not* in any way take on the language of Soviet bureaucracy to undermine that language. He did *not* do a series of paintings of a mythical kingdom called Perdo."

So what is all the palaver about truth? What is it that was encoded for all those years in such ritual and complex and self-indulgent ways by this group of smart-aleck, troublemaking, egotistical men and women? Some of the ineluctable nature of that truth surfaced for me during the weeks I spent in Sweden in the spring of 1990. I enjoyed my time there as much as I have ever enjoyed any visit to a foreign country. I took abundant pleasure in the elegant eighteenth-century buildings of Stockholm, and more in the reunion with friends who were there for *Isskonstvo;* but this was most significantly a time in which that friendship and the import behind it came vividly together.

We were lucky with the weather in Stockholm. Each morning broke radiant and bright, the sky pale blue and infinitely far away, the pale-colored buildings of the city like rare spring blooms in the clear northern light. In the parks, the flowers were out, and the air smelled of lilacs and white blossoms and the sea. In the course of my stay, I taped more than twenty-eight hours of interviews with the Soviet artists. I was struck first in Sweden, and then again in London, when I sat transcribing these interviews in the chill gray of British springtime, by the sheer scale of the events being recounted, and by how smoothly these events had gone sliding almost into irrelevance during the two years it had taken me to get to know these people. In attractive little restaurants with fresh fish and sprigs of dill and crisp table linen, Sven told me of his experience with the KGB, Kostya of his time in the army, Nikita and Dima of their imprisonment in mental hospitals. As I sat in London, I could not help being struck by the sounds that interrupt the recitation of these adversities on tape: the sounds of people chatting in Swedish, of cordial waiters wondering whether we have finished our drinks and would like more, of friends stopping by to ask whether we want to take a boat later on to see the Archipelago.

In 1985, the Mukhomors were in the army, undergoing grueling and unrelenting punishment, being dragged every week to the tribunals of the military KGB for intimidation sessions that often lasted for twelve hours or more. "One day, after eighteen months in the army," Kostya told me, "I was called in by the colonel and told that if I completed one more task I could go home. I set to work on that task, but I didn't do it as quickly as I might have. Because by that time, I understood that the army was all right for me, and that if I had had to stay there for the rest of my life, that also would have been all right." I was struck, in Stockholm, by the fact that though the artists were doing their utmost to avoid the eventuality of a return to life under dictatorship, they were profoundly prepared for it. Which of the great cultural or artistic figures of the West would have ventured to create their works knowing that by doing so they risked their ways of life, indeed their lives themselves? What does it mean to create a work of art under such circumstances, rather than with a government grant? That question lies only at the edge of the Soviets' dignity. More difficult, perhaps, to wonder which Western artists would be prepared to, would be able to turn their gifts inward, to illuminate themselves with the private incandescence of their own insight in order to endure such eventualities, for which Westerners the effort of communication, even when that communication had no object, would validate a life stripped of all other satisfactions.

In Stockholm, we talked a lot about this book, and everyone was full of ideas. "Be sure to make it funny," they all said to me. "Tell all the stories, all the funny things that have happened to us. Try to tell about the games we played, the jokes, the humor." I have tried to do that; but I could not dismiss the reverse side of that humor, the centrifugal seriousness for which it stands. That seriousness has been changed, distorted, transformed by the events of the last few years; but it has not been invalidated. There is much discussion now about who is a competent artist in our Western terms, but the strength of these artists in their own terms has not disappeared, and the moral rectitude of their decision to be artists remains an undimmed gesture of optimism not about politics, but about humanity itself. This is no less true if that decision shimmers in and out of focus against old values—the need for a supportive community, the will to stir up trouble for sport—and new values—fame, money, and glory. Perhaps moral courage is neither more nor less than the willingness to act on such optimism. Did Kabakov lead the generations down a path inexplicably shaped by mysticism? He could not have done otherwise. Is Soviet art ultimately deeply engaged with spirituality? Is it religious art? The very belief in good and evil is a mystical thing, and the strength to lead a crusade for the good, whether that good is social or mythological, internal or external, is religious and spiritual.

Money is now being sought to build a center in Paris (Nikita Alexeev and Julia Tocaier are the driving forces) for the Soviet artists, a place where they can store work they do not wish to import to Moscow, a place where they can live in the intervals between gallery exhibitions in the West, a place where they can be sure of meeting one another, a place where they can curate exhibitions of their own or of one another's work without regard to the market. The facility would be also a library, an archive, a center for mutual understanding, a place that would be home when the artists do not have time to go home. Very little is said about the underlying other agenda of this place: that when things fall apart in Moscow, it will be a haven, a place for everyone to live, a Furmanny-by-the-Seine from which to negotiate whatever new citizenships prove necessary.

To live always in a state of preparedness, of knowing instability, is so profoundly difficult as to be beyond the telling. But like all difficulties endured until they become habit, it is ultimately accepted to the point of being ignored. Malicious, competitive, and immature though they have variously been since the dawn of perestroika, these artists have sustained their underlying moral fiber, and if the worst scenario were to take place, if these men and women were shipped off to the salt mines, there can be no question that they would manage to remain true to themselves even there. To what extent they can sustain such integrity in the glorious opulence of the West, however, we are only beginning to see.

A Note on Spelling

The correct spelling of Russian words and names in English is constantly debated, and most of the artists mentioned in this book have used various spellings for catalogues and exhibitions since they came into contact with the West. In the cause of consistency, all Russian names here have been transliterated according to the system of the U.S. Board on Geographic Names with the exception that the Cyrillic letter "e" has been consistently rendered as "e" except when it is the opening letter of such names as "Yelena" and "Yevgeniy." The primary advantage to this system is that it avoids diacritical marks, which are difficult to read and which make the names even more obscure to Western readers than they otherwise would be.

I have, however, made two exceptions to this agenda. The first is that I have accepted the established spellings of Russian words commonly used in English and of the names of famous historical figures; so I have used "ruble" rather than "rubl," "perestroika" rather than "perestroyka," "Rachmaninoff" rather than "Rakhmaninov," and "Mayakovsky" rather than "Mayakovskiy." The second is that I have accepted spellings adopted by artists who have emigrated to the West as the correct spellings of their names. So I have used "Chelkovski" rather than "Shelkovskiy," "Alexander Melamid" rather than "Aleksandr Melamid," and "Alexeev" rather than "Alekseev."

Index

Andrew Solomon was educated at Yale and Cambridge universities and now lives in New York and London. He is a contributing editor for *Harpers and Queen*, and a regular contributor to *The Spectator*, *Artforum International*, *HG*, and other periodicals in the United States and Great Britain. *The Irony Tower* is his first book.

A NOTE ON THE TYPE

The text of this book is set in Garamond No. 3. It is not a true copy of any of the designs of Claude Garamond (1480–1561), but an adaptation of his types, which set the European standard for two centuries. This particular version is based on an adaptation by Morris Fuller Benton.

Composed by Dix Type, Inc., Syracuse, New York. Printed and bound by Halliday Lithographers, West Hanover, Massachusetts.

Designed by Peter A. Andersen